DOR · PLAN ·
1/16" = 1:0"
ELEVATION

30'-0"

25'-6¼"

23'-4"

46'-6½"

36'-0"

28'-4"

21'-0"

10 14 18 112 116 120 124 128 132 136 140 144 148 152 156 160 164 FEET
· SCALE · FOR · PLAN ↑ ELEVATION ·

NOTE:
FOLLOWING · ISSUE · OF ·
THE · MONOGRAPH · SERIES ·
WILL · CONTAIN · MEASURED ·
DRAWINGS · OF · THE · INTERIOR ·
OF · THE · BRICE · HOUSE ·

MEAS ↑ DRAWN · KENNETH CLARK ·

E V A T I O N ·

· S E C T I O N ·

E · H O U S E ·
· M A R Y L A N D ·

BLUEPRINTS FOR AMERICA'S PAST

Architectural Treasures of Early America

BLUEPRINTS FOR AMERICA'S PAST

From material originally published as
The White Pine Series of Architectural Monographs
edited by
Russell F. Whitehead and Frank Chouteau Brown

Lisa C. Mullins, Editor

Roy Underhill, Consultant

A Publication of
THE NATIONAL HISTORICAL SOCIETY

Library of Congress Cataloging-in-Publication Data

Blueprints for America's past.
    (Architectural treasures of early America; 11)
      1. Architecture, Colonial — United States — Themes, motives. 2. Architecture, Modern — 17th–18th centuries — United States — Themes, motives. 3. Architecture — United States — Themes, motives. I. Mullins, Lisa C. II. Underhill, Roy. III. Series: Architectural treasures of early America (Harrisburg, Pa.); 11.
NA707.B58 1988   720′.973   88-1361
ISBN 0-918678-33-1

CONTENTS

INTRODUCTION

The 1910's and 1920's saw the climax of the Colonial Revival that took hold in the 1880's. Throughout America, architects were besieged by clients wanting Cape Cods, salt boxes, Dutch colonials, and Federal mansions. Restoration projects of colonial villages and towns recreated the past for a new audience. Colonial Williamsburg received a new lease on life during this period.

The White Pine Series of Architectural Monographs began in 1916 in the midst of all the hoopla. In the fourth monograph published by the White Pine Bureau, Russell Whitehead commented on the popularity of the Monograph Series, a popularity that far exceeded the founders' hopes of success. Architects subscribing to the series used the monographs as idea books and as practical building guides, following the precedent of colonial builders who turned to Builder's Handbooks for inspiration or guidance during the early years of the new nation. "The keen interest expressed throughout the country in the early architecture of America had prompted the thought," Whitehead wrote, "that something more of real value might be accomplished if architects were given an incentive to vie with one another in the creation of a really American house of a given size." The competition's objective would be the "study of the wood-house problem, especially of the type where delicacy of detail and refinement of molding can be best executed in White Pine."

Thus, the annual White Pine Architectural Competitions were born. Sponsored by the White Pine Bureau, judged by well-known experts in the field, and advertised through the Monograph Series, these competitions garnered the interest of the top architects of the period. All entries were assigned a number and the identity of the author was a mystery to the judges until the winners were chosen. The first competition challenged each entrant to build a house that would "meet a particular need in every American suburb, and therefore should be in all respects a distinct improvement over the average house erected by the speculative builder." An obvious call for excellence in homebuilding—one that was heeded by a substantial number of architects. As with the series itself, the response to the competition to build a "Suburban House and Garage to Cost $10,000" was overwhelming.

Over the next seven years, Whitehead and his staff sponsored other architectural competitions that dealt with common building concerns encountered by most professional architects during their careers. Always mindful of the need to maintain a standard of excellence while creating practical, comfortable homes and buildings, the Jury of Award was not afraid to admonish the architects who contributed designs that did not meet both requirements. "One of the lessons to be learned in competitions," wrote one Jury of Award, "is the development of good judgment in analysis and in an intelligent and interested weighing of the relative importance of the several elements of the problem, whether these be formally set forth in a competitive programme or stated orally by a client in one's private office."

This volume of the Architectural Treasures of Early America is a compilation of the eight architectural competitions held by the White Pine Bureau. It is our hope that in looking through them the reader will gain a greater appreciation of the elements involved in designing a building or home and the myriad ways that an architectural problem can be solved when a little imagination and thought is applied. These competitions will prove invaluable to those interested in recreating the early American look. House plans and detail sheets provide all the information needed to produce your own early American home.

CAR CULTURE AND THE COLONIAL

The years around the Great War saw revolution in America. In millions of automobiles, waves of a new suburban aristocracy poured out from the cities. The automobile spread homes and highways over the farmlands of old America. The American popular culture of the 1920's valued the mechanical efficiency that gave them their new wealth—even in the arts. William Strunk remarked on this attitude when pinpointing his *Elements of Style* in 1919: "A sentence should contain no unnecessary words, a paragraph no unnecessary sentences, for the same reason that a drawing should have no unnecessary lines and a machine no unnecessary parts."

But, if the test of a classic is that it remains eternally modern, then American Colonial architecture has proven a timeless winner. Colonial Revival architecture in the twenties was not simply a reaction to, or a retreat from, modern times. It embodied the values of the age. The efficiency-oriented, gasoline-powered culture of the twenties found Colonial architecture a vital form. The suburban elite adopted the rational, efficient designs of Colonial architecture for their new American country houses. The twenties saw some of the finest achievements in both Colonial Revival architecture and in the preservation of their sources of inspiration.

By 1916, when the first of these White Pine competitions, the design for "A Suburban House and Garage" was published, the restoration of many early American homes was well underway. Wealthy but displaced Southerners began to buy and restore homes on the James River in Virginia. The Great War interrupted the trend, but the boom quickly revived in the twenties. Work was underway on Monticello by 1923, and the American Wing of the Metropolitan Museum of Art opened in 1924, with a score of rooms taken from early American houses.

William Lawrence Bottomley, an architect from New York, was responsible for some superb expressions of the Colonial Revival style in the Richmond, Virginia, area during this time. He began with English models, but slowly came to depend on local sources. One of the first of his Richmond homes is considered much "more English than American Georgian" in significant details. Designers relied on books, and, in 1916, when this house was designed, early European architecture was far better documented than American. Architectural historian Mark R. Wenger has identified the source of the door pediment of this house as being from a seventeenth-century English building illustrated in Ware's *The Georgian Period*.

Prosperity was no stranger to Richmond in the twenties, and on the West End there grew a prime example of Anglo-Colonial suburban development. New money brought old mansions from neighboring counties into the more fashionable area. When the supply of local mansions ran out, a few went shopping abroad. In 1925, Agecroft Hall, an early English home, was re-erected on the hills overlooking the James to become the focal point of the new suburb of Windsor Farms. The half-timbered, Tudor Revival architecture was very popular at the time. It became so common that by 1920 the style became known as Stockbroker Tudor. Agecroft Hall was to be surrounded by homes designed in the Tudor style, but, even here, the indigenous Colonial home soon took hold.

In 1923, Bottomley undertook the design for the great mansion, Nordley, in Windsor Farms. The client told Bottomley that she was "leaning to the English Cottage type of architecture," but the architect carefully steered her towards the Virginia manor house that he wanted to build. He cited the excessive cost of the "picturesque English style."

> . . . to be properly carried out, [it] requires very heavy slates or tiles in the roof, it needs steel casements and leaded glass, it needs solid timber hand-adzed and it needs patine, all which things are dreadfully expensive at the present time to use . . .

The client soon agreed with Bottomley's preference for an American design. She wrote that she wanted "a house which fifty years from now will not be out-of-date but more beautiful with time." Bottomley saw that her wish was granted.

One of Bottomley's later mansions, Redesdale, built in 1925 typifies the growing acceptance of regional American sources. Although he modeled the dining room and the library on rooms displayed in the American Wing of the Metropolitan, Bottomley also began to do more of his own fieldwork. In the spring of 1925, he took his client on a trip to see Williamsburg, Carter's Grove, and the Nelson House in Yorktown, Virginia. The immediate result was the construction of a superb "Virginia Manor House." But all these years of energy and attention had longer-term effects as well. The growing focus on colonial America made possible one of the great architectural achievements of the time.

Wealth and suburban development made possible by the automobile fueled the interest in the Colonial. Yet it was the automobile that was contributing to the destruction of the survivors of the colonial past. Dr. William Goodwin, the Rector of Brouton Parish Church in Williamsburg felt that the forces of destruction should also bear the responsibility of preservation. He presented his case, first to Henry Ford, and then, successfully, to John D. Rockefeller, Jr. In 1926, Rockefeller began to fund the restoration and preservation of the entire town of Williamsburg. This most ambitious project in historic preservation had many of its roots in the 1916 "Suburban House and Garage." It was the product of a remarkable decade of unparalleled enthusiasm for the enduring quality of our American architectural heritage.

ROY UNDERHILL
MASTER HOUSEWRIGHT
COLONIAL WILLIAMSBURG

A Suburban House
and Garage

Report of the Jury of Award
Given May 12 and 13, 1916
Originally published in 1916 as White Pine Monograph
Volume II, Number 4

PERSPECTIVE VIEW OF ENTRANCE SIDE

FIRST FLOOR PLAN

SECOND FLOOR PLAN

PLOT PLAN

DESIGN FOR A SVBVRBAN HOVSE AND GARAGE TO BE BVILT OF WHITE PINE

ESTIMATED COST

	CVBIC FEET
MAIN HOVSE	34.398
BOTH WINGS [THE PORCH BEING FIGVRED AT ITS FVLL CVBAGE]	10.897
GARAGE	2.430
PERGOLA [FIGVRED AT ¼ ACTVAL CVBAGE	608
TOTAL CVBAGE	48.333
ESTIMATED COST	·20
TOTAL COST	$9.666

FIRST PRIZE DESIGN
Submitted by R. S. Raymond and H. Brookman, New York, New York

A SUBURBAN HOUSE AND GARAGE

Report of the Jury of Award of the First Annual White Pine Architectural Competition

Judged at the Biltmore, New York, NY, May 12 and 13, 1916

THE PROBLEM : The subject is the design of a Suburban Residence with a Garage to accommodate one car, both to be built of wood, the outside finish, consisting of siding and corner boards ; window sash, frames and casings; outside doors, door frames and casings; outside blinds; all exposed porch and balcony lumber; cornice boards, brackets, ornaments and moldings; and any other outside finish lumber—*not* including shingles—to be built of White Pine. The house is to be located on a rectangular lot with a frontage on the highway of 100 ft. and 200 ft. deep, the Northerly end of the lot facing the highway. Running South from the highway for a distance of 50 ft. the lot is approximately level, but from this point takes a 10% grade to the South. There is facing the South an unobstructed river view. It is assumed that the adjacent lots are of similar dimensions and that a restriction covering all this block provides that no house be erected nearer than 30 feet from the highway property line. The architectural style, plan arrangement, gardens, and the location of the house and garage upon the lot, are left to the designer. Provisions should be made for a living-room, dining-room, kitchen, pantry, laundry, four master's rooms and two baths, and one maid's room with toilet, and should also include a piazza. The total cubage of the house, garage, and porches must not exceed 50,000 cubic feet, and for the purpose of this Competition the price per cubic foot is set at 20 cents, this being the estimated cost at which houses of the type specified can be built in almost every part of the country.

THE problem proposed seems to have been particularly interesting to the competitors if the number and excellence of the submitted designs may bear testimony. There were three hundred and sixty-six contestants and when the nom de plume envelopes were opened they disclosed the names, not only of leading designers and draughtsmen the country over, but of principals whose names are by-words in connection with residence architecture.

The very precise and clear conditions and requirements given in the program left no doubt as to the intention of its author, who wished above all to present a definite problem, which while it gave all possible variety in scope and treatment was still governed by specific conditions so that the judges might consider the various plan solutions upon an exact parity. It was considered unjust to permit the contestant to assume his own points of the compass and different grade relations. It is interesting to note that even when the contestants were restricted to exactly one problem a wide variety of plans were developed.

Your jury in making the awards based their judgment, as prescribed by the program of the competition, upon the effect of the design as a whole, its appropriateness to the given site, the degree of ingenuity shown in the plans; and the fitness of the design to express the wood-built house. The drawings, however, were considered not alone from the design point of view but rather design combined with the requirements of a good, common-sense, livable house, and the jury at all times endeavored to balance their ideas between the artistic and the practical.

After carefully considering all the designs submitted, the judges agreed upon about one hundred from which to select the four prize and six mention drawings. This next task proved much more difficult than the first step and consumed the better part of two days. Designs which exceeded the prescribed cubage were of course eliminated from consideration as well as those which, for some reason or another, failed of uniform excellence. Either the plan was weak or the competitor failed to regard his house as a suburban dwelling built upon a lot with improved property on either side. Then, too, there were designs which were distinctly country house in type and therefore unsuitable for a suburban district where the close building on adjoining property would ruin their livableness. There were many schemes which, although they came within the cubage, were obviously too pretentious to be built for anywhere near the prescribed cost. All these defects were carefully analyzed and regretfully taken into consideration in eliminating the designs.

While the prize drawings and those admitted to mention are each most creditable to the authors, none were without faults and the object of this report is to give constructive criticism as well as praise.

FIRST PRIZE. The requirements of the program were met in a most direct manner, the general plan allowing of ample space both to the east and the west, an important consideration especially in a comparatively narrow lot if the house is to feel the freedom the location suggests, and taking full advantage of the exposure to the south. The plan is excellent, giving liberal space on the first floor, indoors and out.

Every room of importance has a southerly exposure. A feature of the second floor plan is that each bedroom has two exposures and that the four rooms connect directly with baths, with possible privacy for the owner. The position of the stairs to the attic is unfortunate, making it necessary to pass through the main second floor hall to reach them from the back stairs. This, however, in a small house of this type is not of great importance.

The exterior speaks of its material—wood. The design is simple in form and construction and most frankly expressed the Ten Thousand Dollar house. The jury was particularly pleased with the presentation of the design and the beauty of the detail. The garage is nicely isolated by service yard fence and would not interfere with the morning sun.

SECOND PRIZE. The design is most excellent, particularly the north elevation, and the details show great refinement and a feeling for beautiful proportion. Here again the exterior is unquestionably wood, with the exception of the entrance door, which suggests stone rather than wood. The house is well placed on the lot, with possible criticism of the garage so near the side line. It was thought that the design was too pretentious in feeling for the prescribed cost. The plan is very livable but not as thoughtful and as well arranged as the first prize. The porch and balcony arrangement is admirable. It is to be regretted that the author took two corners on the second floor for maid's room and one for closet. The matter of opening study into porch is optional and has advantages and faults either way, equally true of opening bedroom over study on to balcony. There is no entrance to attic.

THIRD PRIZE. This house has a very charming exterior of good wood design. The street elevation is much more interesting, however, than the garden elevation and the house takes up too much width of the lot. The garage is also placed too near the property line. The plan is well arranged on the first floor but noticeably lacking of cross draft in bedrooms on the second floor. Only two of the master's bedrooms face to the south, and only one of these has two exposures. Making a passage of the child's room from the maid's room to front hall is questionable. No means of getting to the attic, where much storage space is available, has been provided.

FOURTH PRIZE. The exterior of the house shows a marked appreciation of good wood detail, and is altogether very finely done. The position on the lot may be criticized as it forces the garage to the front. The garage is not successfully placed in relation to the house, and in design is ordinary and far below the standard of the house. The sloping roof to the south, although charming exteriorly, was done at the expense of the bedrooms. The plan of the first floor is good,—the wide opposite openings from hall into dining-room and living-room are, however, noticeably bad features, spoiling the privacy of a good room. The second floor suffered by the use of only three dormers, the practical solution perhaps calling for a sacrifice on the exterior. Cross draft is lacking in all bedrooms, with only one dormer in each. There is no stairway to attic, where much room is available.

MENTIONS. The six drawings are presented as of equal merit. They are of a high standard of excellence, but from a practical standpoint were not considered as good as the prize designs. No attempt was made to place them in any sort of order.

It is the opinion of your jury that the contestants in the White Pine Architectural Competition are to be congratulated on the thought which they gave to their work. It was very satisfactory to the jury to be privileged to consider so many designs of unquestionable architectural quality and superb draughtsmanship. There must be a personal benefit to be derived by the care and time which each one gave to the consideration of the problem and the material in which it was to be executed.

RICHARD B. DERBY
BENNO JANSSEN
HARRIE T. LINDEBERG   } Jury
FRANK B. MEADE   of
FREDERICK W. PERKINS   Award

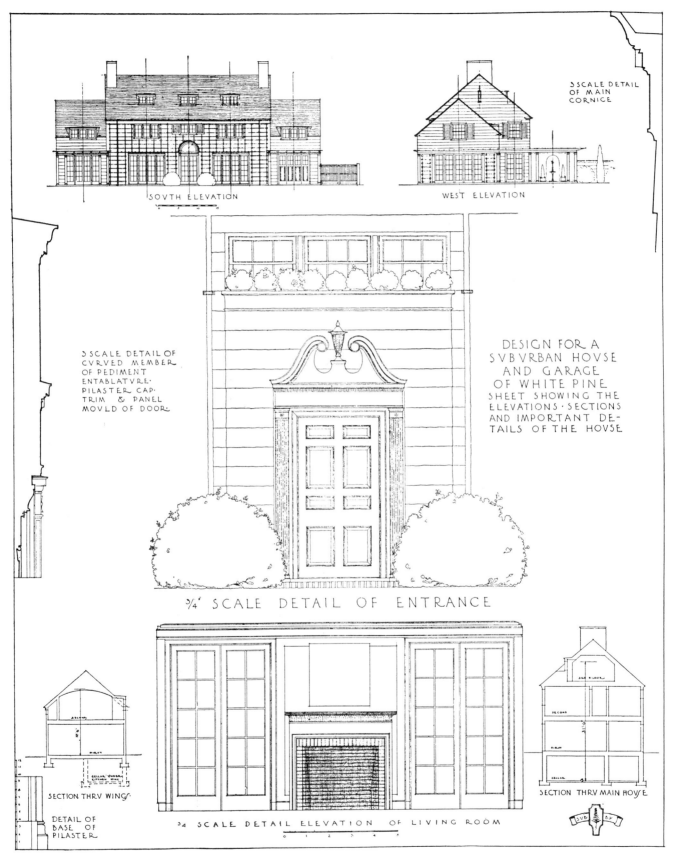

FIRST PRIZE DESIGN, Detail Sheet
Submitted by R. S. Raymond and H. Brookman, New York, New York

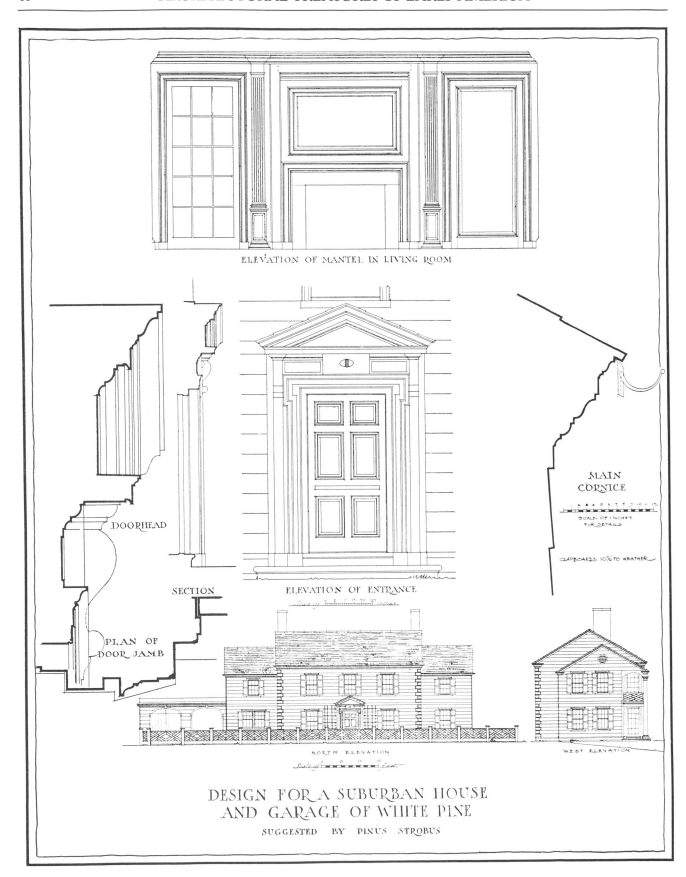

ELEVATION OF MANTEL IN LIVING ROOM

DOORHEAD

SECTION

ELEVATION OF ENTRANCE

PLAN OF DOOR JAMB

MAIN CORNICE

SCALE OF INCHES FOR DETAILS

CLAPBOARDS 10½ TO WEATHER

NORTH ELEVATION

WEST ELEVATION

DESIGN FOR A SUBURBAN HOUSE
AND GARAGE OF WHITE PINE
SUGGESTED BY PINUS STROBUS

SECOND PRIZE DESIGN, Detail Sheet
Submitted by Alfred Cookman Cass, New York, New York

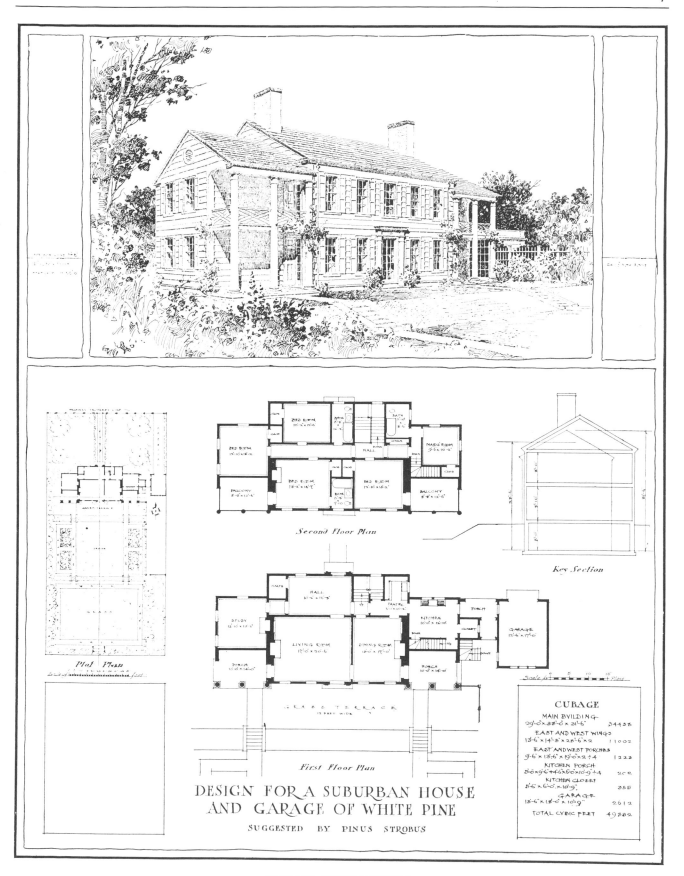

Second Floor Plan

Key Section

Plot Plan

First Floor Plan

DESIGN FOR A SUBURBAN HOUSE AND GARAGE OF WHITE PINE

SUGGESTED BY PINUS STROBUS

CUBAGE

MAIN BUILDING
29'-0" x 35'-0" x 34'-6"   34438

EAST AND WEST WINGS
13'-6" x 14'-0" x 28'-6" x 2   11002

EAST AND WEST PORCHES
9'-6" x 18'-6" x 13'-0" x 2 + 4   1223

KITCHEN PORCH
8'-0" x 9'-6" + 6'-0" x 10'-9" + 4   202

KITCHEN CLOSET
5'-6" x 6'-0" x 10'-9"   355

GARAGE
18'-6" x 13'-0" x 10'-9"   2612

TOTAL CUBIC FEET   49832

SECOND PRIZE DESIGN
Submitted by Alfred Cookman Cass, New York, New York

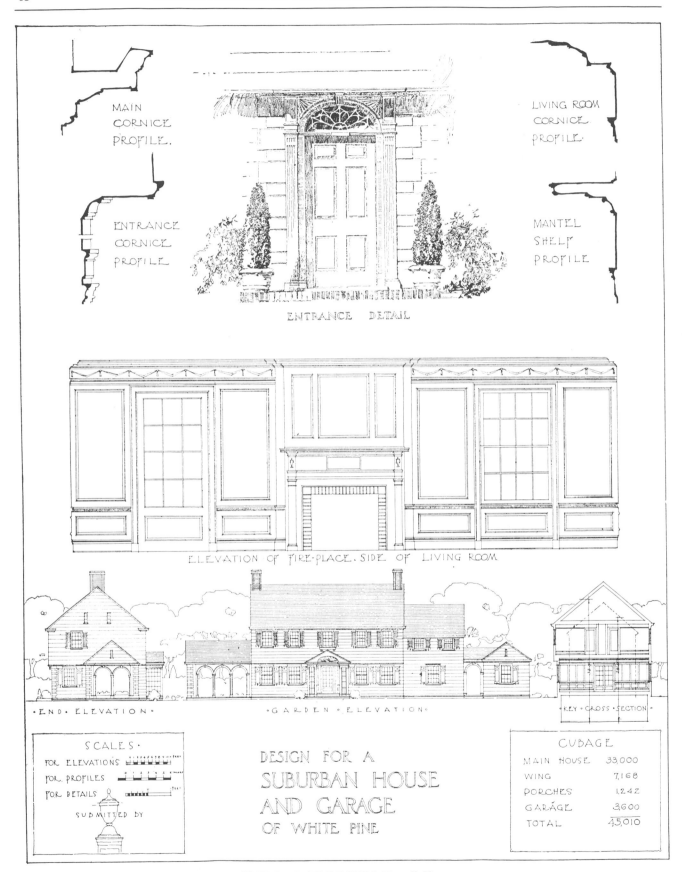

MAIN CORNICE PROFILE.

ENTRANCE CORNICE PROFILE

LIVING ROOM CORNICE PROFILE.

MANTEL SHELF PROFILE

ENTRANCE DETAIL

ELEVATION OF FIRE-PLACE SIDE OF LIVING ROOM

·END·ELEVATION·

·GARDEN·ELEVATION·

·KEY·CROSS·SECTION·

SCALES·

FOR ELEVATIONS
FOR PROFILES
FOR DETAILS

SUBMITTED BY

DESIGN FOR A
SUBURBAN HOUSE
AND GARAGE
OF WHITE PINE

CUBAGE	
MAIN HOUSE	33,000
WING	7,168
PORCHES	1,242
GARAGE	3,600
TOTAL	45,010

THIRD PRIZE DESIGN, Detail Sheet
Submitted by Lewis Welsh and J. Floyd Yewell, New York, New York

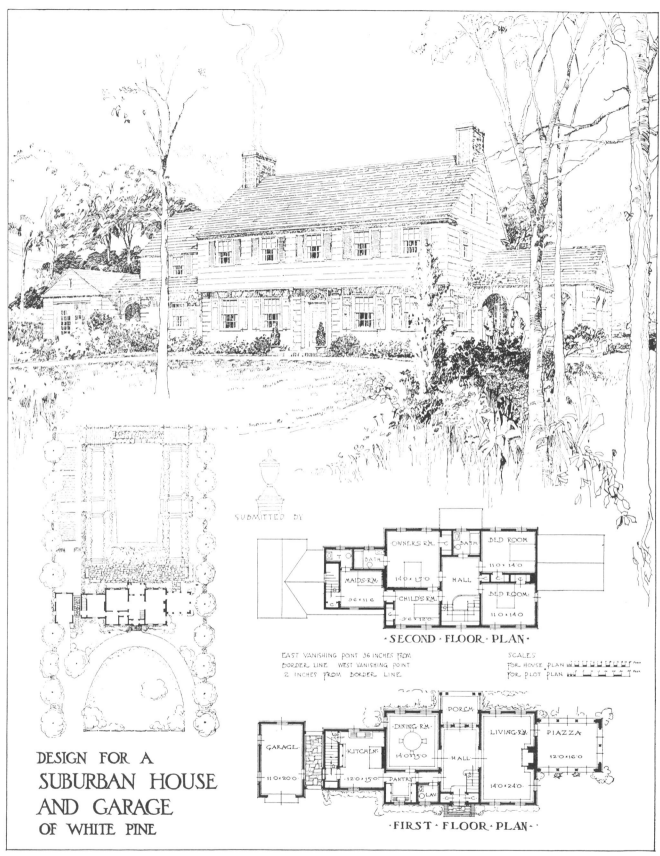

SUBMITTED BY

OWNERS·RM. | BATH | BED ROOM
MAIDS·RM. | BATH | HALL | 11·0 x 14·0
14·0 x 15·0
CHILD'S·RM. | BED·ROOM
9·6 x 11·6 | 9·6 x 12·0 | 11·0 x 14·0

·SECOND·FLOOR·PLAN·

EAST VANISHING POINT 36 INCHES FROM
BORDER LINE   WEST VANISHING POINT
2 INCHES FROM BORDER LINE

SCALES
FOR HOUSE PLAN
FOR PLOT PLAN

PORCH
GARAGE | KITCHEN | DINING·RM. | LIVING·RM. | PIAZZA
11·0 x 20·0 | 12·0 x 15·0 | 14·0 x 15·0 | HALL | 12·0 x 16·0
PANTRY | 14·0 x 24·0
LAV.

·FIRST·FLOOR·PLAN·

DESIGN FOR A
SUBURBAN HOUSE
AND GARAGE
OF WHITE PINE

THIRD PRIZE DESIGN
Submitted by Lewis Welsh and J. Floyd Yewell, New York, New York

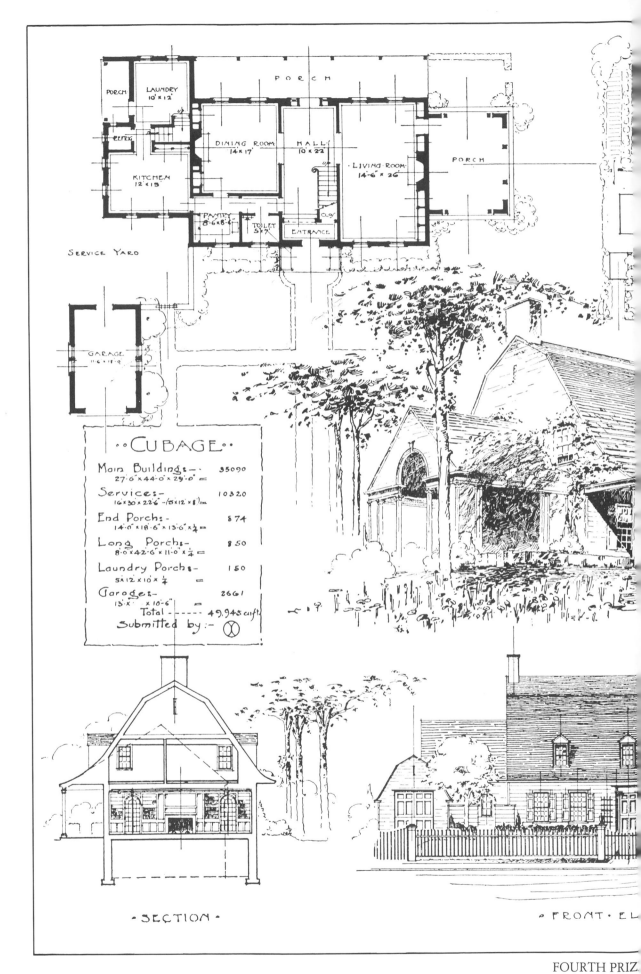

PORCH

PORCH

PORCH

LAUNDRY
10' x 12'

DINING ROOM
14 x 17

HALL
10 x 22

LIVING ROOM
14'-6" x 26

PORCH

REFRIG.

KITCHEN
12 x 15

PANTRY
8'-6" x 8'-6"

CLO.

TOILET
5 x 7

ENTRANCE

SERVICE YARD

GARAGE
11'-6" x 18'-0"

·· CUBAGE ··

Main Buildings:— 35090
27'-6" x 44'-0" x 29'-0" =

Service:— 10320
16' x 30' x 22'-6" -(5 x 12' x 8') =

End Porch:— 874
14'-0" x 18'-6" x 13'-6" x ¼ =

Long Porch:— 850
8'-0" x 42'-6" x 11'-0" x ¼ =

Laundry Porch:— 150
5 x 12 x 10 x ¼ =

Garage:— 2661
13'-x" x 10'-6" =

Total ——— 49,945 cu.ft.

Submitted by:— ⊗

- SECTION -

· FRONT · EL

FOURTH PRIZE
Submitted by R. J. Wadsworth,

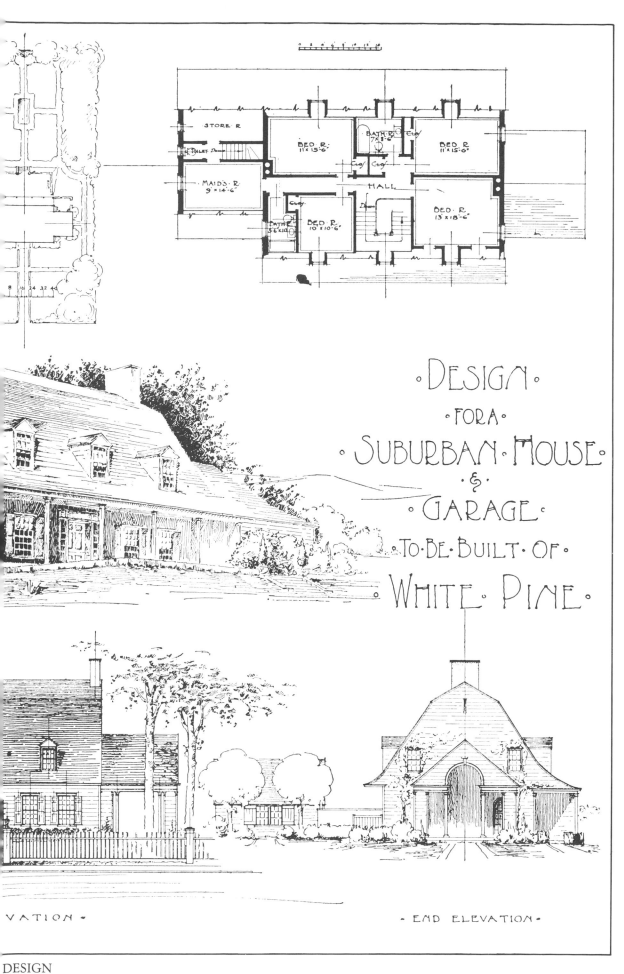

STORE R

BED R
11'x 15'-6"

BATH R
7'x 8'-6"

Clo.

BED R
11'x 15'-6"

TOILET

MAID'S R
9'x 14'-6"

Clo.

Clo.

HALL

Clo.

BATH
5'-6"x10'

BED R
10'x 10'-6"

BED R
13'x 18'-6"

·DESIGN·
·FOR·A·
·SUBURBAN·HOUSE·
·&·
·GARAGE·
·TO·BE·BUILT·OF·
·WHITE·PINE·

· VATION ·

· END·ELEVATION ·

DESIGN

Philadelphia, Pennsylvania

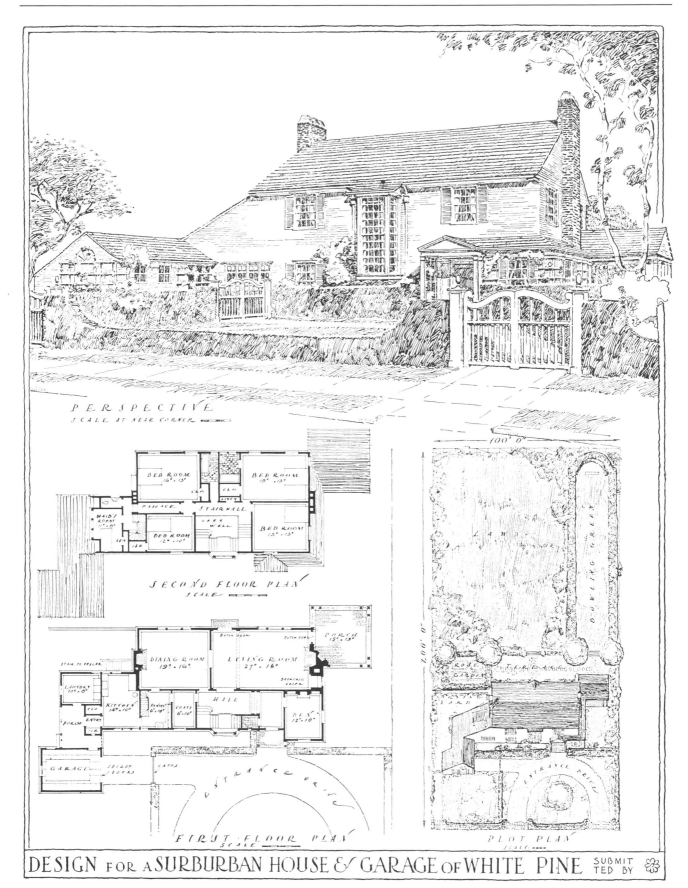

PERSPECTIVE
SCALE AT NEAR CORNER

SECOND FLOOR PLAN
SCALE

FIRST FLOOR PLAN
SCALE

PLOT PLAN
SCALE

DESIGN FOR A SURBURBAN HOUSE & GARAGE OF WHITE PINE SUBMITTED BY

MENTION DESIGN
Submitted by C. M. Foster trand W. M. Smith, New York, New York

LIVING ROOM CHIMNEY BREAST

DETAIL OF LIVING ROOM
SCALE

PORCH CORNICE

MAIN CORNICE

CROSS SECTION
SCALE

GARDEN ELEVATION

ROAD ELEVATION

ENTRANCE PORCH

CUBAGE

CELLAR
.... 12 816 cu.ft.
FIRST STORY
MAIN HOUSE 14 256 " "
SERVICE WING 2 484 " "
PORCHES 1 055 " "
SECOND STORY
AND ATTIC
MAIN HOUSE 17 870 ..
SERVICE WING 1 440 ..
TOTAL 49 921 ..

DESIGN FOR A SURBURBAN HOUSE & GARAGE OF WHITE PINE SUBMITTED BY

MENTION DESIGN, Detail Sheet
Submitted by C. M. Foster and W. M. Smith, New York, New York

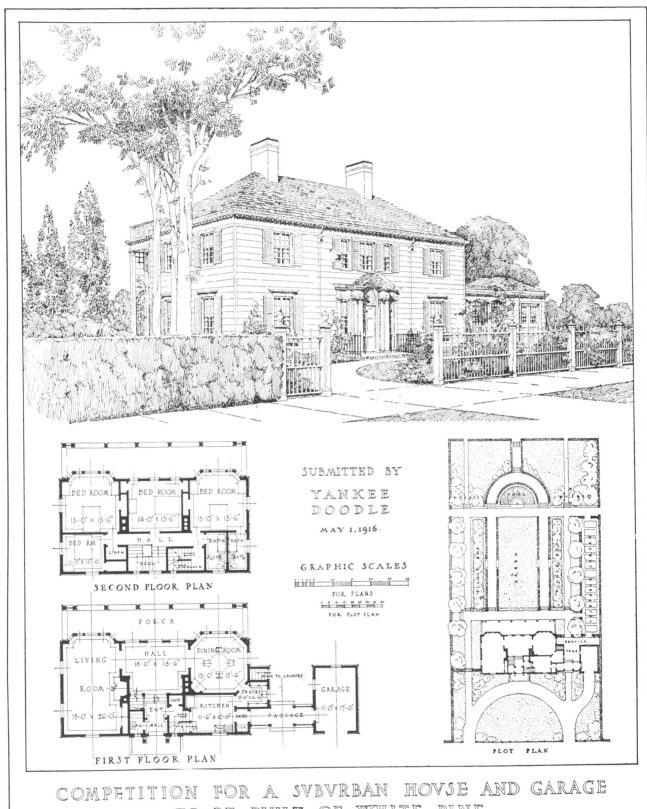

COMPETITION FOR A SVBVRBAN HOVSE AND GARAGE
TO BE BVILT OF WHITE PINE

MENTION DESIGN
Submitted by J. Ivan Dise, New York, New York

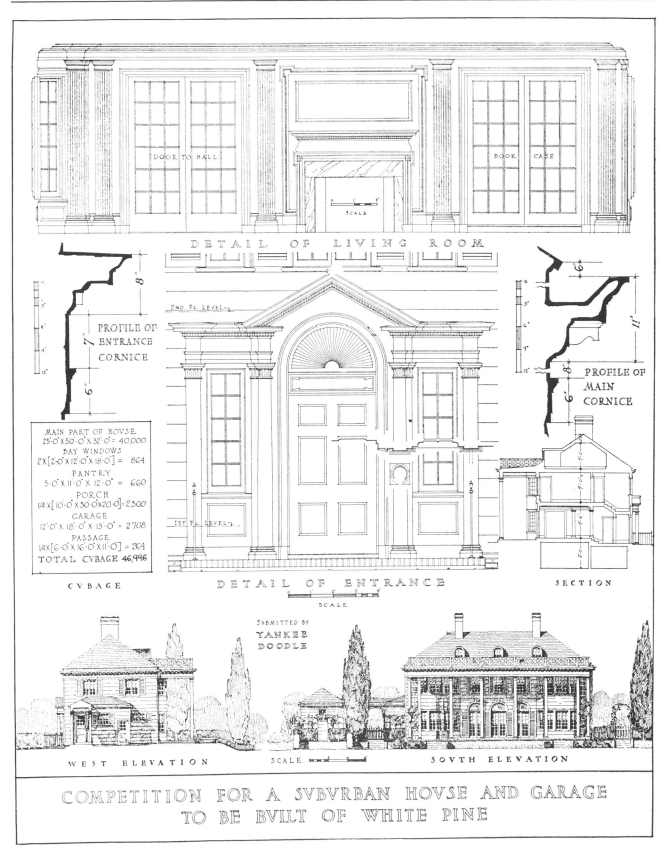

DETAIL OF LIVING ROOM

DOOR TO HALL

BOOK CASE

SCALE

PROFILE OF ENTRANCE CORNICE

2ND FL LEVEL

1ST FL LEVEL

PROFILE OF MAIN CORNICE

MAIN PART OF HOVSE
25'-0" X 50'-0" X 32'-0" = 40,000
BAY WINDOWS
2 X [2'-0" X 12'-0" X 18'-0"] = 864
PANTRY
5'-0" X 11'-0" X 12'-0" = 660
PORCH
1/4 X [10'-0" X 50'-0" X 20'-0"] = 2,500
GARAGE
12'-0" X 18'-0" X 13'-0" = 2,708
PASSAGE
1/4 X [6'-0" X 16'-0" X 11'-0"] = 264
TOTAL CVBAGE 46,996

CVBAGE

DETAIL OF ENTRANCE

SCALE

SECTION

SVBMITTED BY
YANKEE DOODLE

WEST ELEVATION

SCALE

SOVTH ELEVATION

COMPETITION FOR A SVBVRBAN HOVSE AND GARAGE TO BE BVILT OF WHITE PINE

MENTION DESIGN, Detail Sheet
Submitted by J. Ivan Dise, New York, New York

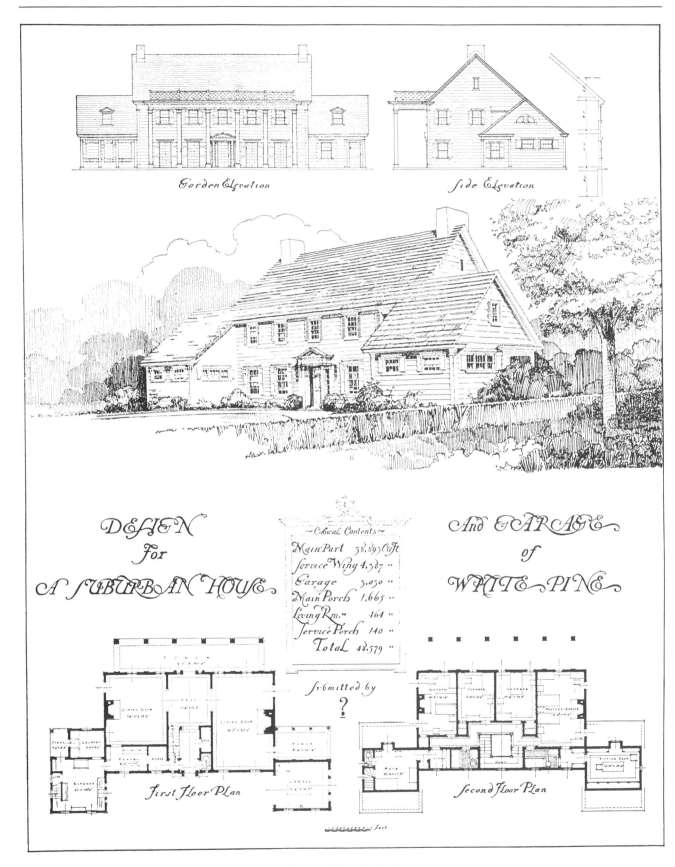

Garden Elevation

Side Elevation

DESIGN For A SUBURBAN HOUSE

And GARAGE of WHITE PINE

~ Cubical Contents ~
Main Part 58,893 Cu ft
Service Wing 4,387 "
Garage 3,030 "
Main Porch 1,665 "
Living Rm." 464 "
Service Porch 140 "
Total 48,579 "

Submitted by ?

First Floor Plan

Second Floor Plan

MENTION DESIGN
Submitted by Conrad A. Albrizio, New York, New York

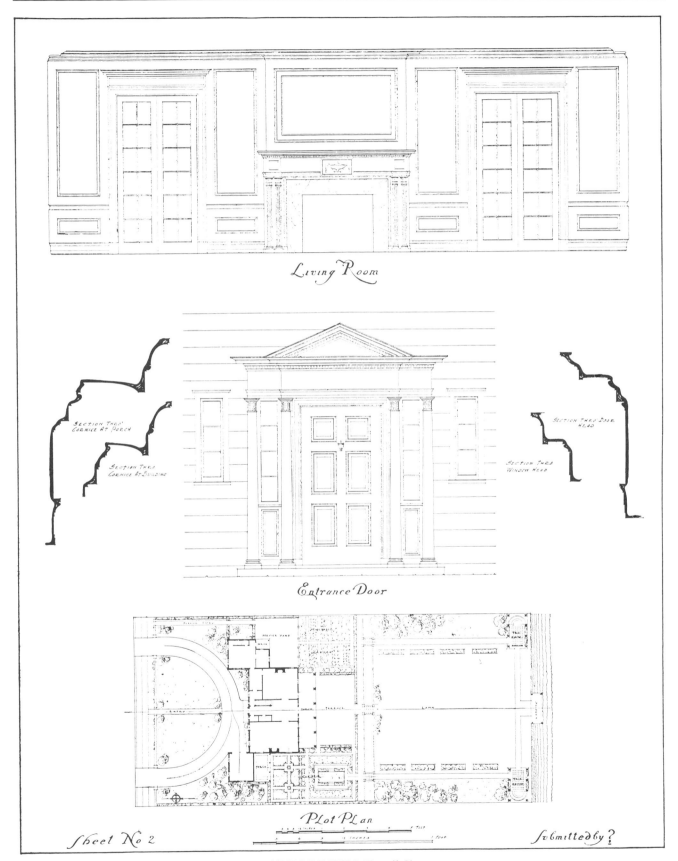

Living Room

Entrance Door

Plot Plan

Sheet No 2   Submitted by ?

MENTION DESIGN, Detail Sheet
Submitted by Conrad A. Albrizio, New York, New York

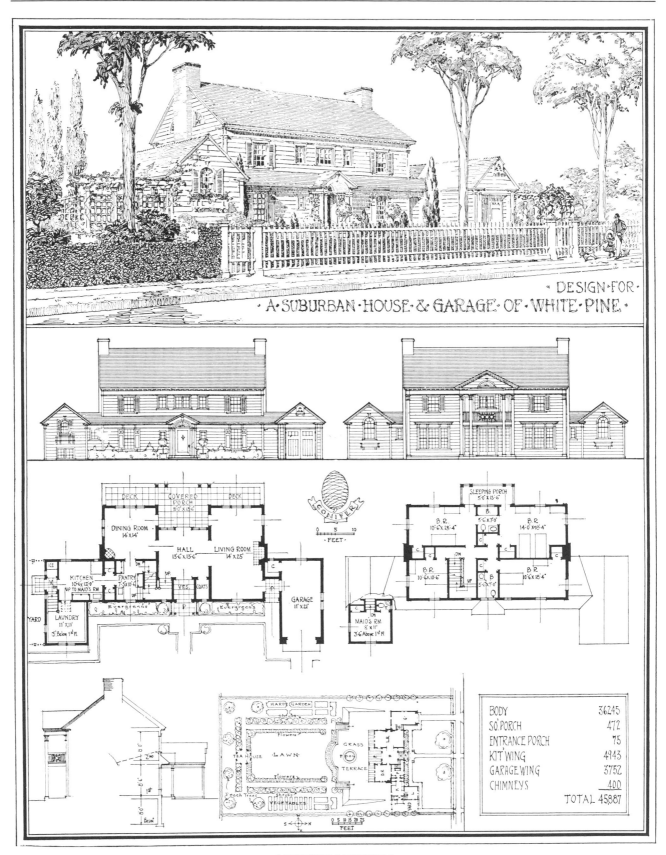

· DESIGN · FOR ·
· A · SUBURBAN · HOUSE · & · GARAGE · OF · WHITE · PINE ·

BODY	36245
SO. PORCH	472
ENTRANCE PORCH	75
KIT' WING	4943
GARAGE WING	3752
CHIMNEYS	400
TOTAL	45887

MENTION DESIGN
Submitted by John A. Tompkins and Harry Brodsky, New York, New York

DOORWAY

MENTION DESIGN, Detail Sheet
Submitted by John A. Tompkins and Harry Brodsky, New York, New York

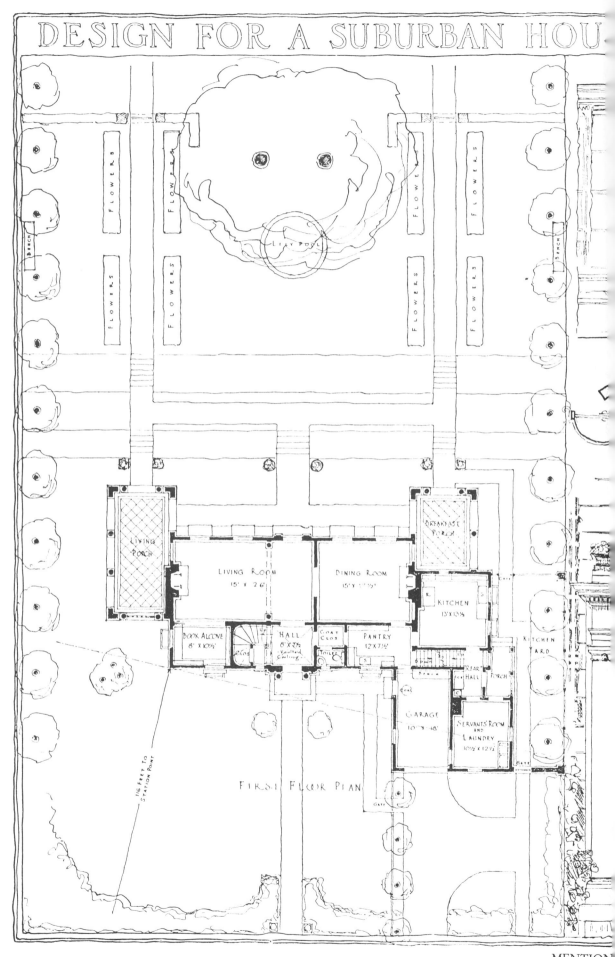

DESIGN FOR A SUBURBAN HOUSE

FLOWERS

LILY POOL

LIVING
PORCH

BREAKFAST
PORCH

LIVING ROOM
15' X 26'

DINING ROOM
15' X 12'6"

KITCHEN
13' X 13½'

KITCHEN
YARD

BOOK ALCOVE
8' X 10½'

HALL
8' X 7½'
Vaulted Ceiling

COAT
CLOS

PANTRY
12' X 7½'

TOILET

REAR
HALL

PORCH

116 FEET TO STATION POINT

GARAGE
10' X 18'

SERVANTS ROOM
AND
LAUNDRY
10½' X 12½'

FIRST FLOOR PLAN

GATE

GATE

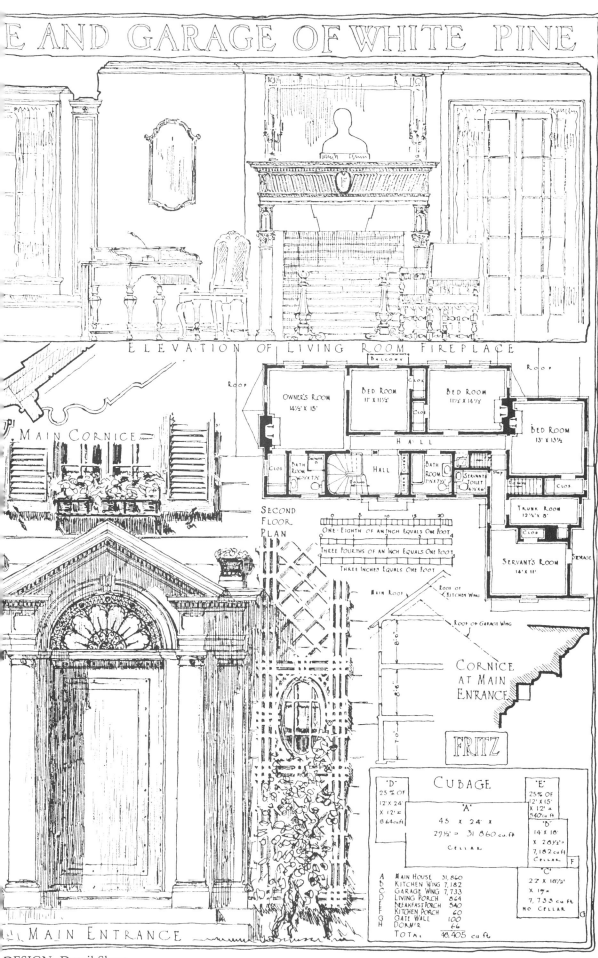

E AND GARAGE OF WHITE PINE

ELEVATION OF LIVING ROOM FIREPLACE

MAIN CORNICE

SECOND FLOOR PLAN

OWNER'S ROOM 14½' X 15'
BED ROOM 11' X 11½'
BED ROOM 11½' X 14½'
BED ROOM 13' X 13½'
BALCONY
CLOS
ROOF
ROOF
HALL
CLOS
BATH ROOM 7½' X 7½'
HALL
BATH ROOM 7½' X 7½'
SERVANTS TOILET 4½' X 6'
CLOS
TRUNK ROOM 12½' X 8'
CLOS
STORAGE
SERVANT'S ROOM 14' X 11'

ONE EIGHTH OF AN INCH EQUALS ONE FOOT
THREE FOURTHS OF AN INCH EQUALS ONE FOOT
THREE INCHES EQUALS ONE FOOT

MAIN ROOF
ROOF OF KITCHEN WING
ROOF OF GARAGE WING

CORNICE AT MAIN ENTRANCE

FRITZ

CUBAGE

'A'
45 X 24 X
29½' = 31,860 cu ft
CELLAR

'D'
25 % OF
12' X 24'
X 12' =
864 cu ft

'E'
25 % OF
12' X 15' =
X 12' =
540 cu ft

'B'
14 X 18'
X 28½' =
7,182 cu ft
CELLAR

'C'
27 X 18½'
X 17' =
7,733 cu ft
NO CELLAR

A	MAIN HOUSE	31,860
B	KITCHEN WING	7,182
C	GARAGE WING	7,733
D	LIVING PORCH	864
E	BREAKFAST PORCH	540
F	KITCHEN PORCH	60
G	GATE WALL	100
H	DORMER	66
	TOTAL	48,405 cu ft

MAIN ENTRANCE

DESIGN, Detail Sheet
umner Schneider, Cleveland, Ohio

DESIGN FOR A SUBURBAN HOUSE AND GARAGE OF WHITE PINE

WEST ELEVATION

GARDEN ELEVATION

MENTION DESIGN

Submitted by Charles Sumner Schneider, Cleveland, Ohio

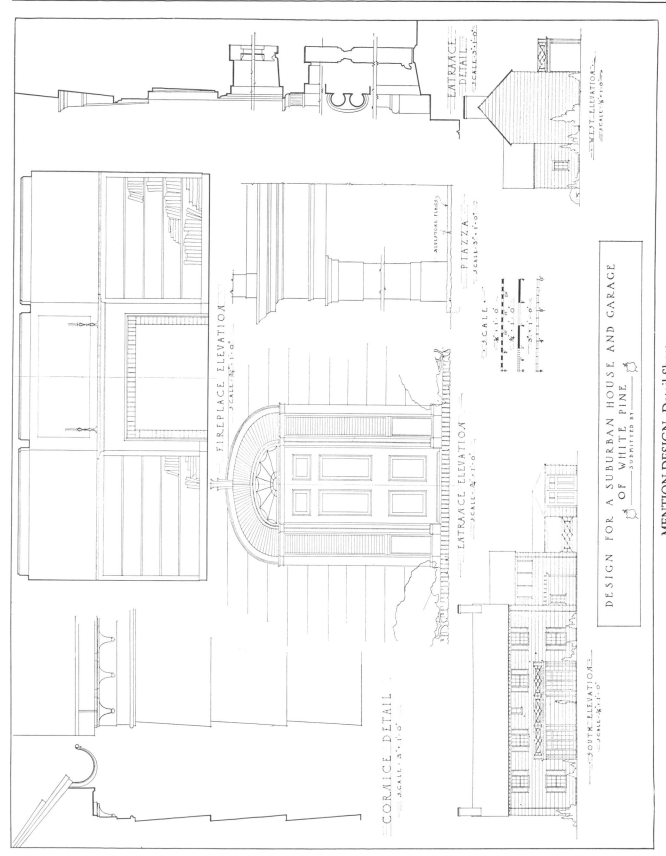

MENTION DESIGN, Detail Sheet

Submitted by Charles H. Umbrecht, East Orange, New Jersey, and L. J. Kaley, Wyncote, Pennsylvania

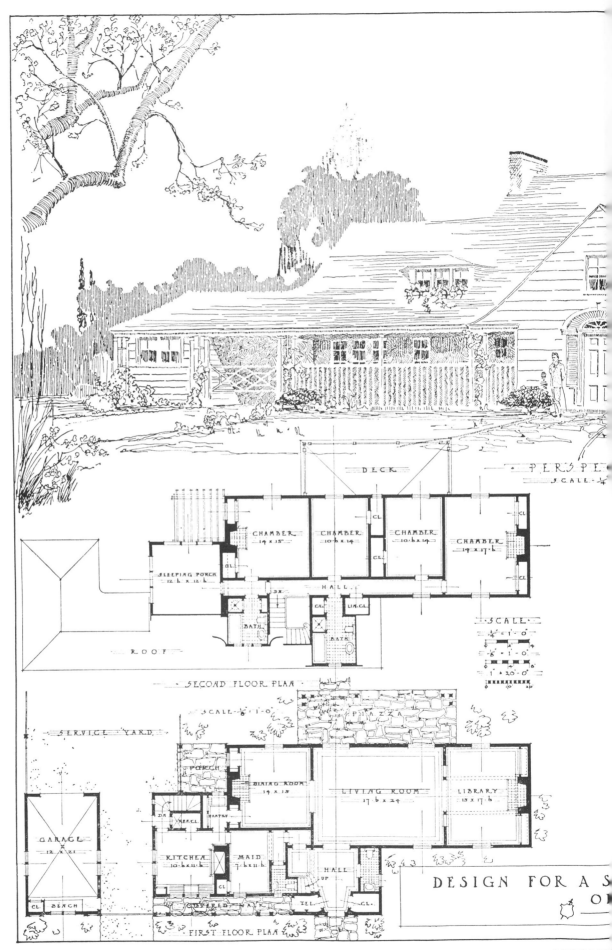

DECK

PERSPE
SCALE - ¼

CHAMBER
19 X 15

CHAMBER
10·6 X 14

CL

CHAMBER
10·6 X 14

CHAMBER
19 X 17·6

CL

CL

SLEEPING PORCH
12·6 X 12·6

CL

CL

HALL

DN

CL

LIN·CL

BATH

BATH

ROOF

SCALE
¼ = 1'-0"
⅛ = 1'-0"
1" = 20'-0"

SECOND FLOOR PLAN
SCALE ⅛ = 1'-0"

SERVICE YARD

PIAZZA

PORCH

DINING ROOM
19 X 15

LIVING ROOM
17·6 X 24

LIBRARY
13 X 17·6

GARAGE
12 X 21

DR

X·CL

PANTRY

KITCHEN
10·6 X 11·6

MAID
7·6 X 11·6

HALL
UP

CL

BENCH

COVERED WAY

TEL

CL

FIRST FLOOR PLAN

DESIGN FOR A S
O

MENTION
Submitted by Charles H. Umbrecht, East Orange,

KEY SECTION
SCALE ¼"=1'-0"

CVBAGE

PART	CV. FT.
BODY of HOUSE 18-6 x 56 x 30	31,080
ENTRANCE WING 16-6 x 12 x 23-6	4,653
SERVICE WING 25-6 x 15-6 x 19	7,510
GARAGE 22 x 13 x 10	2,860
PORCHES ETC.	1,827
TOTAL –	47,930

PLOT PLAN
SCALE 1"=20'-0"

BURBAN HOUSE AND GARAGE
WHITE PINE
UBMITTED BY

DESIGN
ew Jersey, and L. J. Kaley, Wyncote, Pennsylvania

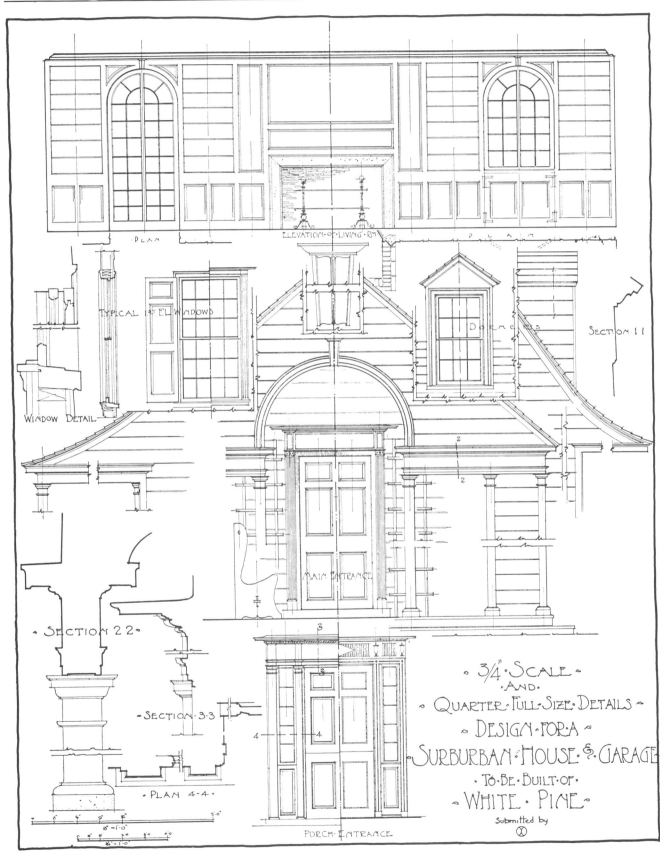

FOURTH PRIZE DESIGN, Detail Sheet
Submitted by R. J. Wadsworth, Philadephia, Pennsylvania

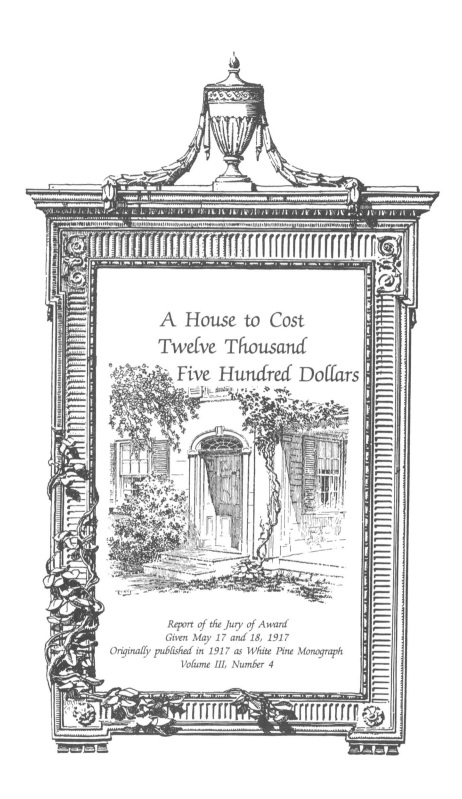

A House to Cost
Twelve Thousand
Five Hundred Dollars

Report of the Jury of Award
Given May 17 and 18, 1917
Originally published in 1917 as White Pine Monograph
Volume III, Number 4

"PARADISE ROW," ONE OF THE OLD RANGES, WHITE SULPHUR SPRINGS, WEST VIRGINIA

Some of the most delightful informal wooden architecture of the South grew up around the "Healing Springs."

A HOUSE TO COST TWELVE THOUSAND FIVE HUNDRED DOLLARS

Report of the Jury Award of the Second Annual White Pine Architectural Competition

Judged at the Greenbrier, White Sulphur Springs, WV, May 17 and 18, 1917

THE PROBLEM: The design of a residence, to be built of wood (all the outside finish, consisting of siding and corner boards; window sash, frames and casings; outside doors, door frames and casings; outside blinds; all exposed porch and balcony lumber; cornice boards, brackets, ornaments and mouldings, etc., *not* including shingles, to be of White Pine), for all-year-round occupancy by an American family with an annual income of $5000. The competitor shall assume that the family is of average size and is one of taste and refinement, and shall provide appropriate accommodations, including out-of-doors sleeping quarters.

The architectural style is optional, and the plan arrangement left to the ingenuity of the designer.

The house is to be located on a rectangular lot at the northeast corner of two streets. The lot measures 125' 0" on the Main street, which runs east and west, and 200' 0" on the Secondary street, which leads to the railroad station. It is assumed that there is a restriction which provides that the house shall not be erected nearer than thirty feet from the Main and twenty feet from the Secondary highway property line, and that no building may be placed within ten feet of the east or five feet from the north lot line. The outlook is equally desirable in all directions, and the neighboring houses of the usual heterogeneous character of design obtaining in towns, small cities or suburbs of large cities.

The total cubage of the house and porches must not exceed 55,000 cubic feet.

The house must be one that can be built for $12,500, and the design must therefore be of such character that there may be no doubt about its cost.

A T the meeting of the Jury, before examining any of the drawings, the Jurors gave careful consideration to the fact that the program did not definitely state the number and sizes of the rooms required; and determined unanimously the permissible latitude in number and sizes of rooms to accommodate the family as described. The Jurors agreed that, on the first floor, two rooms of fairly large size besides the dining room, were necessary to constitute a complete and livable house; that variations in habits of living would make permissible considerable differences in the character of these rooms; they also agreed that an adequate service portion was a necessity. On the second floor a minimum of three bedrooms and two baths, one of the bedrooms to be large enough for the comfortable permanent accommodation of two persons, was thought requisite, together with a sleeping porch for at least two persons, besides either one or two maids' rooms and bath, depending upon the size and character of the house. They decided also that a cellar under the main part of the house was essential to good construction.

This interpretation of the program was faithfully observed in the consideration of the drawings.

Unfortunately, a number of the competitors did not seem to consider that the requirements of the program as to the use of color and diluted ink meant anything, and eleven drawings were removed from consideration for one or the other of these reasons. Some of the competitors managed to figure the cubage of their buildings within the requirements, by excavating the cellar for a small part only; but where the result of such tabulation of contents produced a house which manifestly could not have been built for $12,500 in any portion of the country or at any recent time, these plans were omitted from consideration. Also, where competitors, by deceptive figuring of the cubic contents, made their drawings appear to conform to the terms of the program, where in reality they did not, the designs were not considered. The total number

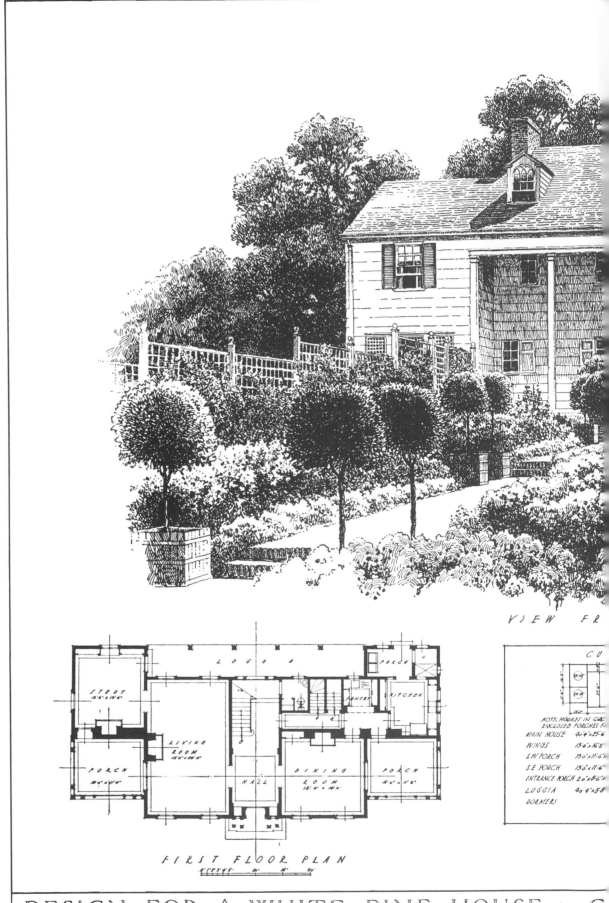

VIEW FR

FIRST FLOOR PLAN

DESIGN FOR A WHITE PINE HOUSE to C

FIRST PRIZE

Submitted by Winchton L. Risley and

M G A R D E N

GE

INDICATE HEIGHTS
D 2 o BELOW GROUND

6"	34455
x2	12120
o	3065
o"	3289
1/2	38
o"x1/2	1141
	184
TOTAL	54292 C.F.

SECOND FLOOR PLAN

CHAMBER
12'6" x 16'6"

BATH   LINEN

BATH

CHAMBER
12'6" x 16'6"

HALL

SLEEPING
PORCH
13'0" x 16'0"

CHAMBER
14'2" x 15'8"

CHAMBER
14'5" x 15'2"

SLEEPING
PORCH
13'0" x 16'0"

ft $12,500 ~ ~ Submitted by Prospectus Apricus

Design No. 204
James Perry Wilson, New York, New York

of drawings eliminated for these reasons was seventeen and the Jury regrets exceedingly the implication of these competitors that it would not faithfully discharge its obligation in this important respect.

In making the judgment, the Jury, in accordance with the terms of the program, considered first the architectural merit of the various designs, and found to their regret that by so doing most of the houses which were located on the plot in the position which the Jury deemed to be the best were not of sufficient architectural excellence to be considered. The Jury was unanimous in believing that the house should be located toward the rear of the plot, with the service wing and a possible garage at the interior corner; the main rooms and the gardening or other development of the grounds toward the Main Street to the South, with the entrance road to the house and garage at the North. This would have given convenient access for automobile traffic to the station, and would also have given proper light, air and outlook to the principal rooms. The plans finally selected by the Jury for the first and second places were those which were placed toward the front of the lot, with the gardens at the rear, but were so arranged that certain of the rooms had both good light and air to the South and in part a good outlook to the North over the garden.

The Jury, after two sessions, were finally able to reduce the number of plans under consideration to twelve, and from these selected four which seemed, in respect to all the qualities mentioned under the heading "Judgment" in the program, to be of all-round superiority. The Jury found themselves unable to discriminate between the eight remaining designs and therefore decided to award all eight Mentions, instead of six, as specified in the program.

FIRST PRIZE, *Design No. 204:* In regard to the first requirement of the judgment (the architectural merit of the design) the Jury considered that this competitor shows the combination of imagination and good taste essential to successful country house design in a greater degree than any other competitor. The placing of the house on the property is excellent, though not ideal; the treatment of the grounds, both as shown in perspective and as on the plot plan, is admirable. The details both of interior and exterior show intelligence and knowledge, and are of a type suitable to the limitation of cost. The plan of the first floor as regards the principal rooms and the placing of the porches is excellent. The space allotted the service portion is much too small and the arrangement is not good, but weighing these matters against similar features in other plans, this point was not

thought sufficient to vitiate the other good qualities of the plan. The second floor is one of the best submitted. The rooms are of good size, thoroughly ventilated and the arrangement en suite of pairs of rooms on each end, with connections to bath rooms and to the sleeping porches, is most satisfactory. The waste of space in circulation is small and the treatment of the second floor corridor is such as to shorten its apparent length, as far as possible.

While the Jury thought there were a number of perspectives of at least equal merit from the point of view of rendering, they felt that this factor should not weigh in making a judgment and because this competitor shows a perception of charm and imagination to an unusual degree, the Jury was unanimous in awarding this design first place on all counts.

SECOND PRIZE, *Design No. 224:* This design was awarded the second prize for substantially the same reasons that the first prize was awarded to Design No. 204.

The placing of the house on the property is good and the architecture of the building is excellent. The Jury admired the treatment of the one-story wings extremely, although they regretted a certain heaviness in the dining porch detail, and felt also that the sleeping porch is too narrow. The position of the first-story toilet is undeniably bad, because of its conspicuousness and because it opens on the dining porch. The plan of the entrance hall is unusual and susceptible of extremely interesting treatment, possibly with arches over the entrance to the stairs and the entrance to the dining porch. The connection from the pantry to the front door and also to the dining porch is extremely good, the kitchen arrangement is good and the closets on this floor are sufficient. On the second floor the Committee felt that the proportion of space devoted to each of the principal rooms is correct, and that the arrangement of the bath rooms is satisfactory. The rear and side elevations are good, as are the details of the main entrance and the wing.

Of all the designs submitted there is perhaps none which so fully complies with the spirit of the competition as regards material and cost.

THIRD PRIZE, *Design No. 49:* The principal consideration which influenced the Committee in making the award of third place to No. 49 is the originality shown in the informal handling both of the plot and of the building itself. The house is extremely well placed on the property; the garden scheme is imaginative and interesting and the grouping of the garage with the house is a pleasant feature. By further development of

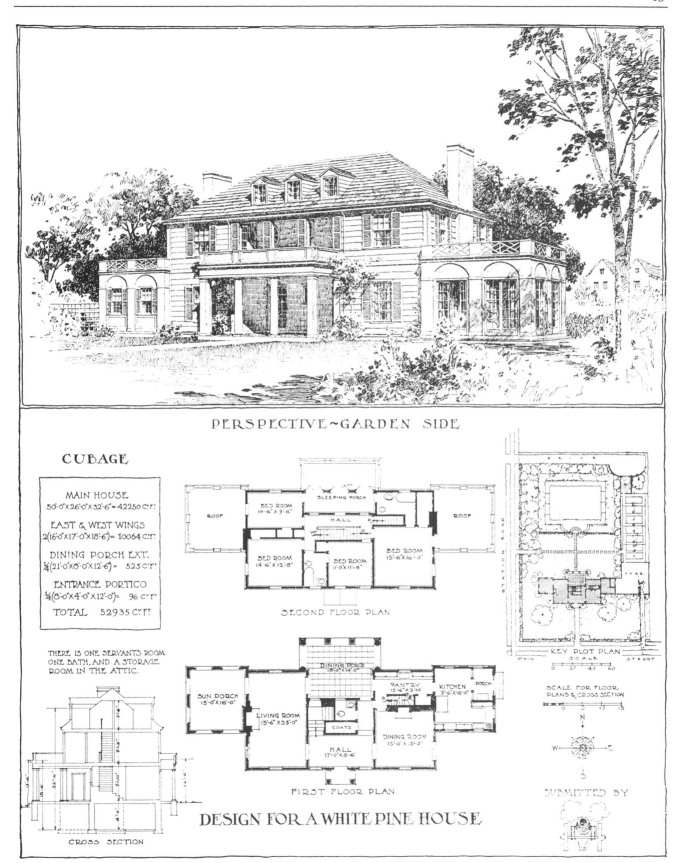

PERSPECTIVE ~ GARDEN SIDE

CUBAGE

MAIN HOUSE
50'-0" X 26'-0" X 32'-6" = 42250 CU'FT

EAST & WEST WINGS
2(16'-0" X 17'-0" X 18'-6") = 10064 CU'FT

DINING PORCH EXT.
½(21'-0" X 8'-0" X 12'-6") = 525 CU'FT

ENTRANCE PORTICO
¼(8'-0" X 4'-0" X 12'-0") = 96 CU'FT

TOTAL 52935 CU'FT

THERE IS ONE SERVANTS ROOM
ONE BATH, AND A STORAGE
ROOM IN THE ATTIC.

SECOND FLOOR PLAN

FIRST FLOOR PLAN

CROSS SECTION

KEY PLOT PLAN

SCALE FOR FLOOR
PLANS & CROSS SECTION

SUBMITTED BY

DESIGN FOR A WHITE PINE HOUSE

SECOND PRIZE, Design No. 224
Submitted by Jerauld Dahler, New York, New York

the scheme the garage could be entered under cover afforded by an arcade. The position of the house conforms fairly well to the Committee's opinion as to the ideal location. The exterior shows an admirable adaptation of English precedent to our materials. The Jury thought that the two weak spots in the exterior were the introduction of a rather unnecessary gable over the amusing double arched entrance to the garden, and the treatment of the sleeping porch, which would cut the East gable badly; but the simple, domestic, almost playful character of the design was sincerely admired. The plan is of a quite different type from most of those presented, and the proportionate spaces allotted to the dining room, the living room and study are good, as are the locations of these rooms with consideration to air, outlook and surroundings. The kitchen is small, but the other service portions are of sufficient size to care properly for the domestic activities. The second floor arrangement shows rooms of irregular shapes, but with a proper proportion of space to the probable requirements of the family for whom the house is designed.

FOURTH PRIZE, *Design No. 86:* The design placed fourth, in rendering is disappointing, but a careful study of the elevations and of the details convinced the Jury that the house would build better than is indicated by the perspective. The sleeping porch, always a difficult problem, is well managed. The arrangement of the servants' quarters on both the first and second floors is admirable, although the disposition of space on the first floor is not so happy as in many other cases, and the Jury felt that it was unnecessary to reduce the size of the den to permit a service passage from the pantry to the front entrance. The layout of the property is satisfactory and in general the scheme shows a careful consideration of all points and a just balance of the several factors.

MENTION DESIGNS

The Jury felt that the Mention designs were so nearly equal in merit that it would be undesirable to attempt to place them in order, and felt likewise that all show qualities of one kind or another of great interest, and that a failure to appreciate the relative importance of all factors was the sole reason for any one of them not having been ranked higher.

Design No. 115: The competitor submitting this drawing shows a knowledge of his architecture and a power in classic Colonial which is unequaled by any other contestant, and the Jury greatly regretted the fact that neither the first nor the second floor plan is up to the standard exhibited in so many of the other designs. This competitor has placed his house in the front of the lot with a garden at the rear, affording an outlook over the garden from only one of the principal rooms (the library, which is the smallest of the three), and on the second floor from the dressing rooms and bath rooms only. The plot plan in itself is one of the best submitted, and had it been completely revised so that the principal rooms could have faced both to the South and the garden, the design would unquestionably have been considered for one of the prizes. The division of the space in the second story into four small bedrooms of equal size is manifestly incorrect, and the balancing of a living room and dining room of equal size in the first story does not seem to the Jury proper or appropriate.

The Jury has gone thus far into the reasons for its refusal to give this drawing higher standing, because of its very great liking for the architecture of the building as a whole, and because of its regret that this should have been nullified by the facts as above stated.

Design No. 195: The architecture of this design especially impressed the Jury. They found practically nothing to criticise in the exterior excepting that the design shows a quality of stone rather than of wood. The plot plan is fair, but the forcing of the plan to meet the requirements of exterior is objectionable. The separation of the breakfast porch by the thinnest possible screen from a service porch opening on so formal a garden is not admired, nor is the division of space in the first story into a living room and a dining room of equal sizes considered good. The service part is well managed in the first story, but the Committee felt that the house demands a possible second servant's room, and did not feel that the main bedrooms are as good as is necessary for a house of this size.

The presentation of these drawings was most masterly, especially in the rendering of the elevations and perspective.

Design No. 44: In this house again the Jury found the elevation to be superior to other points. The quaintness and charm of the exterior were very cordially admired, although the North elevation shows a multiplicity of motives which is disturbing, and the head room in the bedroom No. 4, bath room and maid's room is entirely insufficient. The disposition of the house on the lot is only fairly satisfactory. The property has been deliberately cut in two, and while the treatment of the exterior is such as to permit of an amusing handling of the garden close to the building, the property as a whole has not been used to the fullest ad-

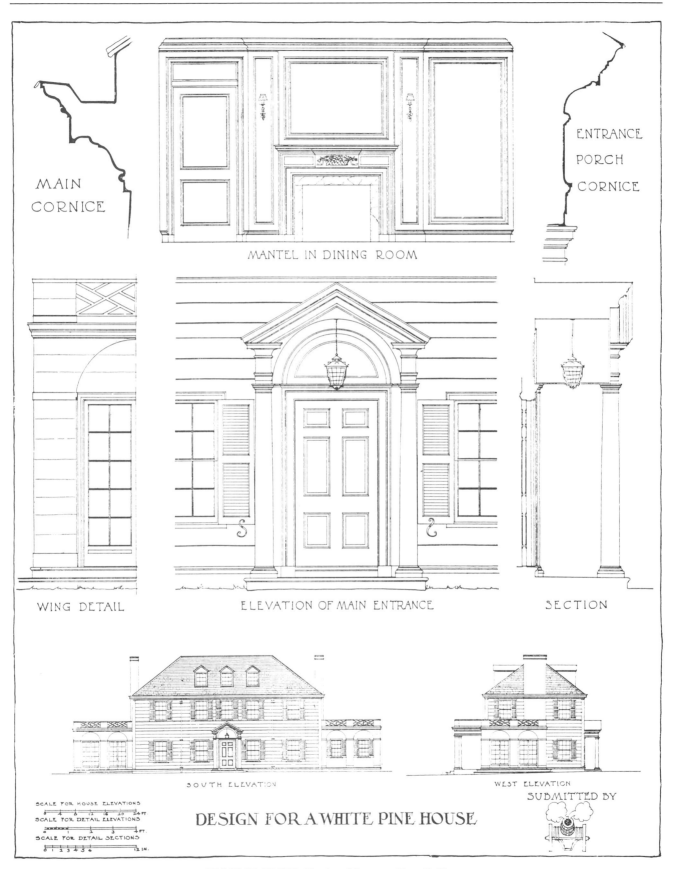

MAIN CORNICE

MANTEL IN DINING ROOM

ENTRANCE PORCH CORNICE

WING DETAIL

ELEVATION OF MAIN ENTRANCE

SECTION

SOUTH ELEVATION

WEST ELEVATION

SUBMITTED BY

SCALE FOR HOUSE ELEVATIONS

SCALE FOR DETAIL ELEVATIONS

SCALE FOR DETAIL SECTIONS

DESIGN FOR A WHITE PINE HOUSE

SECOND PRIZE, Design No. 224, Detail Sheet
Submitted by Jerauld Dahler, New York, New York

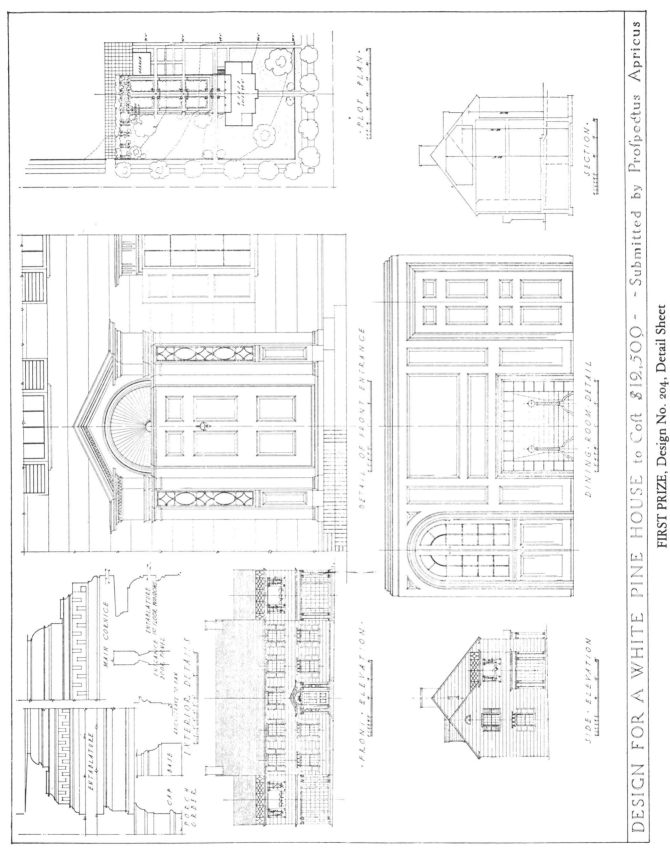

· PLOT · PLAN ·

· SECTION ·

DETAIL OF FRONT ENTRANCE

DINING · ROOM · DETAIL

MAIN CORNICE

ENTABLATURE

INSTANCE IN FLOOR PANEL

INSTANCE TO JAN

CAP

BASE

ENTABLATURE

PORCH
ORDER

INTERIOR DETAILS

· FRONT · ELEVATION ·

· SIDE · ELEVATION ·

DESIGN FOR A WHITE PINE HOUSE to Cost $12,500 ~ Submitted by Prospectus Apricus

FIRST PRIZE, Design No. 204, Detail Sheet
Submitted by Winchton L. Risley and James Perry Wilson, New York, New York

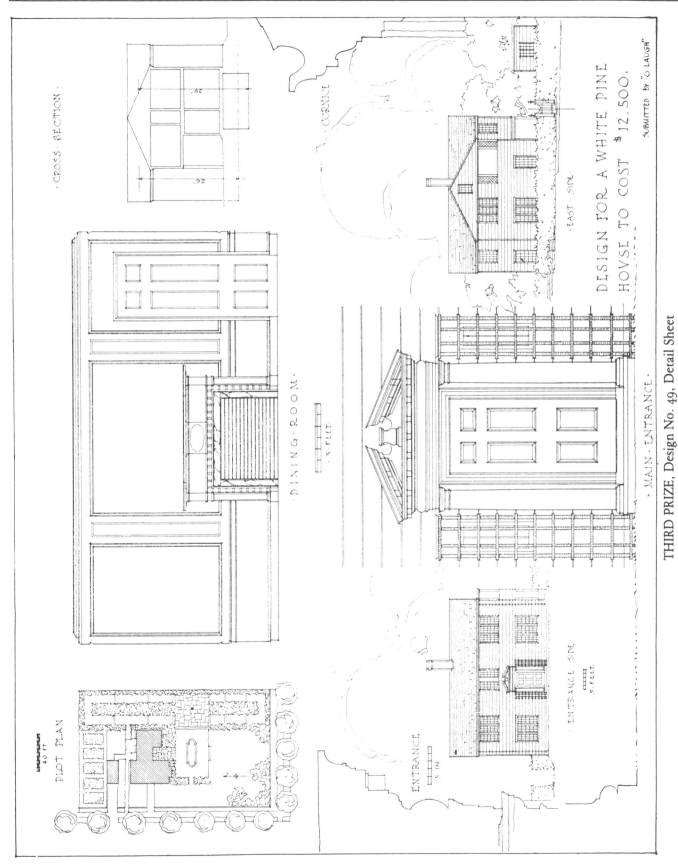

THIRD PRIZE, Design No. 49, Detail Sheet
Submitted by Olaf William Shelgren, Buffalo, New York

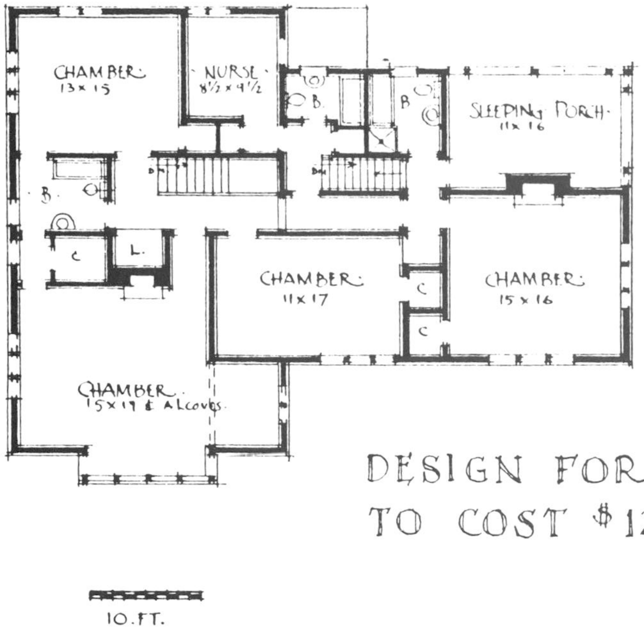
CHAMBER
13×15
NURSE
8½×9½
B.
B
SLEEPING PORCH
11×16
B.
C
L.
CHAMBER
11×17
C
C
CHAMBER
15×16
CHAMBER
15×19 & ALCOVES
10. FT.

·CVB

25 × 41 × 26(

31.5 × 27 × 29

2.5 × 12 × 23 (

5 × 8 × 16 ÷

TOTAL CV. F

DESIGN FOR A WHITE PINE
TO COST $12,500

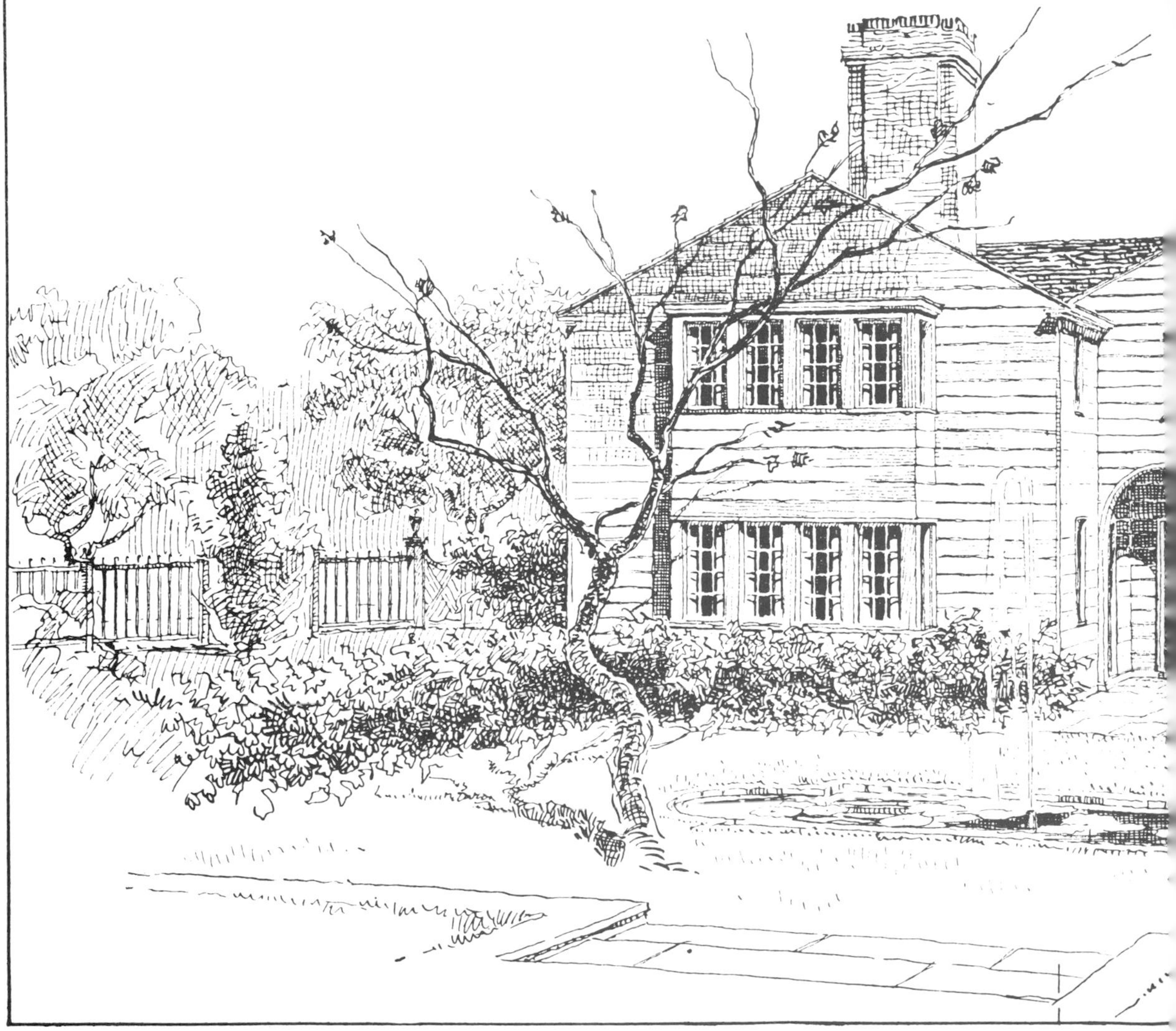

THIRD PRIZE

Submitted by Olaf William

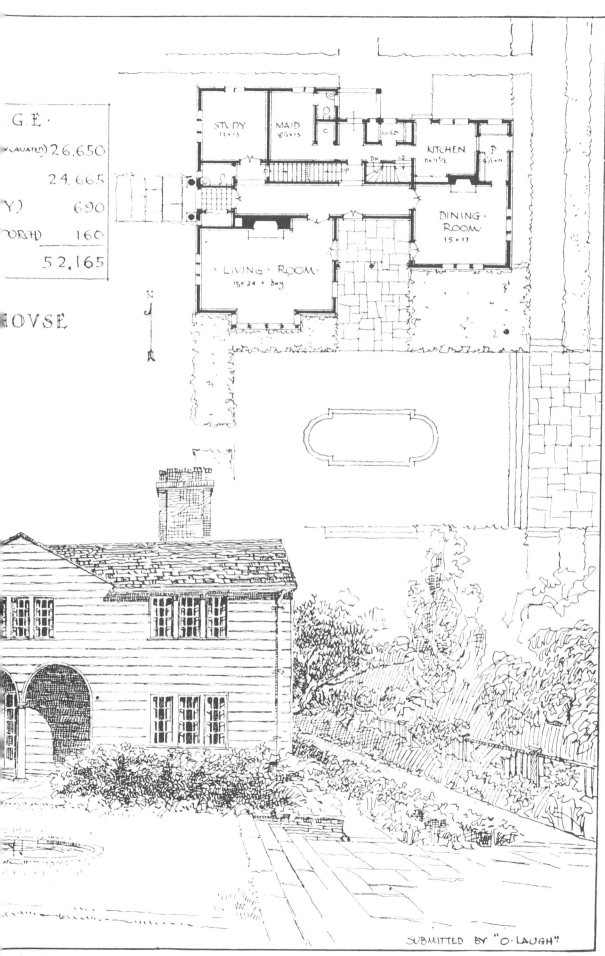

G.E.

(AVATED) 26.650

24.665

Y) 690

ORCH) 160

52.165

HOVSE

STVDY
12×13

MAID
8½×13

KITCHEN
11×11½

DINING·
ROOM·
15×17

LIVING·ROOM·
15×24 + bay

SUBMITTED BY "O·LAUGH"

Design No. 49
helgren, Buffalo, New York

vantage. The details throughout are admirable and would indicate that the house could be developed fully as well in reality as it appears in the perspective.

Design No. 226: The architecture of this house is of a character quite different from that of most of the drawings submitted and the effort made by the author to get away from the formal and stereotyped motives was appreciated and commended. The details of the building as well as its elevations were admired, with the exception of the treatment of the sleeping porch and the open porch below, which are, in the opinion of the Committee, quite too light and frail to be properly coördinated with the architecture of the balance of the building. The North elevation with the inadequate door and dissymmetrical treatment does not show the proper balance necessary to good design. The plot plan is good, but the location of the entrance door and path is not satisfactory, especially since the service yard is in full sight of a person entering the property.

Design No. 241: This design has an exterior architecture as pleasing as any in the competition, but the disposition of the house on the lot, while unusual, was considered by the Jury as not properly utilizing so limited a space, since the garden would necessarily be crowded and difficulties would arise in adjusting natural grades to the conditions indicated. The author has endeavored to include too many units in the plan, with consequent loss of space and loss of value in each. This applies equally to both floors. The single servant's room without a bath room is manifestly inadequate for a house of this type, nor is it possible to reach the attic in the manner indicated.

The things which especially pleased the Committee in this plan are the delightful architecture and the capable manner in which the most was made of details of a simple and admirable type.

Design No. 199: The architecture, both as indicated by the perspective of the garden side and by the elevations as shown on the detail sheet, is unusual, interesting and admirable. The treatment of the property is good, assuming that no vehicular entrance is necessary, which seemed to the Jury a fair assumption. The details, both as to exterior and interior, are excellent, and, except for what the Jury considered a very important feature, the outdoor sleeping accommodations, the plan is in many respects the best submitted. The Jury does not consider an upper deck proper outdoor sleeping accommodations, but otherwise the competitor has

fully recognized in plan the requirements for what was stated to be in the program "The average American family of taste and refinement."

The service portion is especially good, and one of the two maid's rooms is sufficiently large to accommodate two persons, a desirable feature not commonly found in the plans. The second floor has an excellent principal bedroom, two fair-sized bedrooms for children, and a good guest bedroom. The enlargement of the hall in front of the staircase in the second story relieves the house from any cramped appearance, and the locations of the bath rooms are good. The Jury liked the exterior, but especially commended the plan.

Design No. 194: The perspective shows a house of agreeable proportions and admirable shape, and had the competitor treated the rear of his building with the same restraint shown in the front he would have achieved a far more successful result. The porch at the rear of the living room and the garden porch should not, in the opinion of the Jury, have been added at all; they are obviously included to secure more space in the second story, which should have been done by better planning. The treatment of the sleeping porches is the best, both as to architecture and plan, which appears in the competition, and the Jury felt that the treatment of the sleeping porches indicated on these drawings is the correct solution of what has hitherto been a very difficult problem. Such porches are coming to be practically rooms with a large proportion of openings and a waterproof floor, and this competitor was one of the few who appreciated the fact.

The arrangement of the plot plan with the garage at the rear of the garden, and the suggestion of garden treatment, is admirable, while the use of the garage as a terminal feature is excellent. The plan of the drive is bad—it unnecessarily cuts up the property on all sides, and would make dust and noise in the dining room, breakfast room and living room.

Design No. 193: The plot plan of this house shows a very interesting utilization of the grade conditions, which permit the competitor to depress his entrance drive so that the house may be entered from vehicles under cover in the rear without interfering with the vista across the lawn. Possibly a reception room in the basement might have improved this feature. The main floor plan is good, the service portion well developed, and the principal rooms of agreeable character. In spite of the irregular form of the first floor plan it is not the opinion of the Jury that the effect would be disagreeable. The exterior is in general good, with the exception of the treatment of the large window on the staircase with a key block of disproportionate scale. The side and front elevations are good, especially with reference to the sleeping porches, and the detail of the exterior is well managed. The detail of the dining room is not considered to be in harmony with the character of the building and is exceedingly disappointing to the Committee.

The Jury extends to the contestants in the White Pine Architectural Competition its sincere congratulations upon the high architectural standard attained by the majority of the designs. Many of the schemes not awarded either Prize or Mention are sufficiently interesting

to warrant study. It is, therefore, gratifying to learn that a selection of these is to be published in *The Architectural Review* in a late fall number.

As a whole the Competition brought forth a collection of drawings which will make an interesting contribution to the general subject of planning and designing small wood houses.

AYMAR EMBURY II
WILSON EYRE
CHARLES BARTON KEEN   *Jury*
JOHN RUSSELL POPE   *of*
ALEXANDER B. TROWBRIDGE   *Award*

"PRESIDENT'S HOUSE" AT WHITE SULPHUR SPRINGS, WEST VIRGINIA

This house was used by President Madison during his visits to White Sulphur Springs. Practically all the old Southern watering-places were built in this manner, the occasional two-story building connected by long one-story ranges, with a piazza so constructed that one could be always under cover. It was, perhaps, from these groups that Jefferson derived his scheme for the University of Virginia. The ranges were never more than one room deep, so that through ventilation was insured, and most of the rooms were not connected, family accommodations being provided by two-story buildings, or by small detached one-story buildings containing three or four small rooms side by side. The dining-room and recreation rooms were in the central building. The architectural interest of what is known to most people as purely a pleasure resort led to the selection of White Sulphur Springs for the Judgment, and not the least pleasing function of the Jury was the examination of this old work, dating as it does from 1760 to 1820, and including many varieties of early wooden architecture.

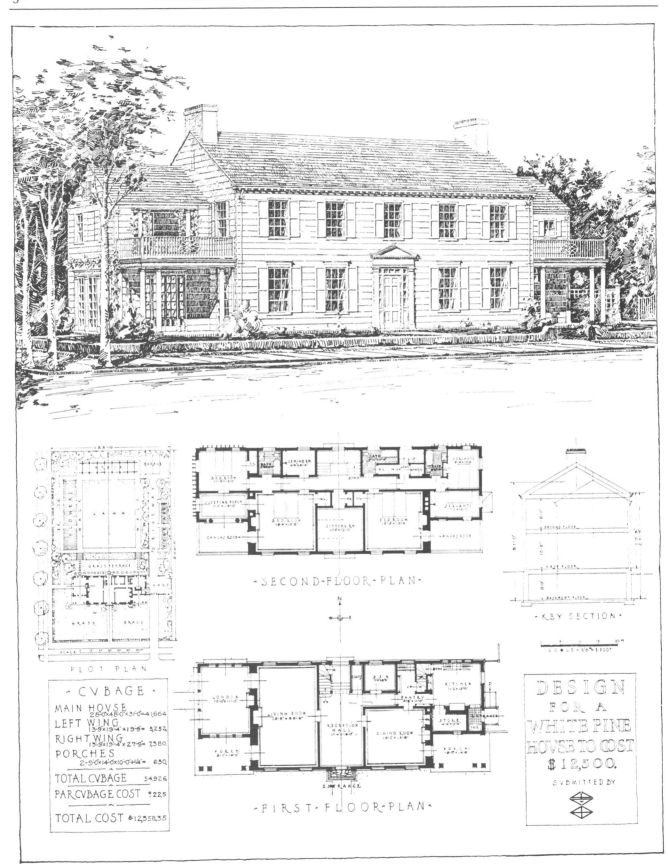

FOURTH PRIZE, Design No. 86
Submitted by Sotaro Y. Ohta, New York, New York

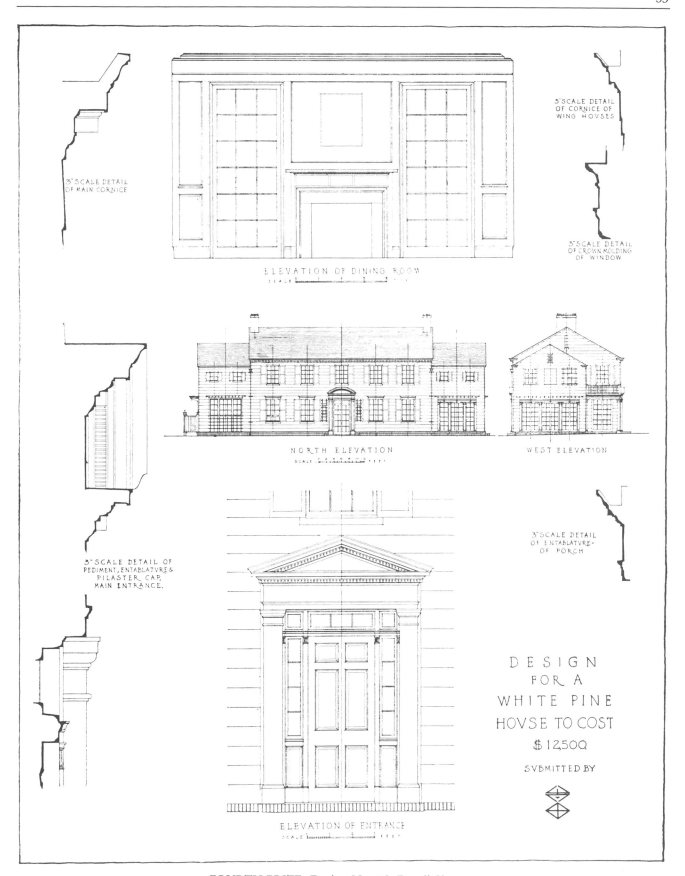

3"SCALE DETAIL OF MAIN CORNICE

3"SCALE DETAIL OF CORNICE OF WING HOVSES

3"SCALE DETAIL OF CROWN MOLDING OF WINDOW

ELEVATION OF DINING ROOM
SCALE

NORTH ELEVATION
SCALE

WEST ELEVATION

3"SCALE DETAIL OF PEDIMENT, ENTABLATVRE & PILASTER CAP, MAIN ENTRANCE.

3"SCALE DETAIL OF ENTABLATVRE OF PORCH

DESIGN FOR A WHITE PINE HOVSE TO COST $12,500

SVBMITTED BY

ELEVATION OF ENTRANCE
SCALE

FOURTH PRIZE, Design No. 86, Detail Sheet
Submitted by Sotaro Y. Ohta, New York, New York

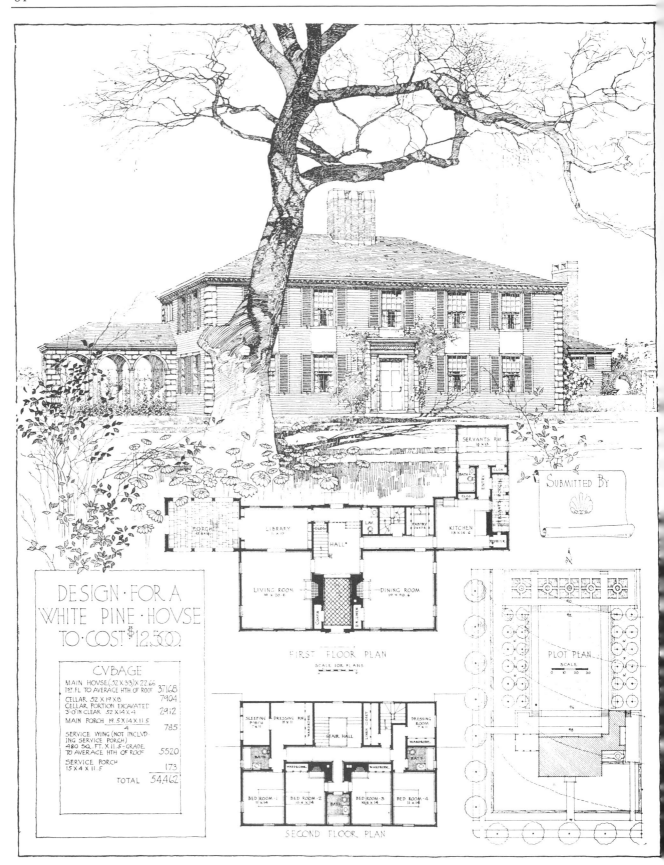

MENTION, Design No. 115
Submitted by Richard M. Powers, Boston, Massachusetts

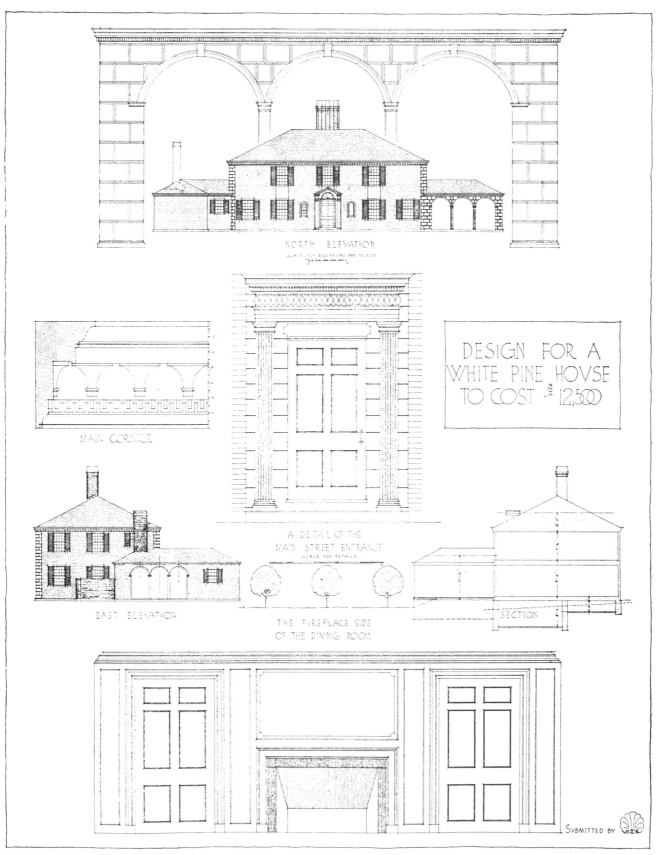

NORTH ELEVATION

MAIN CORNICE

DESIGN FOR A
WHITE PINE HOVSE
TO COST $12,500

A DETAIL OF THE
MAIN STREET ENTRANCE

EAST ELEVATION

THE FIREPLACE SIDE
OF THE DINING ROOM

SECTION

SVBMITTED BY

MENTION, Design No. 115, Detail Sheet
Submitted by Richard M. Powers, Boston, Massachusetts

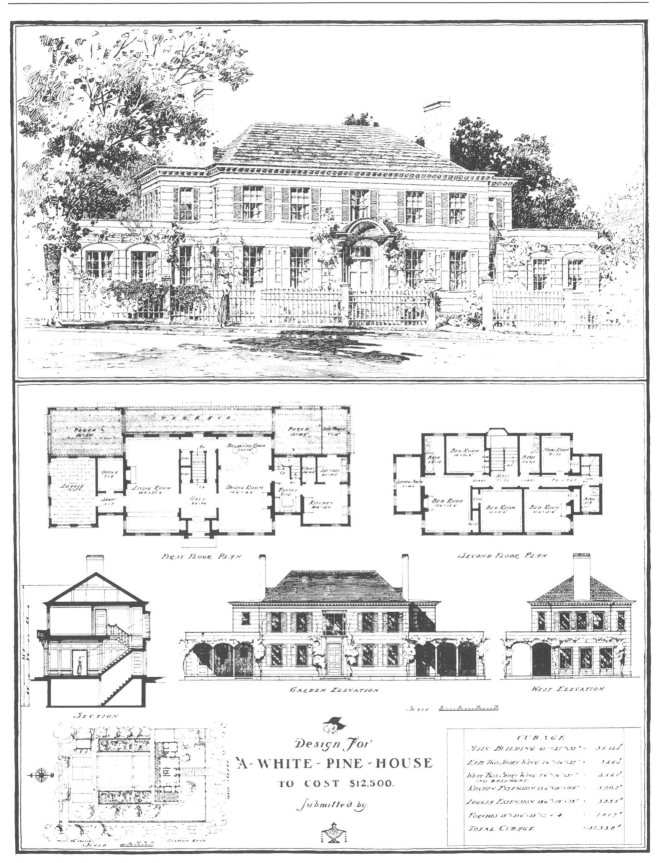

MENTION, Design No. 195
Submitted by Louis J. Farmer, New York, New York

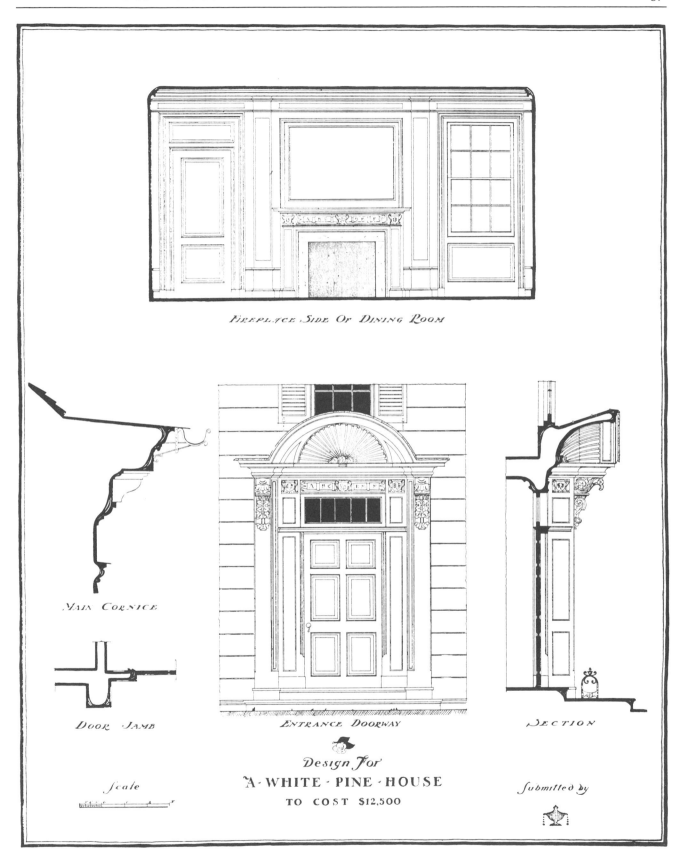

FIREPLACE SIDE OF DINING ROOM

MAIN CORNICE

DOOR JAMB

ENTRANCE DOORWAY

SECTION

Design for
A · WHITE · PINE · HOUSE
TO COST $12,500

Scale

Submitted by

MENTION, Design No. 195, Detail Sheet
Submitted by Louis J. Farmer, New York, New York

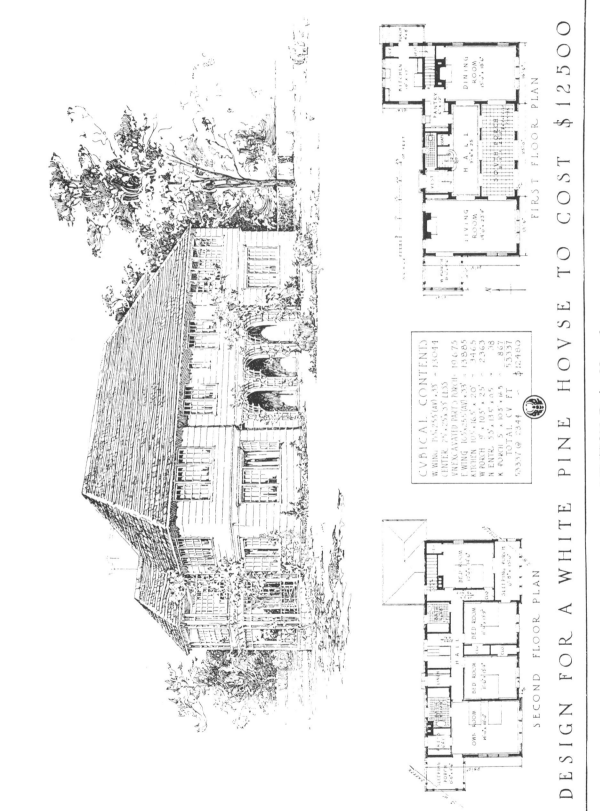

DESIGN FOR A WHITE PINE HOUSE TO COST $12500

MENTION, Design No. 226
Submitted by Chester B. Price, New York, New York

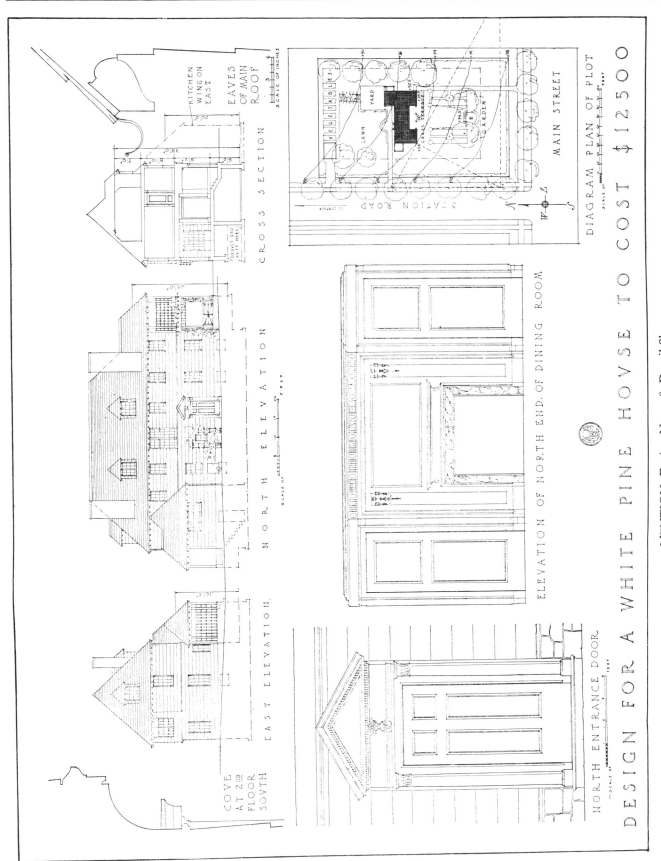

DESIGN FOR A WHITE PINE HOVSE TO COST $12500

MENTION, Design No. 226, Detail Sheet
Submitted by Chester B. Price, New York, New York

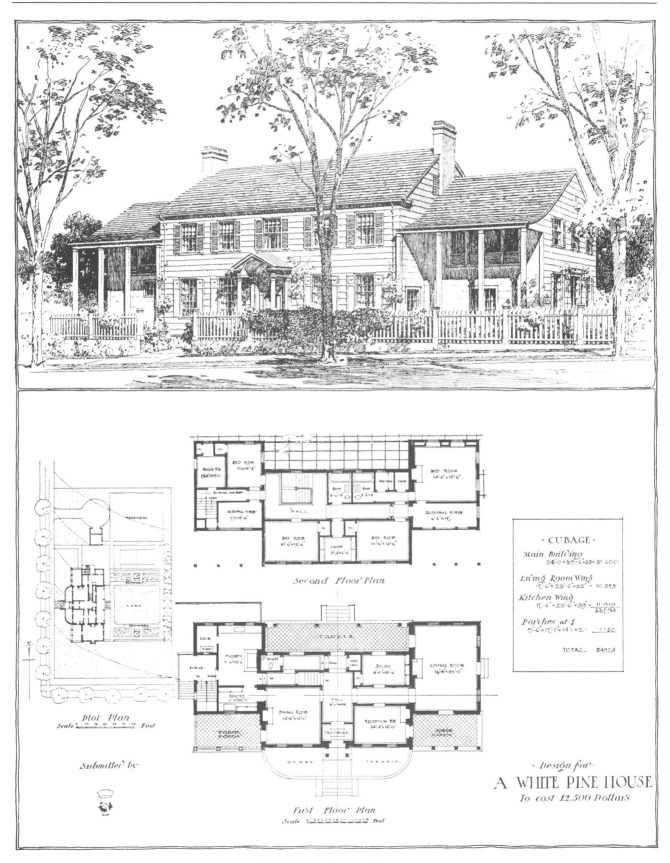

MENTION, Design No. 241
Submitted by Daniel Neilniger, New York, New York

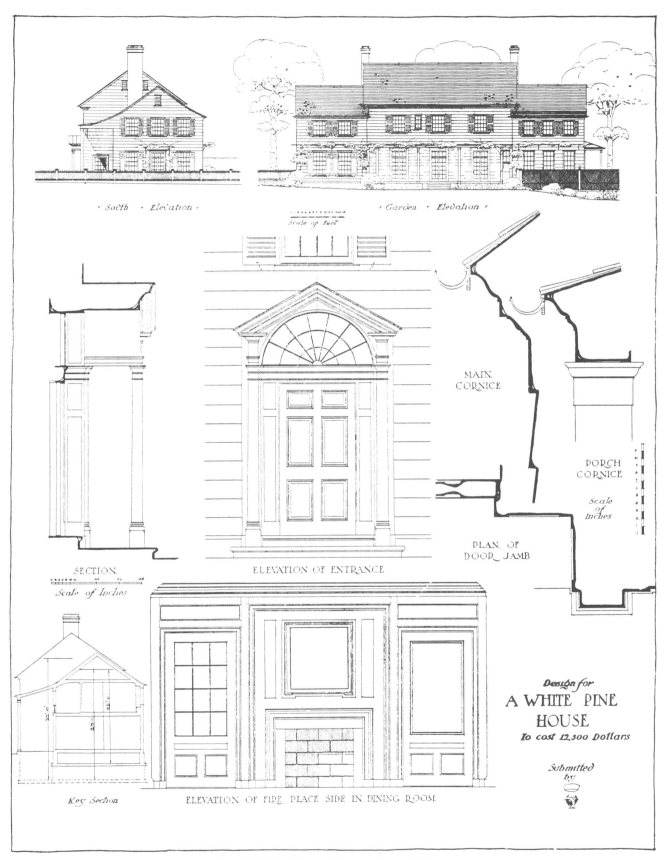

· South · Elevation ·

· Garden · Elevation ·

Scale of feet

MAIN
CORNICE

PORCH
CORNICE

Scale
of
Inches

PLAN OF
DOOR JAMB

SECTION

Scale of Inches

ELEVATION OF ENTRANCE

Design for
A WHITE PINE
HOUSE
To cost 12,500 Dollars

Submitted
by

Key Section

ELEVATION OF FIRE PLACE SIDE IN DINING ROOM

MENTION, Design No. 241, Detail Sheet
Submitted by Daniel Neilniger, New York, New York

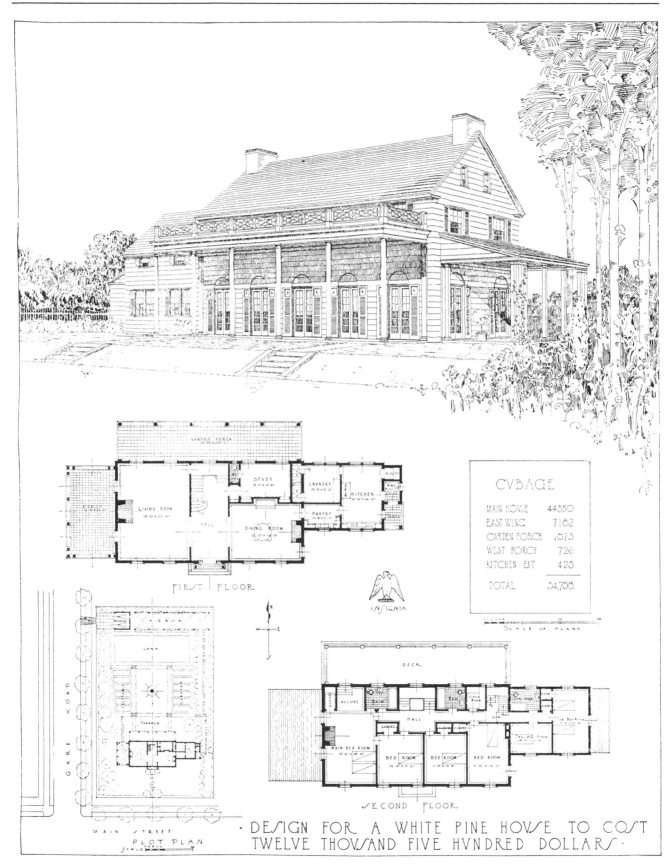

CVBAGE

MAIN HOVSE	44550
EAST WING	7182
GARDEN PORCH	1875
WEST PORCH	728
KITCHEN EXT	425
TOTAL	54,755.

FIRST FLOOR

PLOT PLAN

SECOND FLOOR

· DESIGN FOR A WHITE PINE HOVSE TO COST
TWELVE THOVSAND FIVE HVNDRED DOLLARS·

MENTION, Design No. 199
Submitted by Satterlee & Boyd, New York, New York

SOUTH ELEVATION

EAST ELEVATION

DETAIL OF CORNICE

SCALE OF DETAILS

MAIN ENTRANCE DOOR

SCALE

DETAIL OF COLVMN

EAST END OF DINING ROOM

SCALE

SECTION

SCALE OF ELEVATIONS AND SECTION

INSIGNIA

·DESIGN FOR A WHITE PINE HOVSE TO COST
TWELVE THOVSAND FIVE HVNDRED DOLLARS·

MENTION, Design No. 199, Detail Sheet
Submitted by Satterlee & Boyd, New York, New York

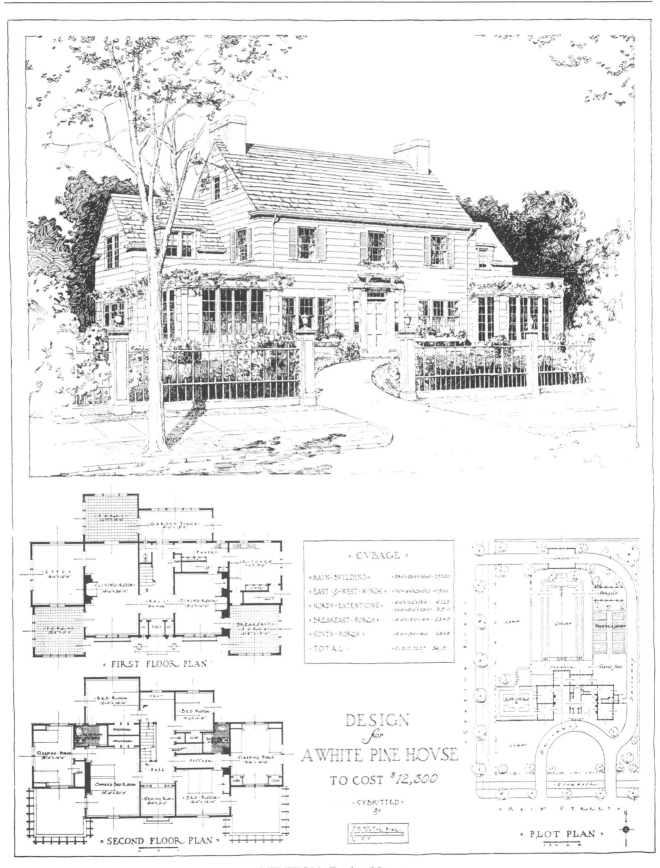

MENTION, Design No. 194
Submitted by Benj. Schreyer, New York, New York

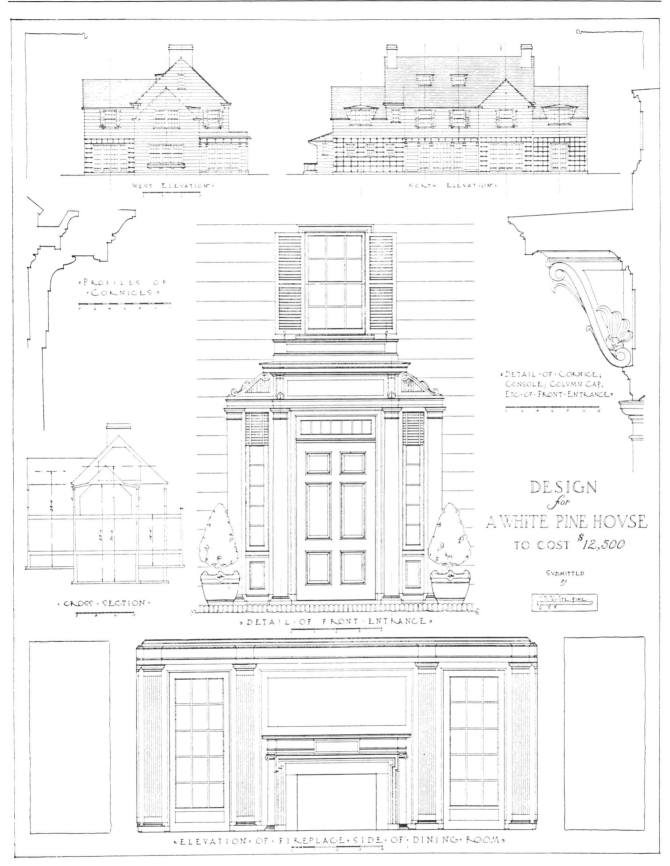

· WEST · ELEVATION ·

· NORTH · ELEVATION ·

· PROFILES · OF · CORNICES ·

· DETAIL · OF · CORNICE ·
CONSOLE · COLVMN · CAP ·
ETC · OF · FRONT · ENTRANCE ·

· CROSS · SECTION ·

· DETAIL · OF · FRONT · ENTRANCE ·

DESIGN
for
A WHITE PINE HOVSE
TO COST $12,500

SVBMITTED
by

· ELEVATION · OF · FIREPLACE · SIDE · OF · DINING · ROOM ·

MENTION, Design No. 194, Detail Sheet
Submitted by Benj. Schreyer, New York, New York

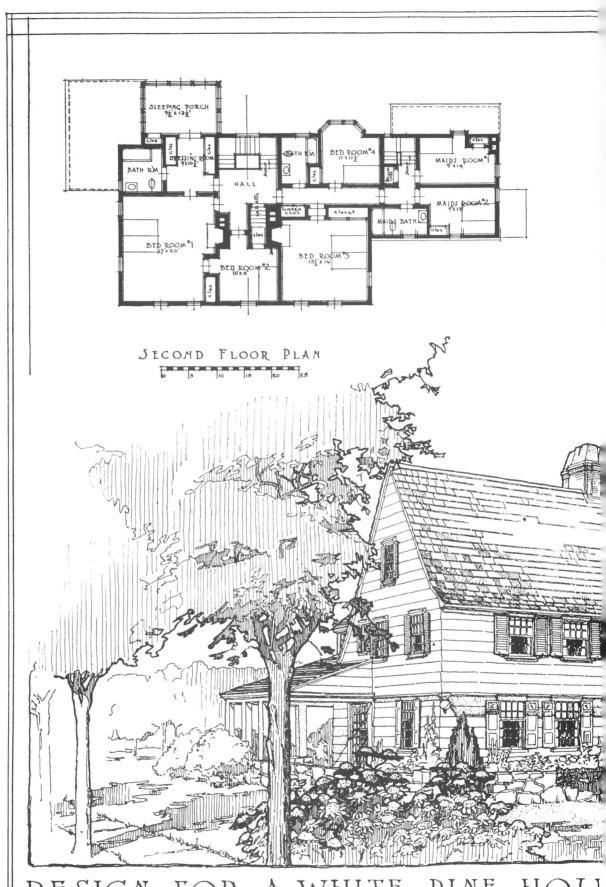

SECOND FLOOR PLAN

SLEEPING PORCH
9½' x 13½'

Clos

DRESSING ROOM
9'x10½'

Clos

BATH R'M

HALL

BATH R'M

BED ROOM #4
11'x11½'

MAIDS ROOM #1
9'x14'

MAIDS ROOM #2
9'x12'

MAIDS BATH

Clos

BED ROOM #1
17'x20'

LINEN CLOS

Clos

CLOSET

BED ROOM #2
10'x11'

BED ROOM #3
15½'x16'

Clos

DESIGN FOR A WHITE PINE HOU

MENTION

Submitted by Stanley B.

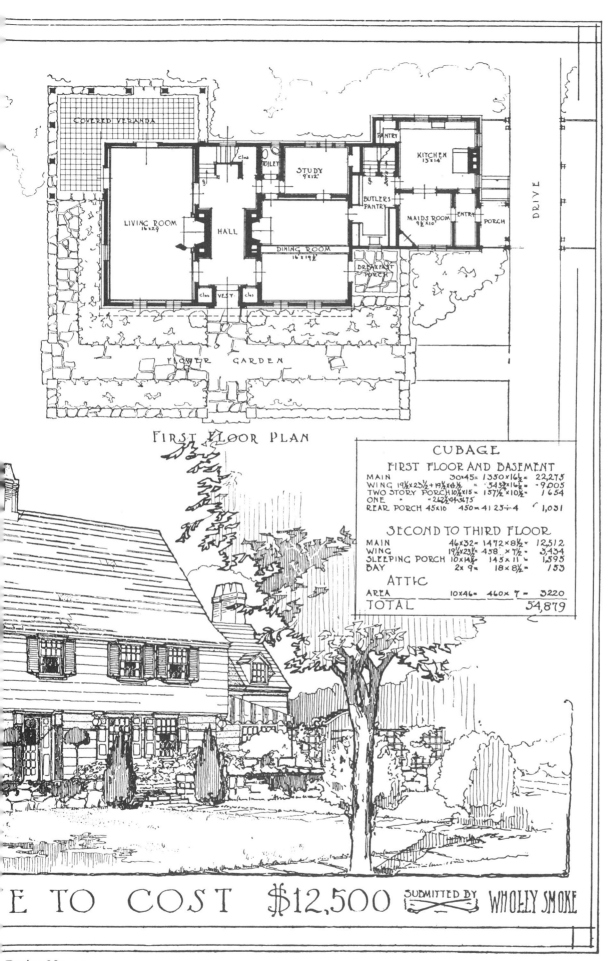

FIRST FLOOR PLAN

Within plan labels:
COVERED VERANDA
LIVING ROOM 16×29
HALL
STUDY 9'×12'
DINING ROOM 16'×19½'
PANTRY
KITCHEN 13×14'
BUTLERS PANTRY
MAIDS ROOM 9½×10'
ENTRY
PORCH
BREAKFAST PORCH
TOILET
clos
VEST·
DRIVE
FLOWER GARDEN

CUBAGE

FIRST FLOOR AND BASEMENT

MAIN	30×45= 1350×16½=	22,275
WING 19½×23½ + 19½×8½	= 543×16½=	9,005
TWO STORY PORCH 10½×15=	157½×10½=	1,654
ONE " = 262½×4=3,675		
REAR PORCH 45×10 450= 4125÷4		1,031

SECOND TO THIRD FLOOR

MAIN	46×32= 1472×8½=	12,512
WING	19½×23½= 458 ×7½=	3,434
SLEEPING PORCH 10×14½= 145×11=		1,595
BAY	2×9= 18×8½=	153

ATTIC

AREA	10×46= 460× 7 =	3,220
TOTAL		54,879

E TO COST $12,500   SUBMITTED BY WHOLLY SMOKE

Design No. 44
Parker, Boston, Massachusetts

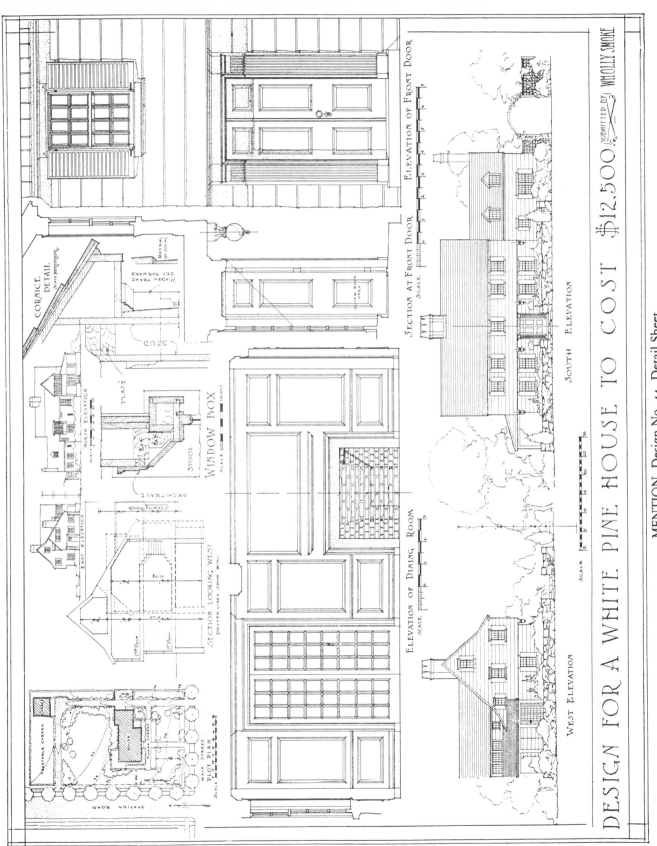

DESIGN FOR A WHITE PINE HOUSE TO COST $12,500. SUBMITTED BY WHOLLY SMOKE

MENTION, Design No. 44, Detail Sheet
Submitted by Stanley B. Parker, Boston, Massachusetts

A House for the Vacation Season

Report of the Jury of Award
Given May 18 and 19, 1918
Originally published in 1918 as White Pine Monograph
Volume IV, Number 4

CUBAGE

MAIN HOUSE	53′×21′×20′-6″ =	22816
MAIN PORCH	53′×10′-6″×18′-6″ ÷ 3 =	3434
BILLIARD RM WING	24′×14′×11′ =	3696
SERVICE WING	50′×14′×11′ =	7700
BAY IN LIVING RM	6′×1′-6″×8′-6″ =	77
	TOTAL	37723

DIMENSIONS FOR LENGTH OF WINGS ARE MEASURED ON THE CENTER LINE, TO POINT OF INTERSECTION WITH MAIN HOUSE.

DESIGN for A WHITE PINE HOUSE for THE VACATION SEASON. SUBMITTED BY

PLOT PLAN
Scale

SECOND FLOOR PLAN

FIRST FLOOR PLAN

SCALE FOR PLANS

FIRST PRIZE, Design No. 161
Submitted by Richard M. Powers, Boston, Massachusetts

A HOUSE FOR THE VACATION SEASON

Report of the Jury of Award of the Third Annual
White Pine Architectural Competition

Judged at the Biltmore, New York, NY, May 18 and 19, 1918

THE PROBLEM: "Here is a survey I have had made of my plot of land by the lake, on which I want to build a White Pine house, for use during the six open months of the year. With the information which I shall give you, you will not need to visit the property. The lake runs north and south. The shore is hilly and fairly well wooded, also somewhat rocky, and you will see that my own plot has those characteristics. My site is on the east side near the north end, and contains a blunt point from which a view is obtained looking southwest, down the lake for several miles; the prevailing breeze is from that direction. The scenery across the lake is also of interest. One approach is by boat, and you will see indicated the place where I have collected stone for a dock foundation, and you may have in mind the general appearance of a boat-house to be built later, to contain a motor-boat, and to have a landing for row-boats, with perhaps a small tea-house or lookout shelter connected with it. This is not to be built now, and I merely mention it because of its prominent position on the property. Just back of my site is a road which runs through a typical American community, and I wish my house to be appropriate to that village, and not to partake too much of the cabin or so-called bungalow design from the mere circumstance that it is on the lake.

"I do not want to spend more than $5000 for the house. If the size and number of rooms which I consider necessary indicate a larger house than it is possible to build for that amount *under normal building conditions*, you may suggest dual use of certain of the rooms. I might say, however, that Mr. Jones told me that his house, built in the neighborhood of my site, contains 38,000 cubic feet and cost approximately what I have to spend.

"I need a good-sized living-room not smaller than 15′×24′, with a fireplace large enough for big logs, and a dining-room, connecting, if possible, with a porch where meals could be served. I would also like to have a small room for books, guns, fishing tackle, etc. If the contour of the land where you suggest placing the house will permit of a room for billiards, etc., without too much excavation, I would like it. I do not object to having two or more levels in the floors.

"My family consists of my wife, two children, a boy (fourteen) and a girl (ten), and myself. We are seldom without guests, and plan to keep 'open house,' so we would like to have five bedrooms, which may be small if well ventilated, and at least two bathrooms. Also additional accommodations for servants. We would have no objection to having sleeping quarters on the ground floor. A sleeping porch is essential. The service portion should have a kitchen, either a porch or a small sitting-room, and of course plenty of closet room.

"Although the house will be used during the open months, some arrangements for heating must be made— either sufficient open fireplaces or space provided for a small heating apparatus.

"The outside finish of the house is to be of White Pine; everything else I leave to you. By outside finish I mean siding and corner boards; window sash, frames and casings; outside doors, door frames and casings; outside blinds; all exposed porch and balcony lumber; cornice boards, brackets, ornaments and mouldings, etc., *not* including shingles. Plastering is not necessary in all the rooms and we shall attend to the wall covering ourselves.

"I have marked the place where a foundation for a garage has been started, but that will not be completed now. It may, however, have some bearing on the entrance from the road."

THE series of competitions instituted by the WHITE PINE ARCHITECTURAL MONOGRAPHS, while frankly part of a campaign to popularize the use of white pine, has nevertheless the ulterior and more altruistic objects of raising the standard of domestic architecture; of discovering and encouraging new talent, and of providing for the prospective house builder a point of departure, at least, in his enterprise. The whole thing is part of a larger movement on the part of the manufacturers and the building trades generally,—a movement which is a hopeful sign of the times, for it is *educative* in the broadest sense of the word.

The third Annual Architectural Competition elicited two hundred and four sets of drawings. The programme called for a different type of house from those previously demanded, and the general failure on the part of most of the competitors to perceive this is the outstanding feature of the competition. The solutions, taken as a whole, indicate an almost painful absence of direct, synthetic, logical thought. The competitors showed a disposition to evade the main issues and stress things non-essential; they overtaxed their fingers and under-exerted their brains; in general, they failed in honesty. Nevertheless, out of so many solutions, it was possible to select a sufficient number to justify the White Pine Bureau in its admirable effort.

As in all such competitions, there was a wide diversity of conceptions and style, and the committee endeavored to show such catholicity of taste as should do justice to these divergent views. It was forced to exclude some sincere and thoughtful efforts on account of a perhaps small but significant indication of a blind spot in the brain, as it was also forced to admit certain others in spite of evident obliquities of intellectual vision. The judges persisted at their task until all were in substantial agreement, their only serious differences of opinion being the result of a difference of point of view as to what particular aspect of the whole matter should be emphasized.

THE FIRST PRIZE of $750 was awarded to Design No. 161, by Richard M. Powers, with full knowledge that the decision would, perhaps, be criticized as having been swayed by the really wonderful adroitness and æsthetic feeling manifest in the rendering. The judges feel, however, that their collective conscience is clear of this charge, because, while the rendering is undeniably beautiful, it is also undeniably true. The house itself is simple, direct and logical. It has an unmistakable wood character, it occupies its point of land as though it had a right there. Moreover, it is clear from the plan and from the scale elevations that the other views would be quite as satisfactory as the particular one chosen, a thing which can be said of very few of the designs submitted. The author has shown an indifference, almost amounting to perversity, for certain economical considerations with regard to the number and construction of the chimneys, and this almost lost him his chance of a prize. His effort to get fireplaces in every bedroom, a thing not called for, expected, or even desired, has led him into structural complications of a wholly unnecessary kind; the judges took the view that in actual execution adjustments and eliminations could be made which would leave the general conception intact. This solution exhibits a high order of ability in planning, designing and rendering. The presentation calls for

the very highest commendation. It is rare that artistic skill of such a quality is combined with such practical good sense as is shown by the floor plans. Most of the practical solutions were painfully deficient in any sense of purely æsthetic values, while the "snappy" drawings too often served only as cloaks for flagrant architectural sins.

THE SECOND PRIZE of $400 was awarded to Design No. 132, by Otto Faelten and Donald Robb. This design composes charmingly and fits the site to admiration. It has just the right character, being neither too rustic nor too formal to comply with the conditions in this respect. The plan is excellent, although it is of a type which would lend itself more naturally to a programme less restricted in the matter of expenditure. Compressed within the limits of the cubage called for, it is too contracted, particularly in its service part. The absorption of the authors in the purely æsthetic aspect of the problem has led them to sacrifice practicality and sound construction here and there. The end gable of the main roof has no sufficient support; the floors of the open sleeping porches coming over the dining room and living room are bad, as is the flat roof on the long dormer. These are matters of which the artistic temperament is always highly impatient, but they are of the greatest moment to people who live in the house. Many of the competitors showed a disposition to sin flagrantly in similar directions. They did not attack their problem honestly and directly, but approached it from the point of view of the *camoufleur* intent upon deceptions.

THE THIRD PRIZE of $250 was awarded to Design No. 23, by Olaf Shelgren. The author of this design did not yield to the temptation to be picturesque, and therefore avoided many of its pitfalls. The result is a design somewhat bleak and bare, but admirably honest and straightforward. This particular design proved a storm center in the deliberations of the committee, one member contending that it was the only solution which deserved any prize at all, on the ground that none of the others could be built for $5000. An analysis of the programme, however, reveals the fact that any plan which comes within the required cubage is eligible for a prize, and that while the economic aspect of the whole matter is never to be lost sight of, it is, after all, only one of several factors. In the last analysis it is perhaps the judges' "estimate of the contestant's real ability" which scores most heavily. The Third Prize design stands high on the first two counts insisted upon in the programme: "The ingenuity shown in the development of the plans to meet

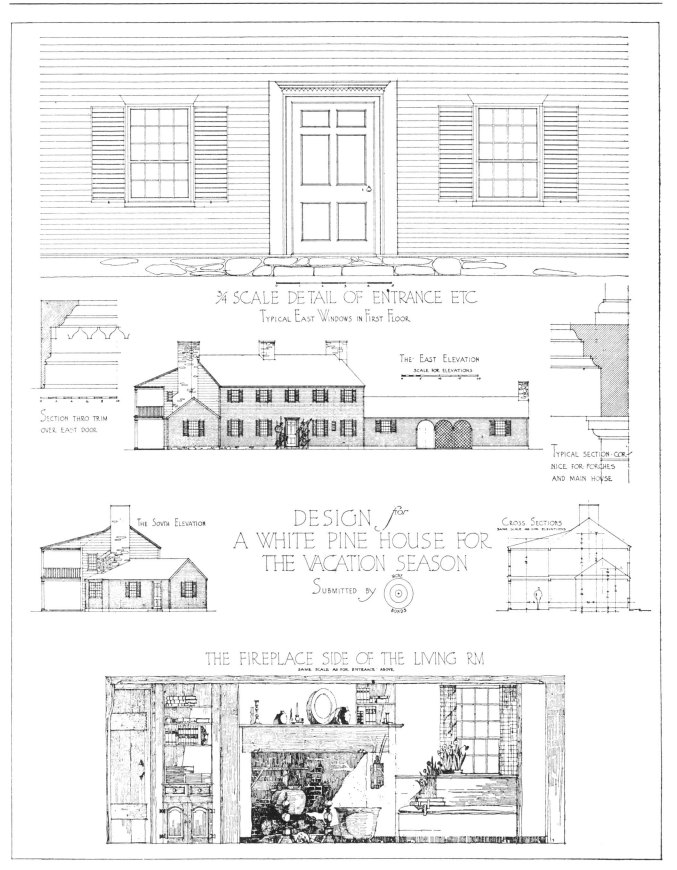

¾ SCALE DETAIL OF ENTRANCE ETC
Typical East Windows in First Floor

THE EAST ELEVATION
SCALE FOR ELEVATIONS

Section thro trim
over East door

Typical section cor-
nice for porches
and main house

THE SOUTH ELEVATION

DESIGN for
A WHITE PINE HOUSE FOR
THE VACATION SEASON
Submitted by

Cross Sections
SAME SCALE AS FOR ELEVATIONS

THE FIREPLACE SIDE OF THE LIVING RM
SAME SCALE AS FOR ENTRANCE ABOVE

FIRST PRIZE, Design No. 161, Detail Sheet
Submitted by Richard M. Powers, Boston, Massachusetts

the client's needs as he has stated them," and "The fitness of the design to express the wood-built house." In meeting the third condition it is less successful, for it has no really vital relation to the given site, of which the perspective gives no suggestion. The recessed piazza with the overhang supported only on slender posts would be unhappy in execution,—almost like a mouth with a missing tooth. The sleeping porch is not expressed on the exterior with sufficient frankness. It would have been better to have made a single feature of the two superimposed porches. The roof is admirably simple and the single chimney a great economical advantage. The honesty of the whole thing, and its respect for the client's interest and wishes, are in sharp and pleasing contrast with the bulk of the solutions submitted. The plan is compact and well arranged, though the maids' rooms are too small, even for a small house.

THE FOURTH PRIZE of $100 was awarded to Design No. 100, by Russell Barr Williamson. This is frankly of that Western school of which Mr. Frank Lloyd Wright is the most popular exponent, and Mr. Louis Sullivan the originator. This type of house, though somewhat *outré* to Eastern eyes, has distinct merits, both from the point of view of practicality and picturesqueness. It does not deserve all of the cheap jokes passed upon it by its detractors. People who live in these houses insist that they do *not* feel as though they were living in a sleeping-car. If we do not want the architectural tree to die of dry-rot, we should welcome these alien grafts, however wild and wanton their growth or however strange their bloom. This Fourth Prize house fits its site to admiration. The plan is distinctly good, the occupants would have, in Irvin Cobb's immortal phrase, "no more privacy than a goldfish," but that is only our happy American way of living openly. Let us be glad that we have so little to conceal. The house suggests all kinds of profound readjustments—in clothes, in furniture and other human accessories—but the committee, with every disposition to change their psychology imaginatively in order to be at home in such a house, could not bring themselves to the point of desiring to sit in front of the living room fireplace.

MENTION DESIGNS

THE Mention designs naturally consist of such as failed, for one reason or another, to get into the winning class. They had their individual advocates on the committee, who one by one were overruled. The following commentary is based upon no order of precedence of one over another:

No. 4, submitted by E. J. Maier and T. E. King, has a charm and originality not easily to be denied. It seems to be in sympathy, however, with a different sort of landscape than the one prescribed. It is too mannered for a vacation house on such a rugged site. The plan, while possessing admirable and unusual features, has grave faults. It would have been better to have thrown the living room and the loggia together. The dormers in the wing are too small, both from an æsthetic and from a practical point of view. The sleeping porch should be accessible from the hall, or, at any rate, from the largest bedroom. The separation of the guests' bedrooms from those of the family is the finest feature of the plan. The rendering deserves especial commendation, even in a competition in which the standard in this particular is extraordinarily high. It was the often-expressed regret of the judges that some of the thought and skill which went into the presentation had not been directed toward the more important matters of arrangement and design.

No. 86, submitted by Paul R. Williams, shows a good grasp of the elements of the problem. It fits the site charmingly, is neither too free nor too formal, but the Palladian feature of the dining porch and the most unhappy dormers of the roof impair the beauty and unity of an otherwise interesting design.

No. 84, submitted by Jerauld Dahler, shows a nice feeling for the essentials of a design, but is somewhat too symmetrical and formal to conform to the spirit of the place. It is urban in feeling and would look better on a level site—as shown—than on the slope of a hill. The author has overstressed that part of the programme which suggests that the design be appropriate to a village as well as to the country. In plan the floor of the sleeping balcony, coming as it does over the living room, shows a disregard for the fundamentals of direct and sound construction in this type of a house.

No. 112, submitted by Antonio di Nardo, exceeds the cubage on a careful recomputation, and according to the terms of the programme should therefore receive no consideration whatever, but the design, plan and presentation are all so good that it forced itself upon the consideration of the judges with a power which could not be denied. In a spirit of regret, but in fairness to the other competitors, the judges cannot give it anything more than this passing word of praise.

No. 118, submitted by T. C. Pomphrey and W. R. Ralston, is interesting and important chiefly on account of its authors' departure from the other contestants in the matter of location. The house is placed far down the hill; in fact, on the beach. This undoubtedly has its advantages, which are made the most of, but such a location would involve expensive and unnecessary fills on the shore side, or else grades too steep to be practical. The two covered porches divide the design unpleasantly and possess no outweighing advantage.

No. 124, submitted by Milton Rogers Williams, also exceeds the cubage, but the judges on that account could not deprive the other competitors of such an admirable example of beauty and restraint as this design shows. Neither No. 112 nor No. 124 exhibit any particular regard for the peculiarities of the site.

No. 165, submitted by L. E. Welsh and J. F. Yewell, makes a truly beautiful picture, but there are grave faults in it, when carefully considered with regard to construction and livableness. The sleeping porch is—to put it brutally—absurd from a practical standpoint. One would get more air and light in any of the bedrooms than in such a sleeping porch. The weight of the second story rear wall and of the main roof come directly upon the ceilings of the hall and gun room. Structural difficulties of this sort can of course be dealt with, but where they are incurred for the sake of mere picturesqueness, they cannot be justified.

No. 167, submitted by J. H. Phillips, is seductively simple and picturesque in the perspective, but the plan has been contorted and the other elevations show that the author had in mind the winning of the competition on these points at the sacrifice of other considerations. The roof lines of the rear are complicated to a degree and in certain respects the plan, the elevations and the section fail to correspond.

ALTHOUGH the duties of the jury cease at this point, there remain a few of the designs relegated to the discard, which, by reason of some special excellence, plead for a word in passing.

No. 3, submitted by Hubert G. Ripley, is wonderfully presented, but its architecture is too pretentious to conform to the spirit of the programme. No. 154, submitted by Porter W. Scott, would have been better if the author had frankly abandoned every attempt at "constructed architecture" in the porches and let the simple spirit of the rest of the design have its way there as well. He has failed to reconcile convincingly these two elements in his design. The rendering of Nos. 3 and 154 are among the best submitted. No. 127, submitted by J. T. Thomson and J. P. Wilson, is in this particular the most remarkable submitted, with the exception of the First Prize design. It owes so much of its appeal to its elaborate system of stone walls, steps and gardens—is, in fact, so largely a thing of masonry rather than of wood, that it could not receive the consideration to which it was clearly entitled on other less essential counts. No. 108, submitted by Edwin J. Schmitt, Jr., is remarkable for its rendering. The style is hard and unbeautiful, but original and strong. No. 123, submitted by Arthur W. Coote, had its advocates for a high place, by reason of the qualities exhibited in the Third Prize design; but the combination of wood and stone is clearly unhappy, besides being unnecessary, and the whole design, though full of merit, is not, after all, convincing. Nos. 105, 174 and 175 are all of the same general type—a good type enough, but rather strained in their particular relations. The authors (Harry L. Skidmore, Eugene D. Monticello and Charles F. Mink, respectively) should rather have sought out a free solution instead of trying to adapt their new libretto to an already popular tune. No. 178, submitted by Carl Bradley and Herman Brookman, is well planned and designed, but the chosen scheme is too ambitious for this type of house; that is, there is too little regard for economy.

CLAUDE BRAGDON
WM. ADAMS DELANO
HUGH M. G. GARDEN   } *Jury of Award*
J. HARLESTON PARKER
HOWARD SILL

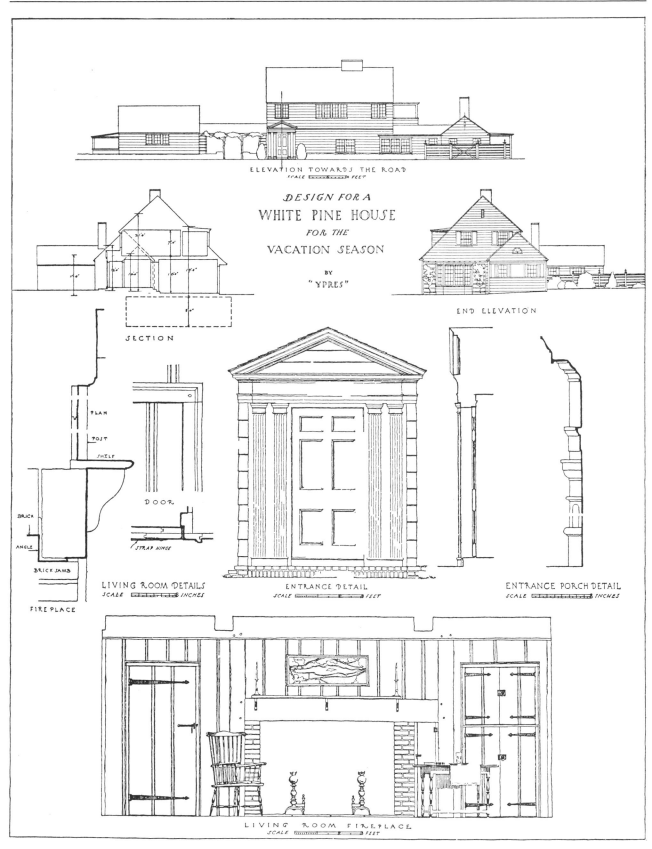

ELEVATION TOWARDS THE ROAD
SCALE _____ FEET

DESIGN FOR A
WHITE PINE HOUSE
FOR THE
VACATION SEASON
BY
"YPRES"

END ELEVATION

SECTION

PLAN

POST

SHELF

BRICK

ANGLE

BRICK JAMB

FIRE PLACE

DOOR

STRAP HINGE

LIVING ROOM DETAILS
SCALE _____ INCHES

ENTRANCE DETAIL
SCALE _____ FEET

ENTRANCE PORCH DETAIL
SCALE _____ INCHES

LIVING ROOM FIREPLACE
SCALE _____ FEET

SECOND PRIZE, Design No. 132, Detail Sheet
Submitted by Otto Faelten, New York, New York, and Donald Robb, Boston, Massachusetts

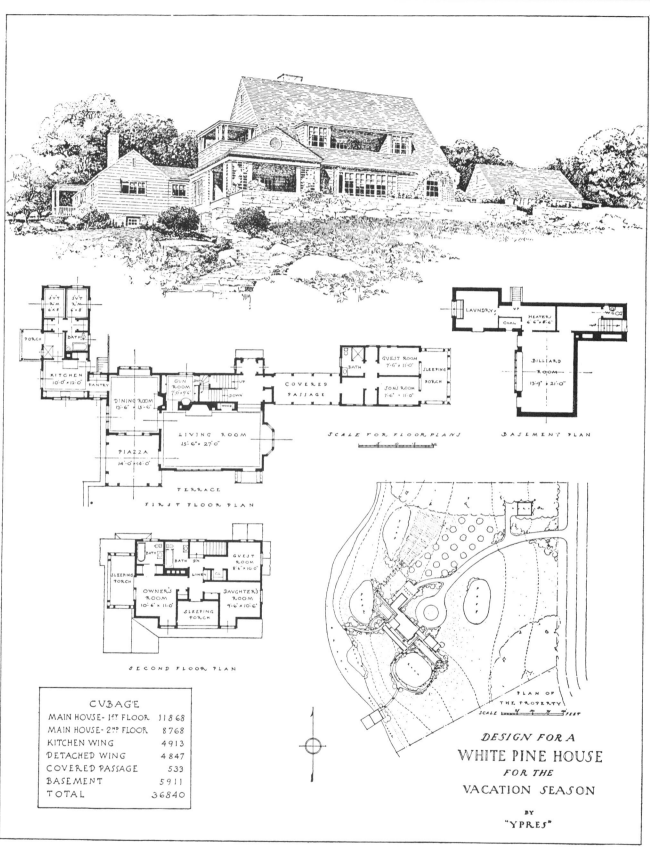

CVBAGE

MAIN HOVSE-1ST FLOOR	11868
MAIN HOVSE-2ND FLOOR	8768
KITCHEN WING	4913
DETACHED WING	4847
COVERED PASSAGE	533
BASEMENT	5911
TOTAL	36840

FIRST FLOOR PLAN

SECOND FLOOR PLAN

BASEMENT PLAN

SCALE FOR FLOOR PLANS

PLAN OF THE PROPERTY
SCALE

DESIGN FOR A
WHITE PINE HOUSE
FOR THE
VACATION SEASON
BY
"YPRES"

SECOND PRIZE, Design No. 132
Submitted by Otto Faelten, New York, New York, and Donald Robb, Boston, Massachusetts

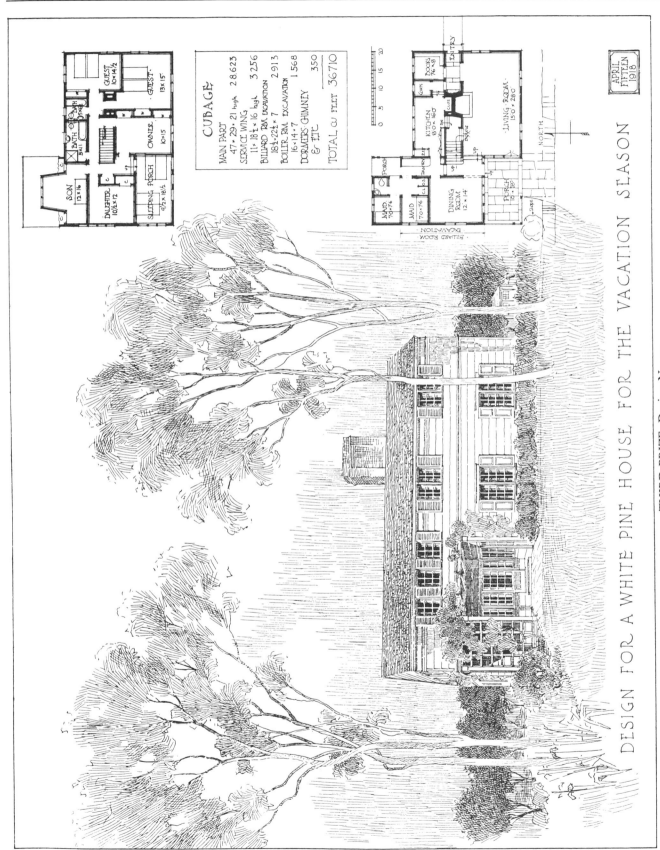

DESIGN FOR A WHITE PINE HOUSE FOR THE VACATION SEASON

THIRD PRIZE, Design No. 23
Submitted by Olaf William Shelgren, Buffalo, New York

THIRD PRIZE, Design No. 23, Detail Sheet
Submitted by Olaf William Shelgren, Buffalo, New York

DESIGN FOR A WHITE PINE HOUSE, FOR THE VACATION SEASON

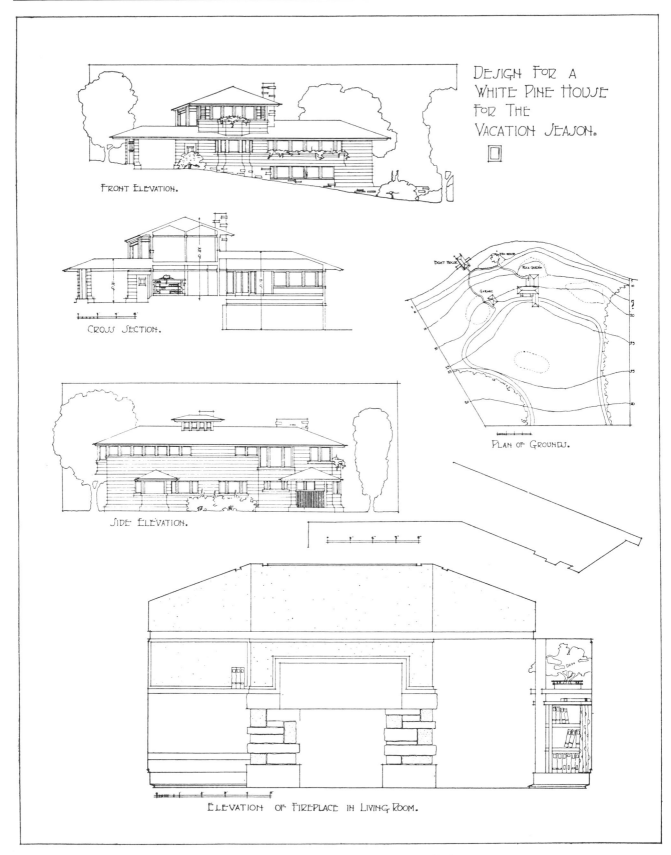

DESIGN FOR A
WHITE PINE HOUSE
FOR THE
VACATION SEASON.

FRONT ELEVATION.

CROSS SECTION.

PLAN OF GROUNDS.

SIDE ELEVATION.

ELEVATION OF FIREPLACE IN LIVING ROOM.

FOURTH PRIZE, Design No. 100, Detail Sheet
Submitted by Russell Barr Williamson, Kansas City, Missouri

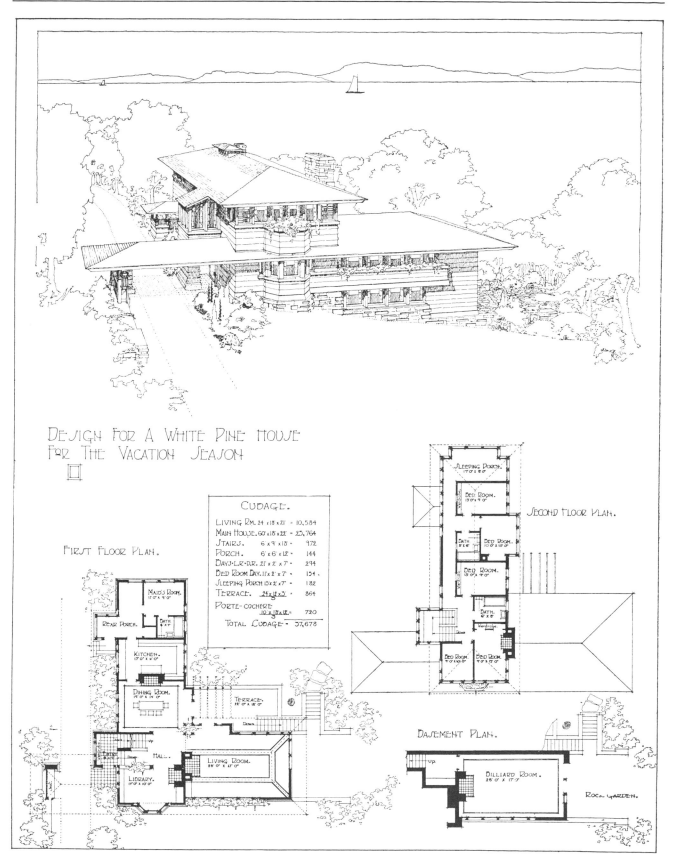

DESIGN FOR A WHITE PINE HOUSE
FOR THE VACATION SEASON

FIRST FLOOR PLAN.

CUDAGE.

LIVING RM. 24 x18 x 21 = 10,584
MAIN HOUSE. 60 x 18 x 22 = 23,764
STAIRS. 6 x 9 x 18 = 972
PORCH. 6 x 6 x 12 = 144
DAYS·L.R·D.R. 21 x 2 x 7 = 294
BED ROOM DAY. 11 x 2 x 7 = 154
SLEEPING PORCH 13 x 2 x 7 = 182
TERRACE. 24 x 18 x 2 = 864
PORTE-COCHERE
10 x 18 x 12 = 720
TOTAL CUDAGE = 37,678

SECOND FLOOR PLAN.

BASEMENT PLAN.

FOURTH PRIZE, Design No. 100
Submitted by Russell Barr Williamson, Kansas City, Missouri

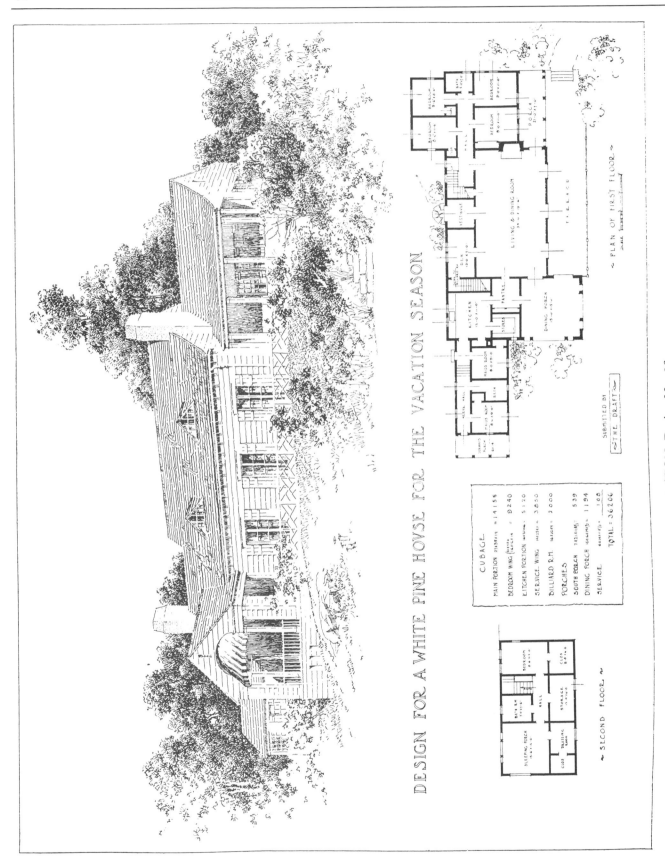

DESIGN FOR A WHITE PINE HOUSE FOR THE VACATION SEASON

MENTION, Design No. 86

Submitted by Paul R. Williams, Los Angeles, California

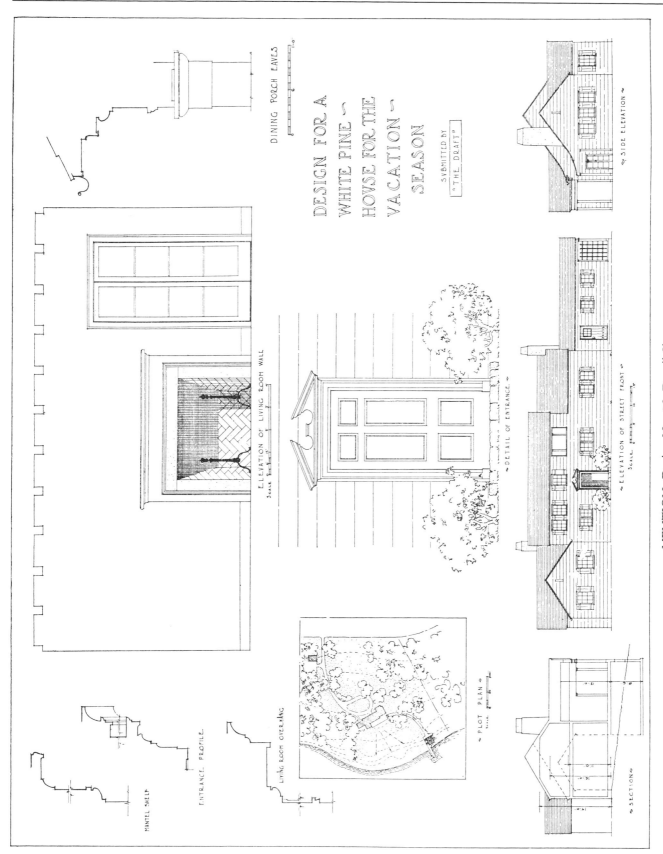

DINING PORCH EAVES

DESIGN FOR A
WHITE PINE ~
HOVSE FOR THE ~
VACATION ~
SEASON

SVBMITTED BY
"THE DRAFT"

~ SIDE ELEVATION ~

ELEVATION OF LIVING ROOM WALL

~ DETAIL OF ENTRANCE ~

~ ELEVATION OF STREET FRONT ~

MANTEL SHELF

ENTRANCE PROFILE

LIVING ROOM OVERHANG

~ PLOT PLAN ~

~ SECTION ~

MENTION, Design No. 86, Detail Sheet
Submitted by Paul R. Williams, Los Angeles, California

MANTEL DETAIL

MAIN CORNICE

ELEVATION IN LIVING ROOM
WHITE PINE PANELING AT THIS SIDE ONLY·

ENTRANCE CORNICE

SECTION

DETAIL ELEVATION OF ENTRANCE.
SCALE FOR DETAIL ELEVATIONS

SCALE FOR DETAIL PROFILES

In Hoc Signo?

ENTRANCE ELEVATION
SCALE FOR ELEVATIONS

SIDE ELEVATION

DESIGN FOR A WHITE PINE HOUSE FOR THE VACATION SEASON

MENTION, Design No. 84, Detail Sheet
Submitted by Jerauld Dahler, Washington, D.C.

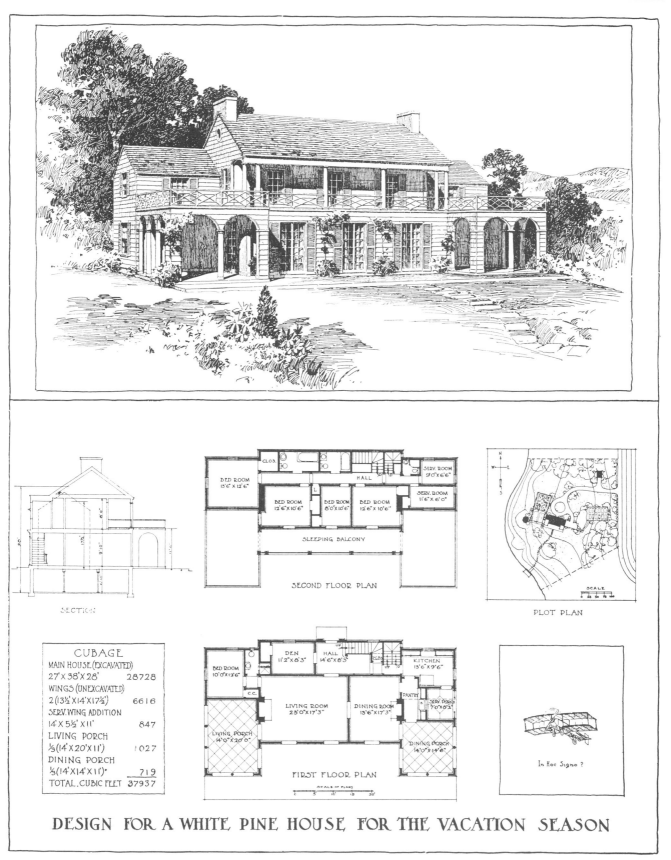

SECTION

CLOS.
BED ROOM
15'6" X 12'6"
HALL
SERV. ROOM
9'0" X 6'6"
BED ROOM
12'6" X 10'6"
BED ROOM
8'0" X 10'6"
BED ROOM
12'6" X 10'6"
SERV. ROOM
11'6" X 6'0"

SLEEPING BALCONY

SECOND FLOOR PLAN

PLOT PLAN

SCALE

CUBAGE
MAIN HOUSE (EXCAVATED)
27' X 38' X 28'   28728
WINGS (UNEXCAVATED)
2 (13½' X 14' X 17½')   6616
SERV. WING ADDITION
14' X 5½' X 11'   847
LIVING PORCH
⅓ (14' X 20' X 11')   1027
DINING PORCH
⅓ (14' X 14' X 11')   719
TOTAL CUBIC FEET   37937

BED ROOM
10'0"X12'6"
DEN
11'2" X 8'3"
HALL
14'6" X 8'3"
KITCHEN
13'6" X 9'6"
C.C.
LIVING ROOM
23'0" X 17'3"
DINING ROOM
13'6" X 17'3"
PANTRY
SERV. PORCH
7'0" X 6'0"
LIVING PORCH
14'0" X 20'0"
DINING PORCH
14'0" X 14'6"

FIRST FLOOR PLAN

SCALE OF PLANS
5   10   15   20'

In Hoc Signo ?

DESIGN FOR A WHITE PINE HOUSE FOR THE VACATION SEASON

MENTION, Design No. 84
Submitted by Jerauld Dahler, Washington, D.C.

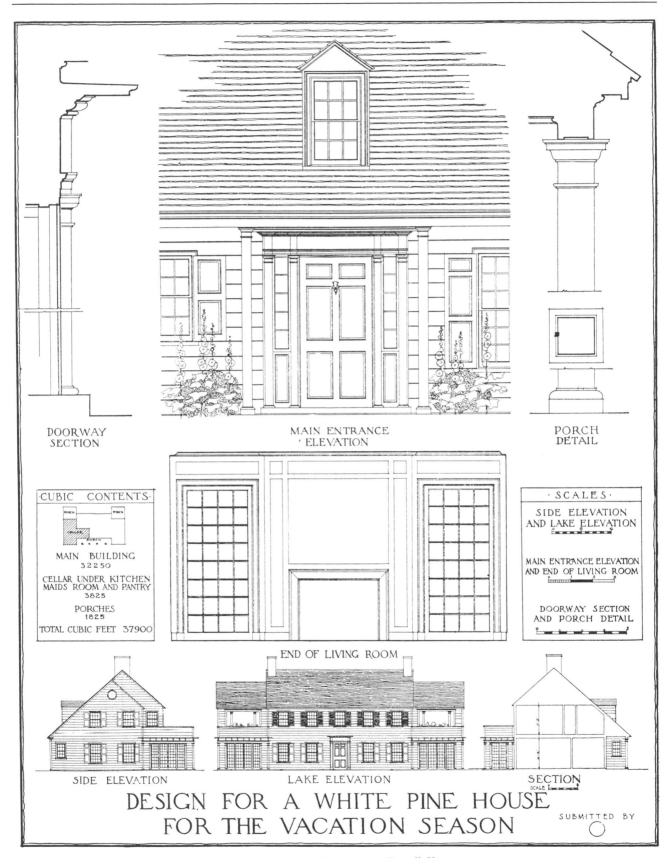

DOORWAY
SECTION

MAIN ENTRANCE
ELEVATION

PORCH
DETAIL

·CUBIC CONTENTS·

MAIN BUILDING
32250

CELLAR UNDER KITCHEN
MAIDS ROOM AND PANTRY
3825

PORCHES
1825

TOTAL CUBIC FEET 37900

END OF LIVING ROOM

·SCALES·

SIDE ELEVATION
AND LAKE ELEVATION

MAIN ENTRANCE ELEVATION
AND END OF LIVING ROOM

DOORWAY SECTION
AND PORCH DETAIL

SIDE ELEVATION

LAKE ELEVATION

SECTION

DESIGN FOR A WHITE PINE HOUSE
FOR THE VACATION SEASON

SUBMITTED BY

MENTION, Design No. 112, Detail Sheet
Submitted by Antonio di Nardo, New York, New York

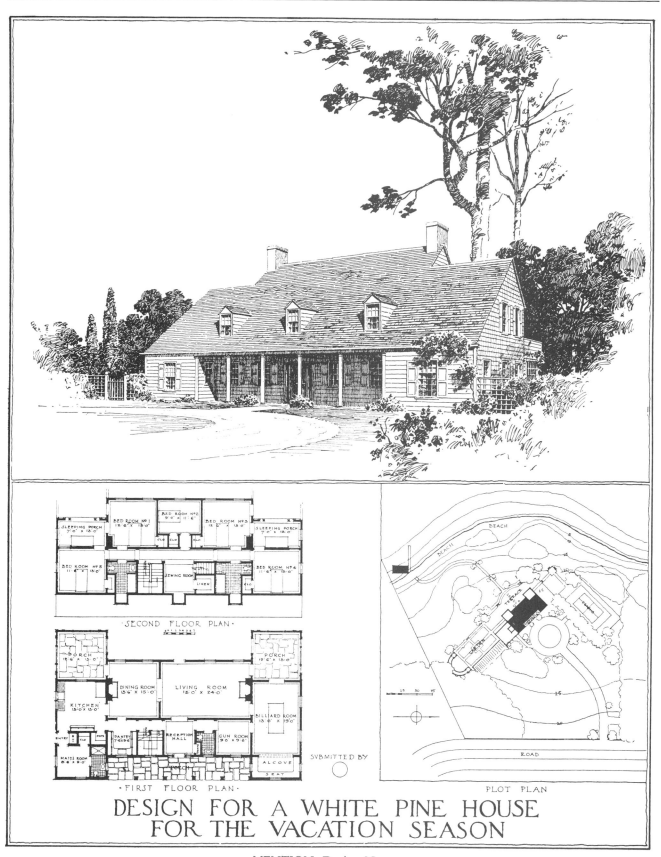

DESIGN FOR A WHITE PINE HOUSE FOR THE VACATION SEASON

MENTION, Design No. 112
Submitted by Antonio di Nardo, New York, New York

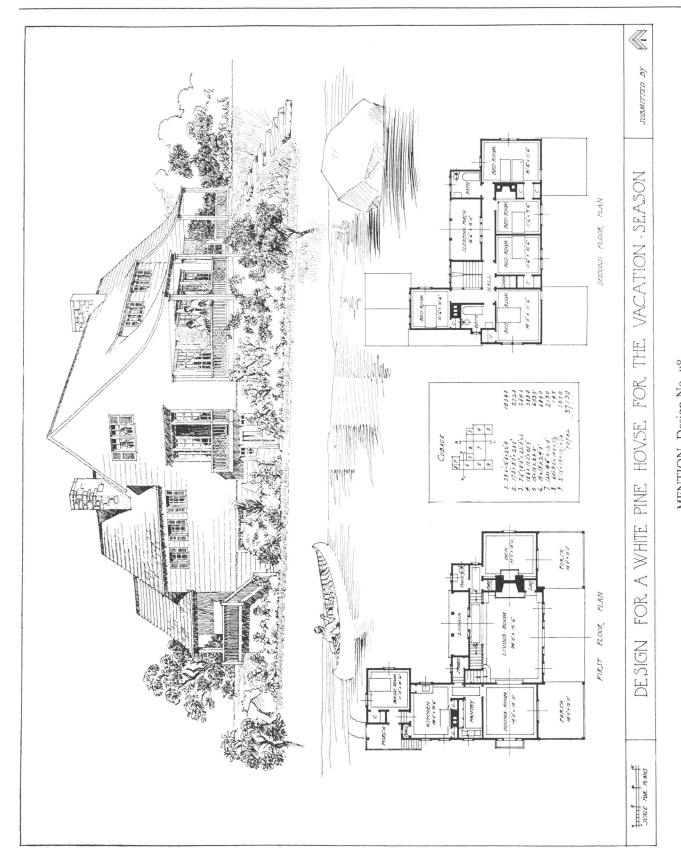

DESIGN FOR A WHITE PINE HOUSE FOR THE VACATION SEASON

MENTION, Design No. 118

Submitted by T. C. Pomphrey and W. Ralston, Toronto, Canada

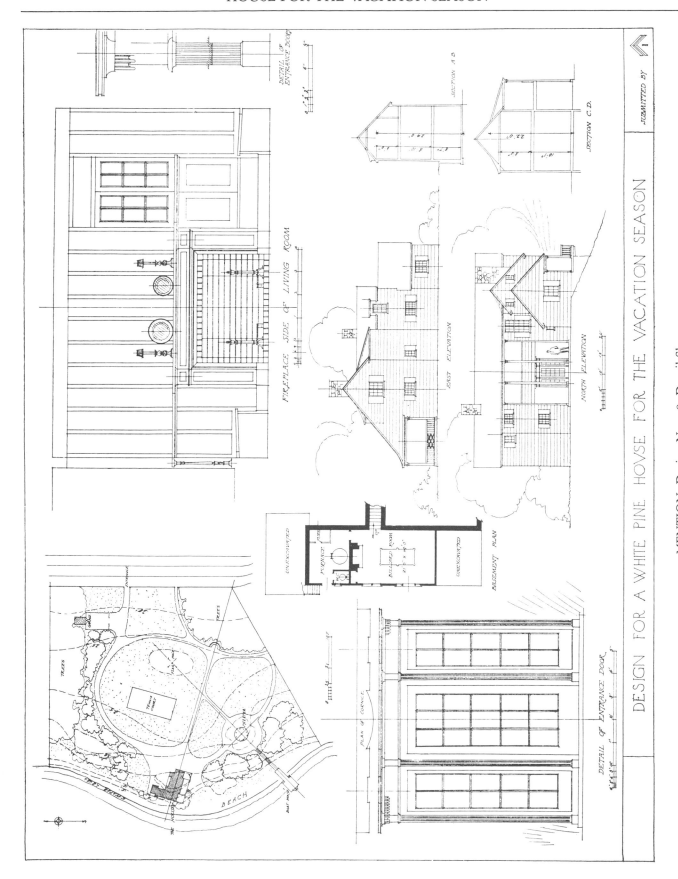

DESIGN FOR A WHITE PINE HOVSE FOR THE VACATION SEASON

MENTION, Design No. 118, Detail Sheet
Submitted by T. C. Pomphrey and W. Ralston, Toronto, Canada

MAIN CORNICE
3 INCH SCALE

MINOR CORNICES
3 INCH SCALE

STAIR WINDOW

BAY
SCALE FOR 3/4 INCH SCALE DETAILS

ENTRANCE

LIVING ROOM FIREPLACE

END ELEVATION

ROAD ELEVATION
1/8 INCH SCALE

SECTION

DESIGN FOR A WHITE PINE HOUSE
FOR THE VACATION SEASON

MENTION, Design No. 124, Detail Sheet
Submitted by Milton Rogers Williams, Highland Park, Michigan

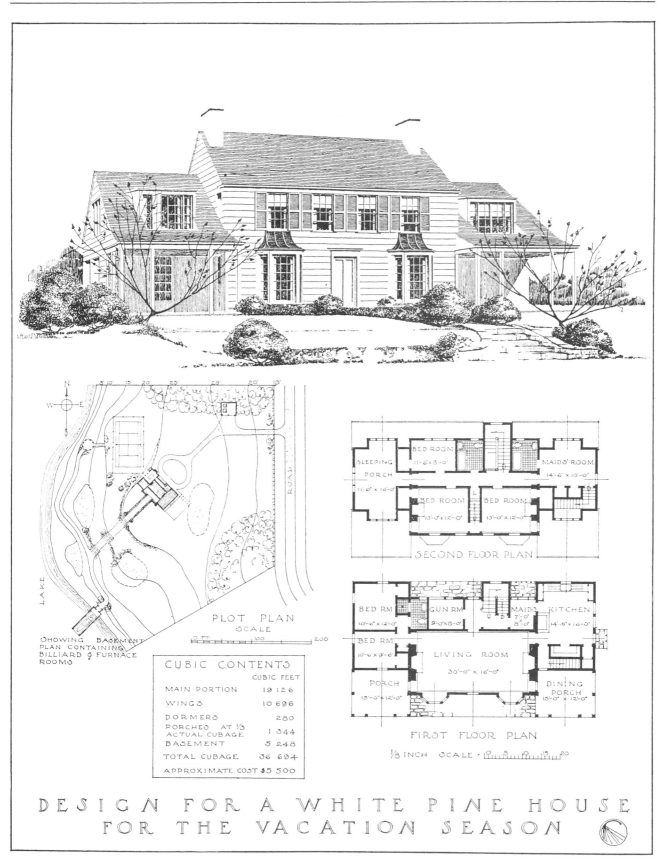

PLOT PLAN
SCALE

SHOWING BASEMENT
PLAN CONTAINING
BILLIARD & FURNACE
ROOMS

CUBIC CONTENTS

	CUBIC FEET
MAIN PORTION	19 126
WINGS	10 696
DORMERS	280
PORCHES AT ⅓ ACTUAL CUBAGE	1 344
BASEMENT	5 248
TOTAL CUBAGE	36 694
APPROXIMATE COST	$5 500

SECOND FLOOR PLAN

FIRST FLOOR PLAN
⅛ INCH SCALE

DESIGN FOR A WHITE PINE HOUSE
FOR THE VACATION SEASON

MENTION, Design No. 124
Submitted by Milton Rogers Williams, Highland Park, Michigan

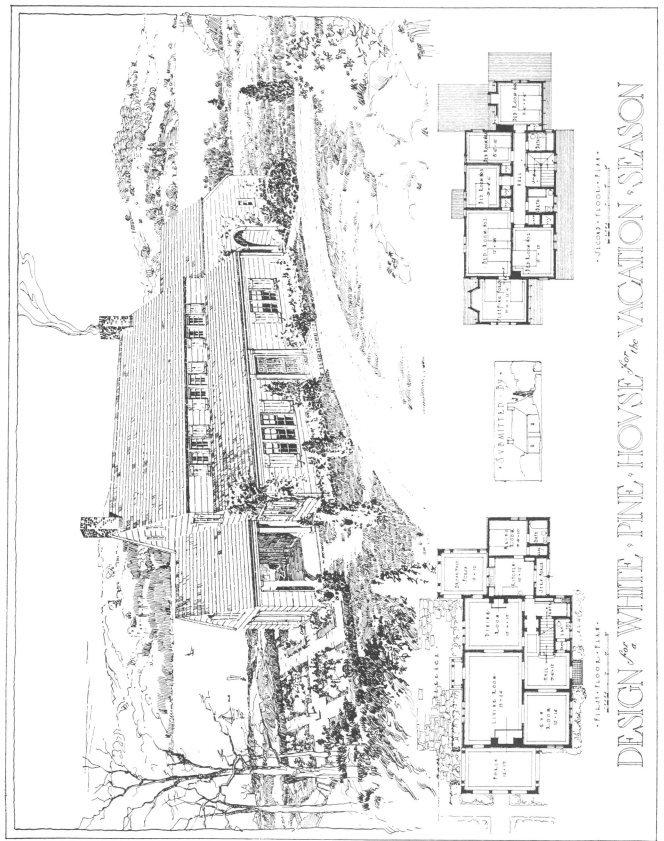

DESIGN for a WHITE PINE HOUSE for the VACATION SEASON

MENTION, Design No. 165

Submitted by J. F. Yewell and L. E. Welsh, New York, New York

DESIGN *for a* WHITE PINE HOUSE *for the* VACATION SEASON

MENTION, Design No. 165, Detail Sheet
Submitted by J. F. Yewell and L. E. Welsh, New York, New York

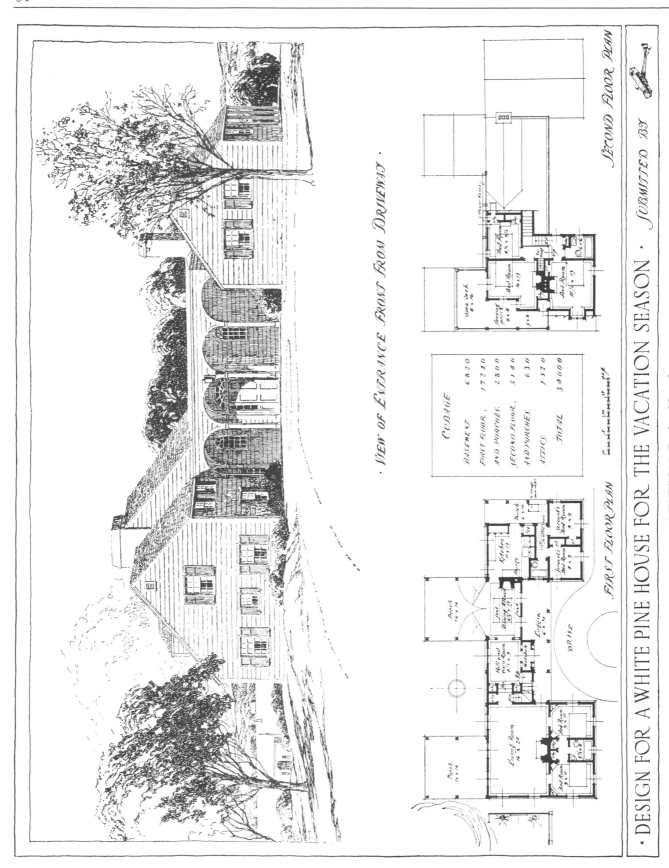

· VIEW OF ENTRANCE FRONT FROM DRIVEWAY ·

SECOND FLOOR PLAN

FIRST FLOOR PLAN

CUBAGE	
BASEMENT.	6820
FIRST FLOOR,	17240
AND PORCHES.	2800
SECOND FLOOR,	5140
AND PORCHES.	630
ATTIC.	1370
TOTAL	34000

· DESIGN FOR A WHITE PINE HOUSE FOR THE VACATION SEASON · SUBMITTED BY

MENTION, Design No. 167

Submitted by J. H. Phillips, New York, New York

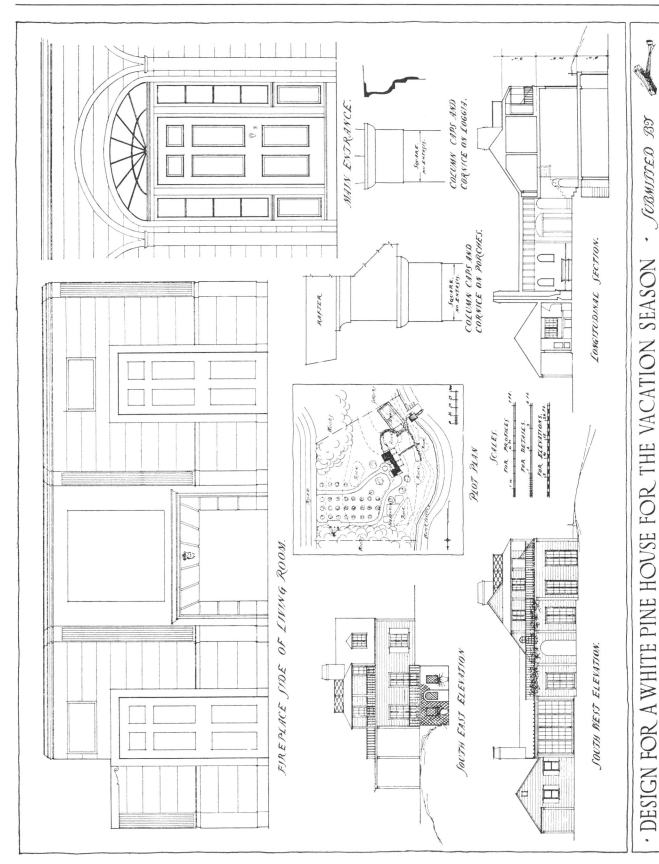

MAIN ENTRANCE.

COLUMN CAPS AND CORNICE ON LOGGIA.

SQUARE. NO ENTASIS.

RAFTER.

SQUARE. NO ENTASIS.

COLUMN CAPS AND CORNICE ON PORCHES.

LONGITUDINAL SECTION.

FIREPLACE SIDE OF LIVING ROOM.

PLOT PLAN.

SCALES.
FOR PROFILES.
FOR DETAILS.
FOR ELEVATIONS.

SOUTH EAST ELEVATION

SOUTH WEST ELEVATION.

· DESIGN FOR A WHITE PINE HOUSE FOR THE VACATION SEASON · SUBMITTED BY

MENTION, Design No. 167, Detail Sheet
Submitted by J. H. Phillips, New York, New York

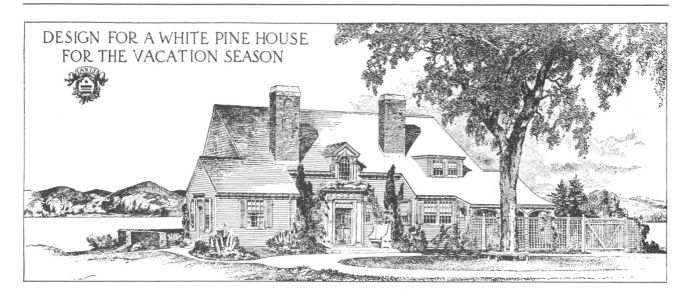

DESIGN No. 3
Submitted by Hubert G. Ripley, Boston, Massachusetts

DESIGN No. 178
Submitted by Karl Bradley and Herman Brookman, New York, New York

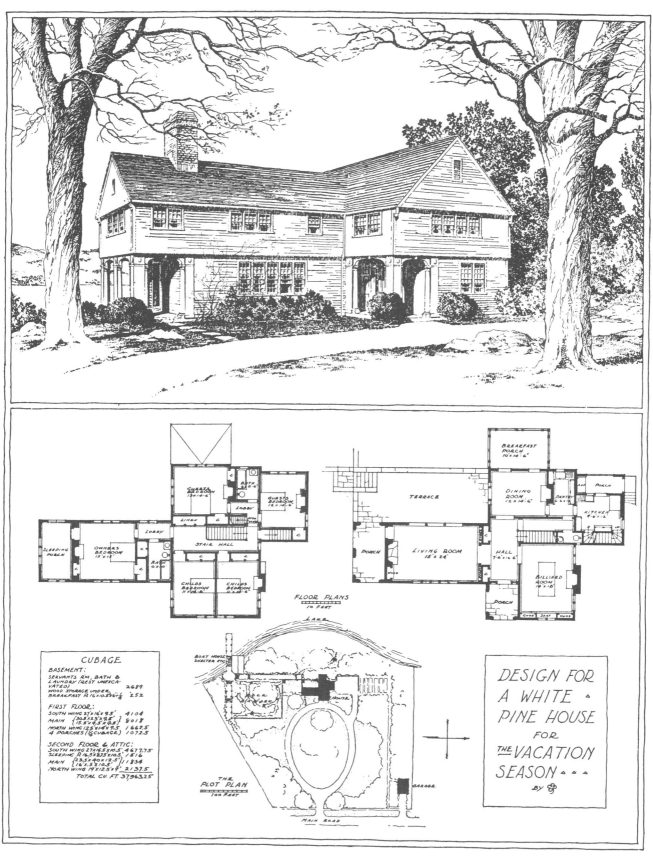

DESIGN No. 154
Submitted by Porter W. Scott, Brooklyn, New York

DESIGN·FOR·A·WHITE·PINE·HOVSE·FOR·THE·VACATION·SEASON

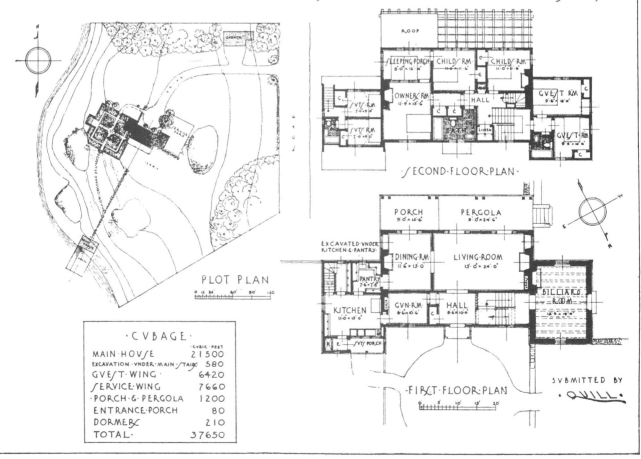

PLOT PLAN

SECOND·FLOOR·PLAN·

·FIRST·FLOOR·PLAN·

SVBMITTED BY ·QVILL·

·CVBAGE·

	CVBIC·FEET
MAIN·HOVSE	21500
EXCAVATION·VNDER·MAIN·STAIRS	580
GVEST·WING·	6420
SERVICE·WING	7660
·PORCH·&·PERGOLA	1200
ENTRANCE·PORCH	80
DORMER	210
TOTAL·	37650

DESIGN No. 127
Submitted by J. T. Thomson and J. P. Wilson, New York, New York

DESIGN No. 108
Submitted by Edwin J. Schmitt, Jr., New York, New York

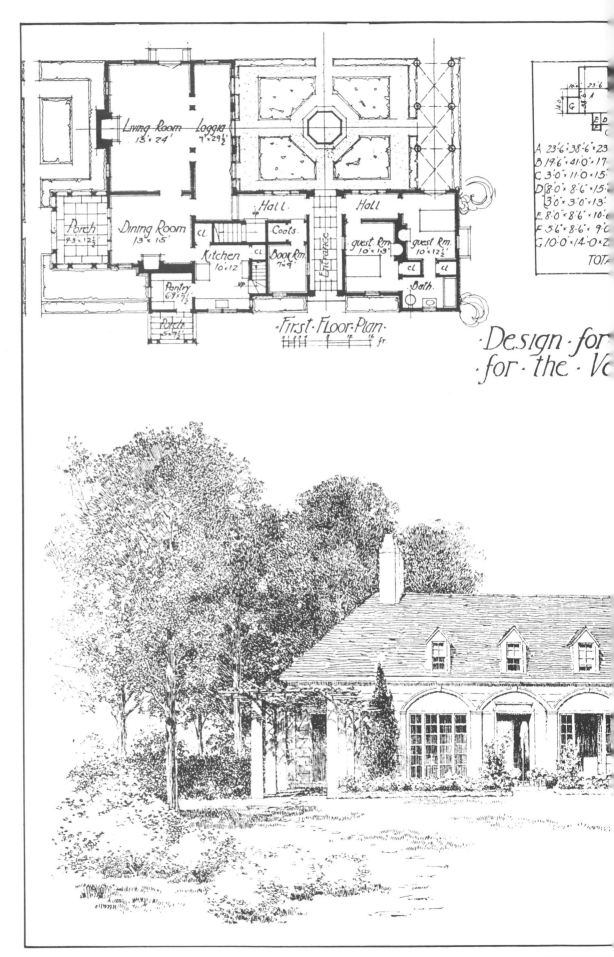

Living Room
13' × 24'

Loggia
7' × 29½'

Porch
9.3' × 12½'

Dining Room
13' × 15'

Hall
up

CL.

Coats.

Kitchen
10' × 12'

Book Rm.
7' × 9'

CL.

Pantry
6.9' × 7½'

up

Porch
5' × 7½'

Entrance

Hall

guest Rm.
10' × 13'

guest Rm.
10' × 12½'

CL

CL

Bath.

·First·Floor·Plan·

A 23'·6 × 38'·6 × 23
B 19'·6 × 41'·0 × 17
C 3'·0 × 11'·0 × 15
D 8'·0 × 8'·6 × 15
3'·0 × 3'·0 × 13
E 8'·0 × 8'·6 × 10
F 5'·6 × 8'·6 × 9'·0
G 10'·0 × 14'·0 × 2

TOTA

·Design·for
·for·the·Ve

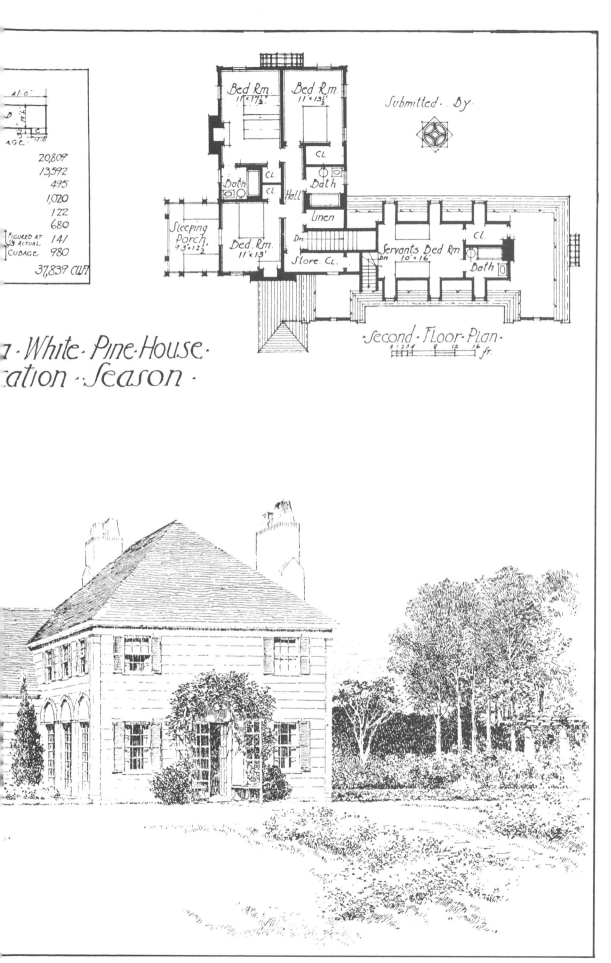

20,809
13,592
495
1,020
122
680
FIGURED AT 1/3 ACTUAL 141
CUBAGE 980
37,839 CU FT

Bed Rm.
11 × 17½

Bed Rm.
11 × 13½

Submitted · By ·

CL

Bath

CL

Bath

Hall

CL

Linen

Sleeping
Porch
9'3 × 12½

Bed Rm.
11 × 13'

Dn.

Store CL.

Dn.

Servants Bed Rm
10 × 16

CL

Bath

Second · Floor · Plan ·

· White · Pine · House ·
· ation · Season ·

Design No. 4
d T. E. King, Toledo, Ohio

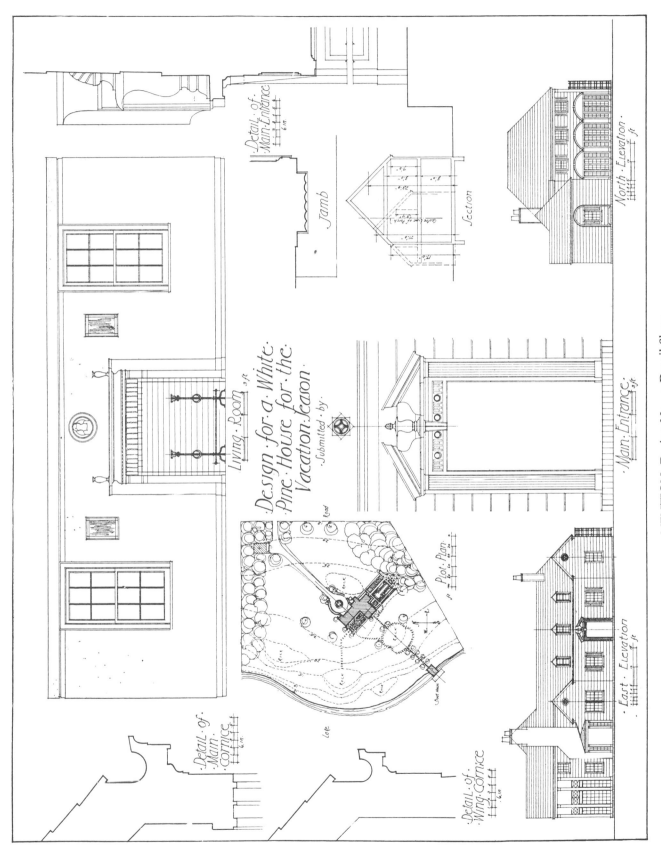

MENTION, Design No. 4, Detail Sheet
Submitted by E. J. Maier and T. E. King, Toledo, Ohio

A Community Center Building

Report of the Jury of Award
Given May 23 and 24, 1919
Originally published in 1919 as White Pine Monograph
Volume V, Number 4

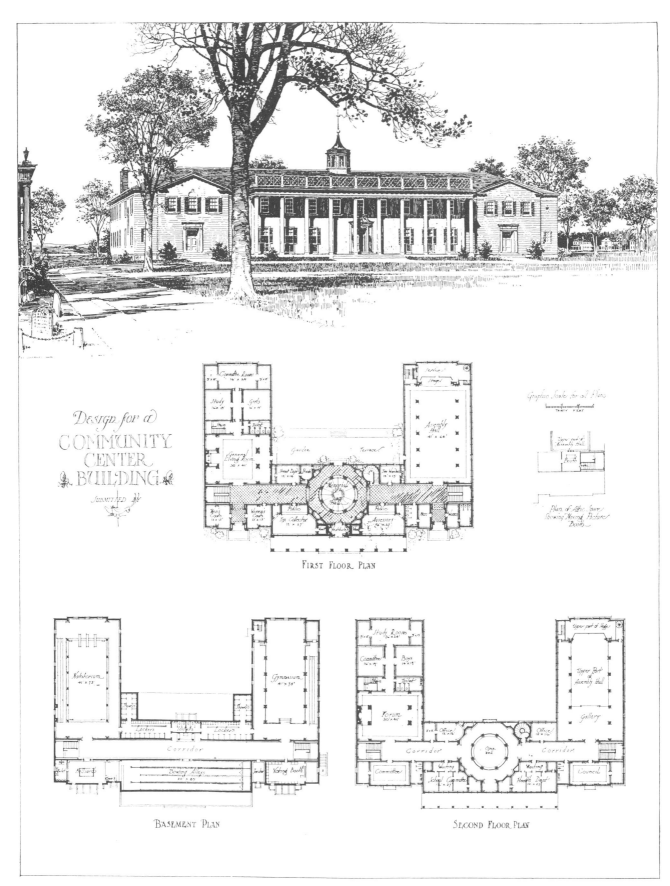

FIRST PRIZE DESIGN

Submitted by Maurice Feather and Niels H. Larsen, Boston, Massachusetts

A COMMUNITY CENTER BUILDING

Report of the Jury of Award of the Fourth Annual White Pine Architectural Competition

Judged at the Biltmore, New York, NY, May 23 and 24, 1919

PROBLEM: The design is for a Community Center Building and a Civic Center Group Plan for a town with a present population of about 5,000 and the probability of steady growth. The town is situated on the shore of a river which flows from east to west. 2,000 feet back from and parallel to the shore line the interurban trolley and the steam railroads are located on contiguous rights-of-way. The Civic Center shall extend from the railroads to the shore line, and shall be of a width determined by the competitor. The town is "somewhere" in New England. The Civic Center is created by the demolition of old buildings not especially valuable, but the remaining structures surrounding the public areas are of painted White Pine, in the character so well developed in that part of our country. Large elm trees predominate. The land slopes gradually down from the railroads to the water level, a descent of about 50 feet in 2,000 feet.

THE COMMUNITY CENTER BUILDING shall contain: A town council chamber, offices for the town officials, and a room for permanent voting booths; an assembly hall to seat 700 persons, equipped with a stage and a motion picture machine. The floor of this room shall be flat to permit dancing and social gatherings. Refreshment facilities shall be provided in connection with the assembly hall. Club rooms for women, which shall include two committee rooms, suitable for small lecture or study purposes. Club room for girls. Club rooms for men, which shall include a forum for the discussion of items of community interest. Club room for boys. A general living-room, provided with tables for current periodicals, desks for writing, etc. A gymnasium and bowling alleys, with accessories; a natatorium with accessories. There shall be a large memorial vestibule or hall to preserve the records and to commemorate the deeds of the local men who served in the Great War.

A GROUP PLAN is required upon which shall be shown the following: Depots for passengers and for freights; an open market; buildings for stores and offices; a high school; three churches; a public library; an art museum and the COMMUNITY CENTER BUILDING—the principal feature of this Competition—a municipal power, heat, light and laundry building; a public space for out-of-door meetings, speaking, band concerts and pageantry; an athletic and public recreation field; automobile parking spaces; and a boat landing.

Not all details are herein listed, particularly in the group plan. The competitor is expected to state his conception of what a Community Center Group should be.

The architectural style of the Community Building is left to the discretion of the contestant. The outside finish is to be of White Pine. By outside finish is meant: siding and corner boards; window sash, frames and casings; outside doors, door frames and casings; outside blinds; all exposed porch and balcony lumber; cornice boards, brackets, ornaments and mouldings, etc., *not* including shingles.

The size and the cost of the building, the equipment which it will contain, and the service which it will perform should be appropriate to the local needs. A sum equivalent to $15.00 per capita has been raised for the building, and it is expected that some special features of the building may be provided for by individual gifts as memorials to men who have lost their lives in the War.

THE Jury of Award begs to report that they have carefully examined the sets of drawings submitted in the Fourth Annual Architectural Competition conducted by THE WHITE PINE SERIES OF ARCHITECTURAL MONOGRAPHS, for a Community Center Building, with a Civic Center Group Plan, and unanimously awarded the prizes and mentions.

Before proceeding to a discussion of the premiated designs, we would offer certain general observations upon the character of the competition as a whole. The programme is admirable in its timeliness, in its broad view of the problem, in the clarity and brevity of its statements; the restrictions imposed upon the competitors are only such as insure equitable conditions and a broad and fair judgment. We feel some surprise, therefore, that there was not a more general participation, especially in view of the liberal prizes offered. If this be due to the fact that the required study of the group plan repelled or failed to interest a sufficient number of men, or that a majority of draftsmen would rather do something of a type with which they are familiar or for which they can readily find precedents to follow rather than to attack a problem which requires the exercise of original thought and of imagination, we would consider this a most unfortunate tendency. We are inclined to believe, from the general weakness shown by most of the group plans, either that the competitors failed to give this feature the importance that it is intended to have, and should have, under the programme, or that the study of a group plan of this nature did not interest them. If the young men who enter these competitions will take the trouble to make a little research, they will find that the prize-winners in practically every competition of any sort which is held, including this, have given careful study to every aspect of their problems. One of the lessons to be learned in competitions is the development of good judgment in analysis and in an intelligent and interested weighing of the relative importance of the several elements of the problem, whether these be formally set forth in a competitive programme or stated orally by a client in one's private office. It may be fairly stated that, with a few notable exceptions, the group plans were very poor and showed no grasp either of the importance of subjects of this sort or of their study and treatment, and we recommend the study of group planning to the careful attention of most of these competitors. On the other hand, taken as a whole, the competitors have very generally, and with comparatively few exceptions, seized what we may term the atmosphere of the subject of the competition so far as the Community Center Building itself is concerned. They have nearly all grasped the essential fact that this building is to be the social focus of a little community of 5,000 people—in short, a village—and nearly all of them have given their buildings the character appropriate to a village. In writing the programme, it was intended to express the idea that the act of voting, one of the most important, even sacred duties of the citizen, should be elevated to the dignity of a ceremony or rite, and that the exercises of the suffrage should take place in a prominent space, such as a memorial room or a forum, not in a dark basement space, which many competitors seemed to think adequate for the purpose.

It is doubtless too much to expect that the group of young men represented by these competitors should at once grasp all the needs of such a building as this, particularly when the problem has in no sense yet become standardized. A few points, however, are evident to any student of the times. One is that women and men must be placed on a practical basis of equality as far as accommodations are concerned, and women must be given absolutely equal rights in and access to such main features as the gymnasium and swimming pool. Another concerns itself with the intensive study which must necessarily be given to the matter of economical administration of an actual building of this sort, which can be brought about only by compact planning and a room arrangement which allows supervision to be done by the least possible number of paid employees.

A study of the different schemes, however, is of interest in showing how the majority of minds would solve the problem. These schemes group themselves into three classes: (A) the T shape, consisting of a front building with a rear wing, perpendicular to it, containing generally the auditorium and possibly the gymnasium or pool underneath; (B) a plan with two separate wings for the larger units of the plan; and (C) all others.

Of the ten designs placed, seven followed with some variations the first scheme, two (of which one gained the first prize) the second, and one the third, a clear majority which seems to establish, as far as may be, the first scheme as a standard form of community house plan. Varying ideas as to sizes of gymnasiums, swimming pools, etc., will, in practice, inevitably modify this arrangement, for a building of this kind is one of the most "pernickety" with which architects have to deal; nevertheless, it is probably the most compact and easily administered plan which can be devised. The two-wing plan would require much more supervision and would meet the needs of a much larger town than one of 5,000 people. The third type of plan, which might be called the "hinge type," is on the whole rather difficult to plan and complicated to construct, so that its general use is not probable.

The studies of these types by bright and enthusiastic young men cannot fail to be of a real and timely usefulness to the profession.

FIRST PRIZE DESIGN. We find the virtues of general grasp, character in mass and in detail, and the atmosphere of the problem preeminent in the drawing we have given the first prize. In the group plan the sense of scale is particularly fine. The authors have realized that they are planning the community center of a village, not a Champs Elysées nor a Mall fit for the City of Washington. It is orderly without being stiff, sufficiently formal in its principal features without frigidity. The position of the Community Center Building itself, standing as it does almost midway between the railway and the river, is admirable. The authors have known when to discard symmetry for balance, and they appreciate the value of curved lines in rural planning. The shops and markets are placed along a broad street running parallel with the railroad and thus do not intrude themselves upon the more important structures in the group plan. The scale of the space around which the principal buildings are grouped is so good and the common sense which it expresses so evident that we highly commend both; instead of using up all of the terrain for one tremendous

(Continued on page 126)

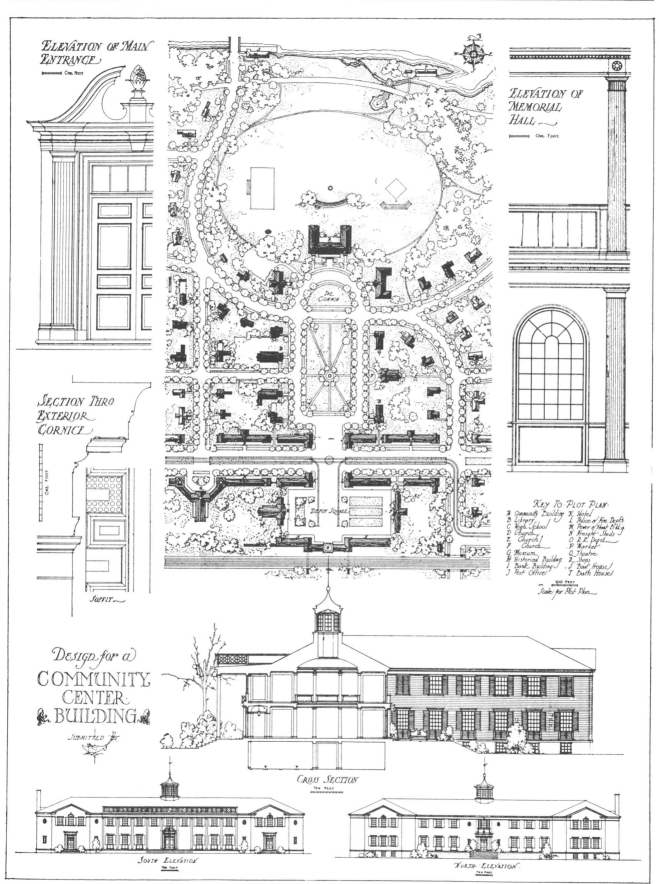

ELEVATION OF MAIN ENTRANCE

ELEVATION OF MEMORIAL HALL

SECTION THRO EXTERIOR CORNICE

SOFFIT

THE COMMON

DEPOT SQUARE

KEY TO PLOT PLAN.
A Community Building K Hotel
B Library L Police & Fire Dept's.
C High School M Power & Heat Bld'g.
D Church N Freight Sheds
E Church O R.R. Depot
F Church P Market
G Museum Q Theatre
H Historical Building R Shops
I Bank Building S Boat House
J Post Office T Bath House

100 FEET
Scale for Plot Plan

Design for a COMMUNITY CENTER BUILDING
SUBMITTED BY

CROSS SECTION
TEN FEET

SOUTH ELEVATION
TEN FEET

NORTH ELEVATION
TEN FEET

FIRST PRIZE DESIGN, Detail Sheet
Submitted by Maurice Feather and Niels H. Larsen, Boston, Massachusetts

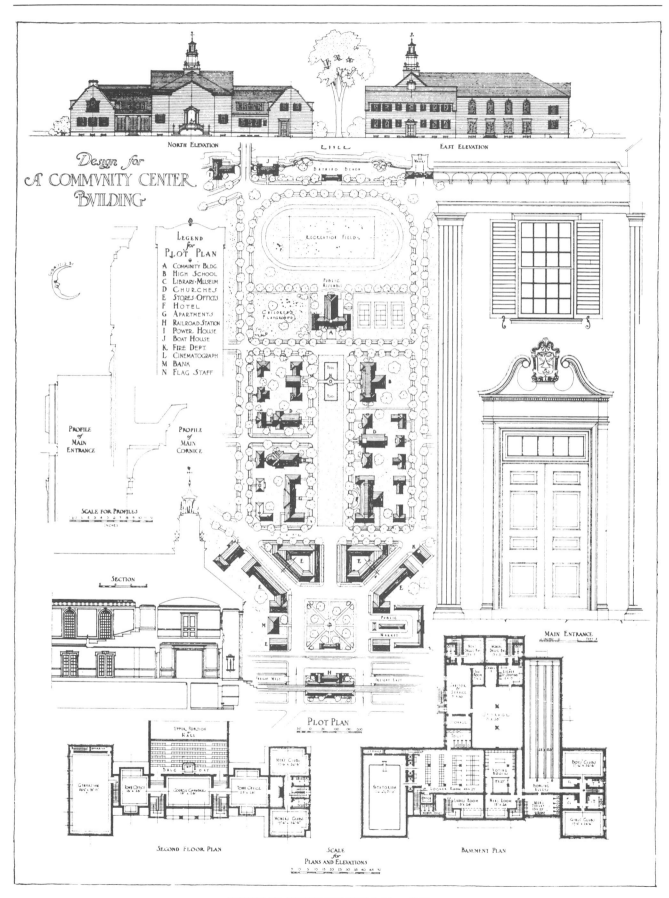

SECOND PRIZE DESIGN, Detail Sheet
Submitted by Wm. J. Mooney, Jamaica Plain, Massachusetts

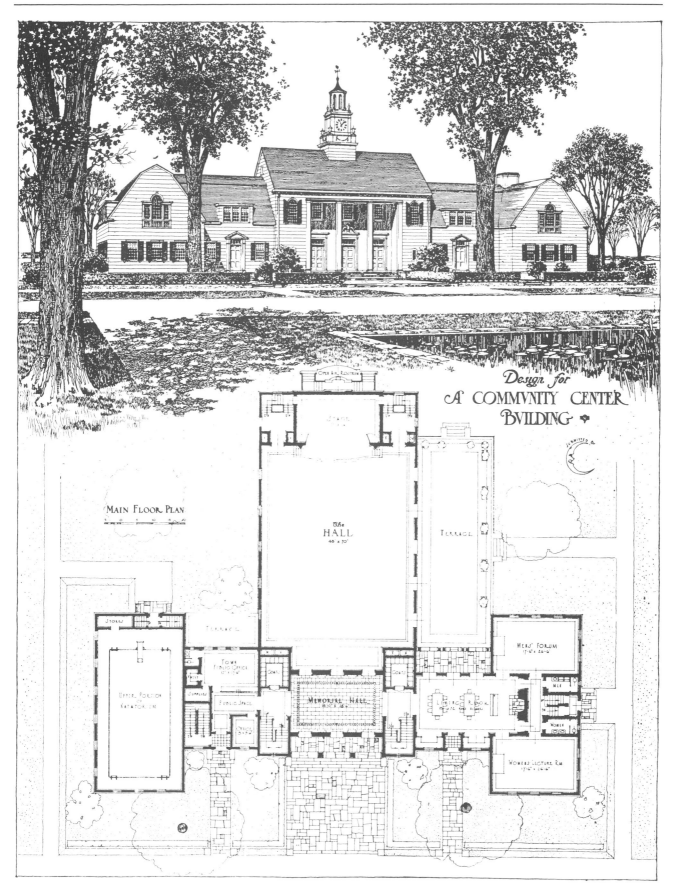

Design for A COMMVNITY CENTER BVILDING

MAIN FLOOR PLAN

The HALL
48 x 70'

TERRACE

MENS' FORUM

UPPER PORTION OF NATATORIUM

TOWN PUBLIC OFFICE

MEMORIAL HALL

LIVING ROOM

WOMENS' LECTURE RM

SECOND PRIZE DESIGN
Submitted by Wm. J. Mooney, Jamaica Plain, Massachusetts

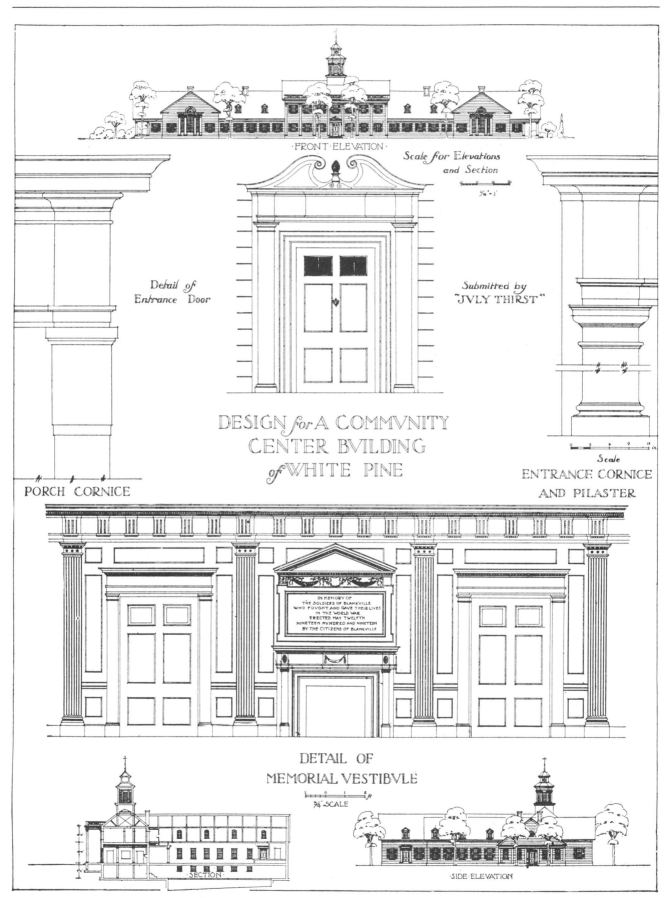

·FRONT·ELEVATION·

Scale for Elevations
and Section

Detail of
Entrance Door

Submitted by
"JVLY THIRST"

DESIGN for A COMMVNITY
CENTER BVILDING
of WHITE PINE

PORCH CORNICE

ENTRANCE CORNICE
AND PILASTER

IN MEMORY OF
THE SOLDIERS OF BLANKVILLE
WHO FOVGHT AND GAVE THEIR LIVES
IN THE WORLD WAR
ERECTED MAY TWELFTH
NINETEEN HVNDRED AND NINETEEN
BY THE CITIZENS OF BLANKVILLE

DETAIL OF
MEMORIAL VESTIBVLE

¾"·SCALE

·SECTION·

·SIDE·ELEVATION·

THIRD PRIZE DESIGN, Detail Sheet
Submitted by Leslie W. Devereux, New York, New York

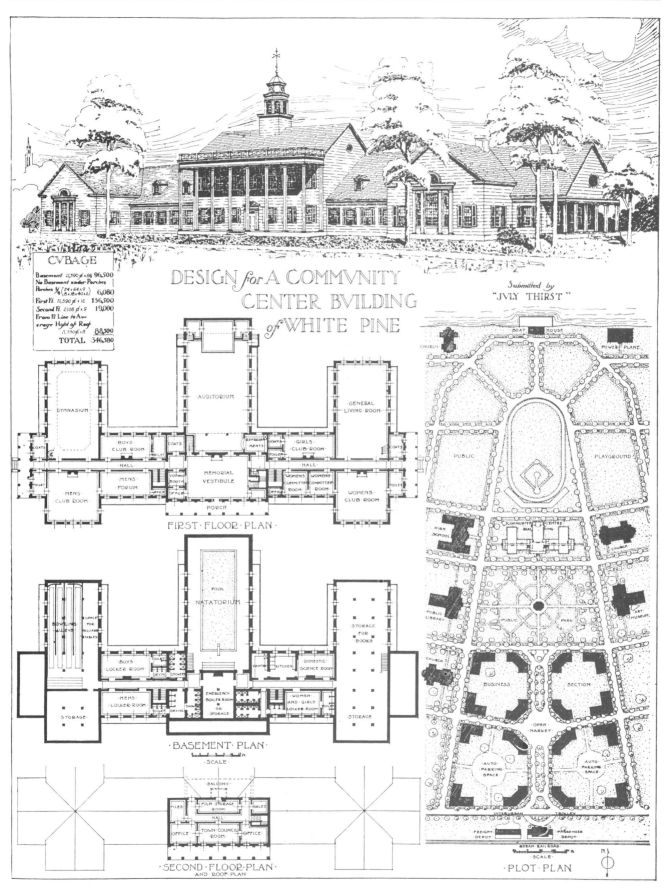

THIRD PRIZE DESIGN
Submitted by Leslie W. Devereux, New York, New York

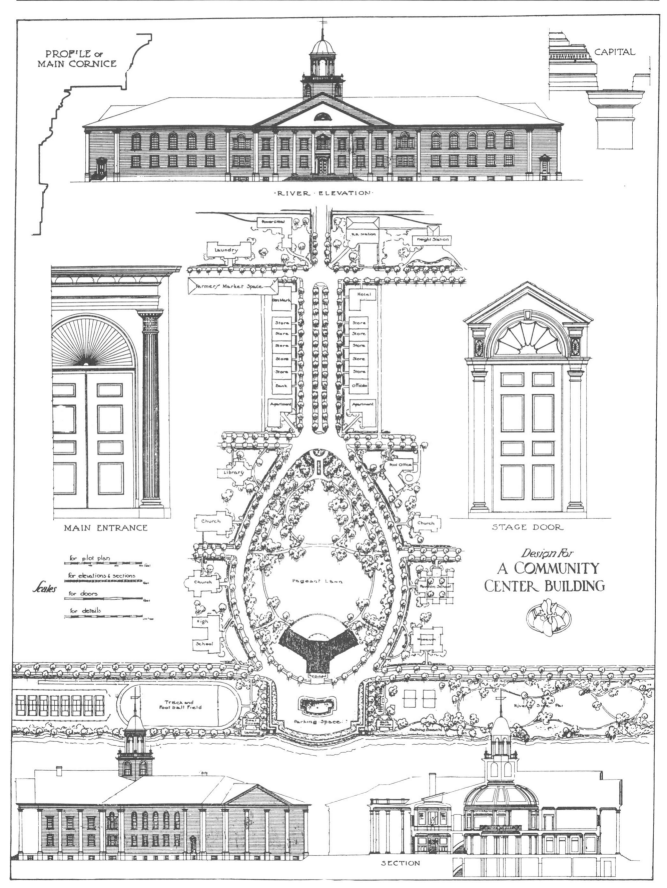

FOURTH PRIZE DESIGN, Detail Sheet

Submitted by Frederick C. Disque, Albert A. Farnham and Maurice E. Kressley, State College, Pennsylvania

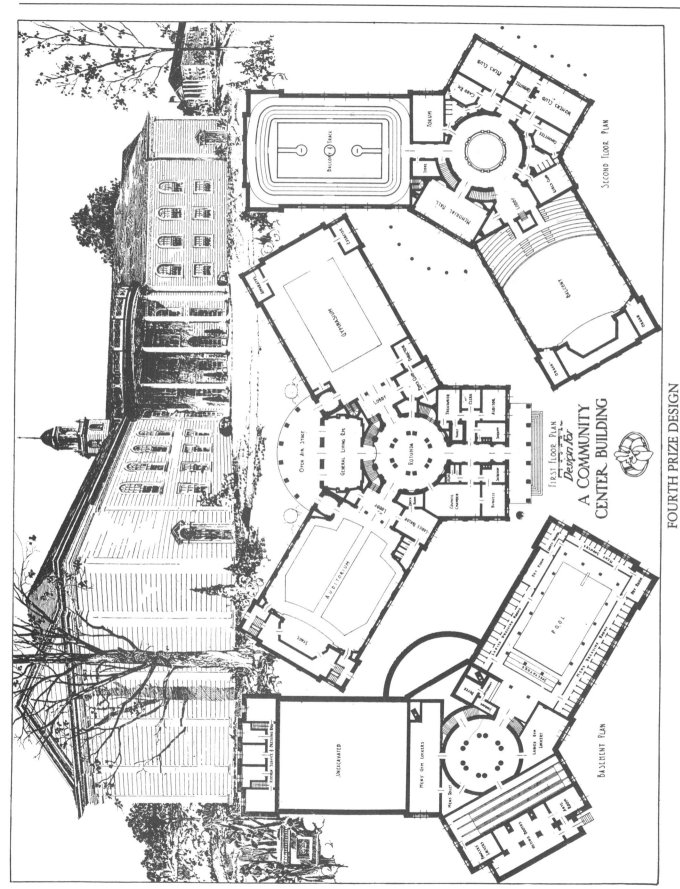

FOURTH PRIZE DESIGN

Submitted by Frederick C. Disque, Albert A. Farnham and Maurice E. Kressley, State College, Pennsylvania

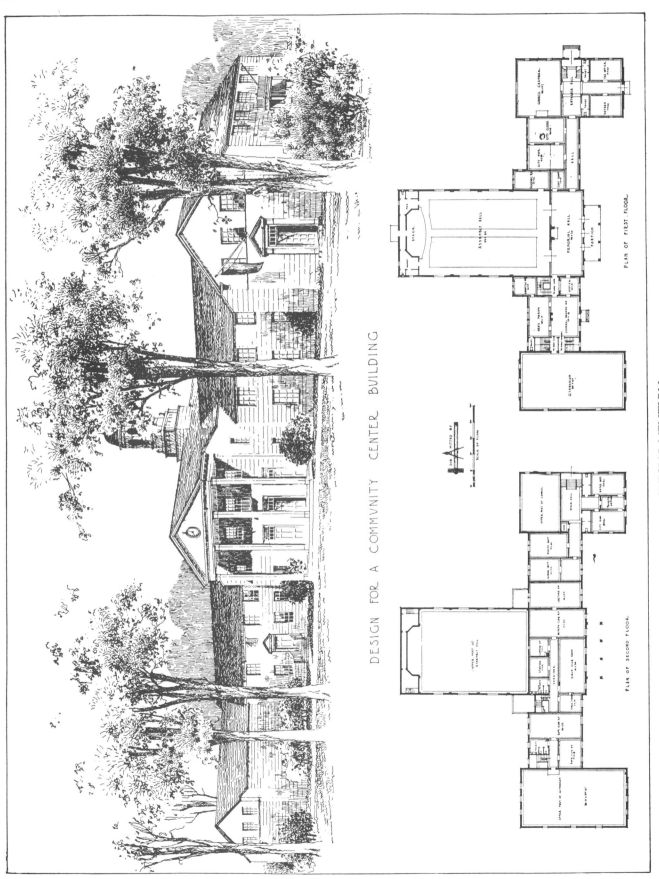

DESIGN FOR A COMMVNITY CENTER BVILDING

SPECIAL MENTION

Submitted by Paul R. Williams, Los Angeles, California

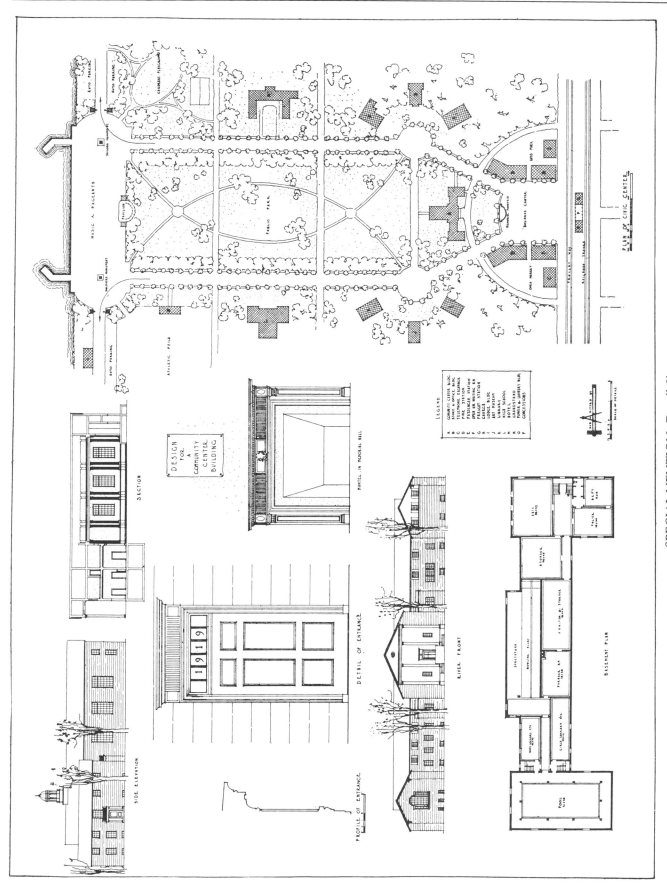

SPECIAL MENTION, Detail Sheet

Submitted by Paul R. Williams, Los Angeles, California

A DESIGN FOR A COMMUNITY CENTER BUILDING

SUBMITTED BY

MENTION

Submitted by Henry Herbert Dean, New York, New York

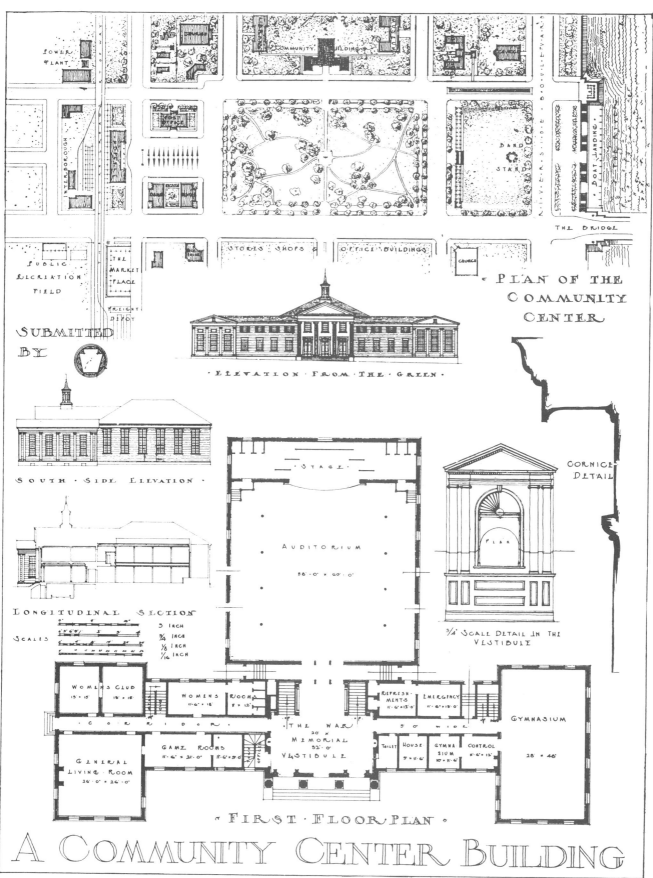

POWER PLANT

INTERBOROUGH

PUBLIC RECREATION FIELD

THE MARKET PLACE

FREIGHT DEPOT

COMMUNITY BUILDING

STORES SHOPS & OFFICE BUILDINGS

CHURCH

BAND STAND

RIVER SIDE BOULEVARD

BOAT LANDING

THE BRIDGE

· PLAN OF THE COMMUNITY CENTER

SUBMITTED BY

· ELEVATION · FROM · THE · GREEN ·

· SOUTH · SIDE · ELEVATION ·

CORNICE DETAIL

· STAGE ·

AUDITORIUM
38'-0" × 60'-0"

PLAN

3/4 SCALE DETAIL IN THE VESTIBULE

LONGITUDINAL SECTION

SCALES
3 INCH
3/4 INCH
1/8 INCH
1/16 INCH

WOMENS CLUB
15' × 15'   18' × 18'

WOMENS ROOMS
11'-6" × 18'   8' × 12'

REFRESHMENTS
11'-6" × 12'-0"

EMERGENCY
11'-6" × 12'-0"

GYMNASIUM
28' × 48'

CORRIDOR

GAME ROOMS
11'-6" × 21'-0"   11'-6" × 56'

GENERAL LIVING ROOM
26'-0" × 26'-0"

OFFICE

THE WAR
20 ×
MEMORIAL
32'-0"
VESTIBULE

5'-0" WIDE

TOILET HOUSE
5' × 11'-6"

GYMNASIUM
10' × 11'-6"

CONTROL
8'-6" × 12'

· FIRST · FLOOR · PLAN ·

A COMMUNITY CENTER BUILDING

MENTION, Detail Sheet
Submitted by Henry Herbert Dean, New York, New York

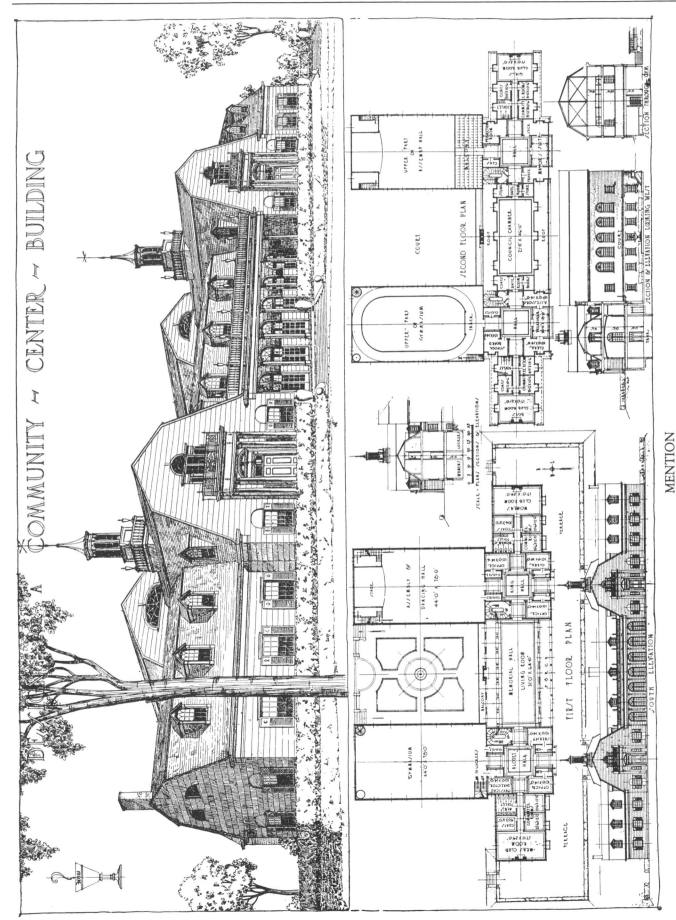

A COMMUNITY CENTER BUILDING

MENTION

Submitted by Clarence E. Wechselberger, Chicago, Illinois

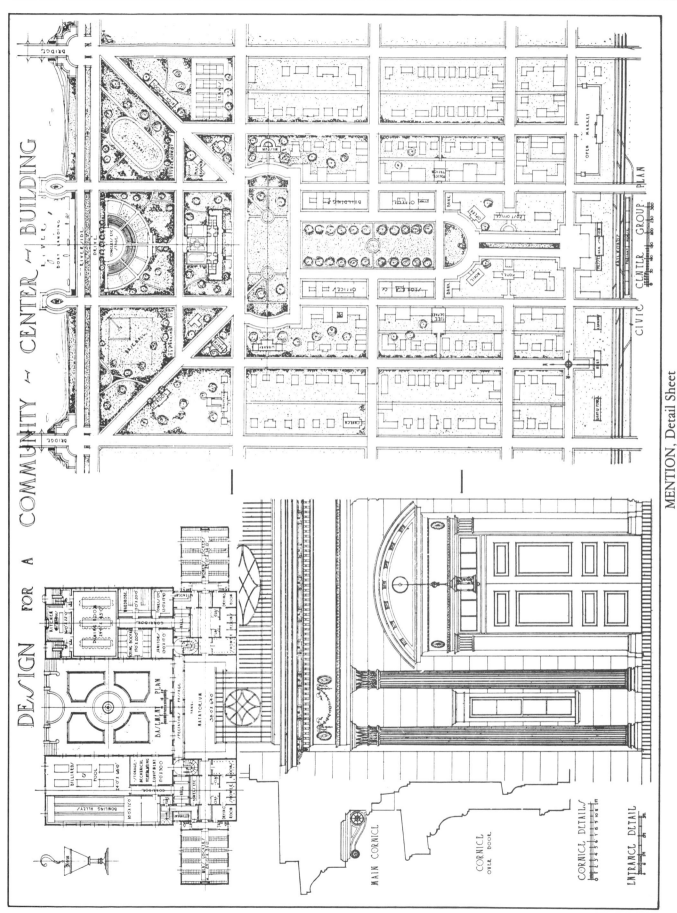

DESIGN FOR A COMMUNITY CENTER BUILDING

CIVIC CENTER GROUP PLAN

MAIN CORNICE

CORNICE
OVER DOOR

CORNICE DETAILS

ENTRANCE DETAIL

MENTION, Detail Sheet

Submitted by Clarence E. Wechselberger, Chicago, Illinois

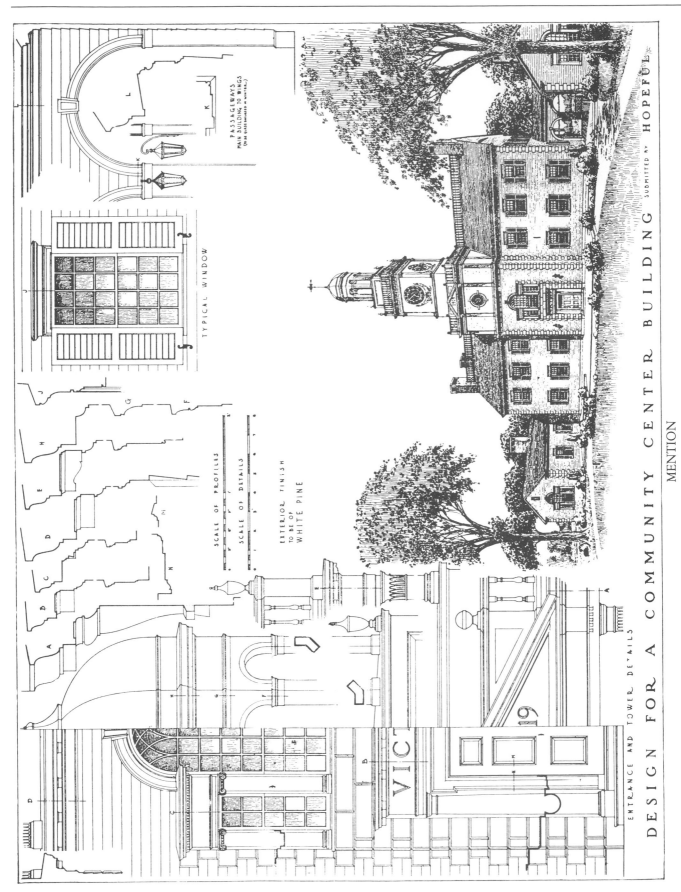

PASSAGEWAYS
MAIN BUILDING TO WINGS
(TO BE GLASS ENCLOSED IN WINTER.)

TYPICAL WINDOW

SCALE OF PROFILES

SCALE OF DETAILS

EXTERIOR FINISH
TO BE OF
WHITE PINE

ENTRANCE AND TOWER DETAILS

DESIGN FOR A COMMUNITY CENTER BUILDING   SUBMITTED BY HOPEFUL

MENTION

Submitted by Carl C. Tallman and R. Douglas Steele, Auburn, New York

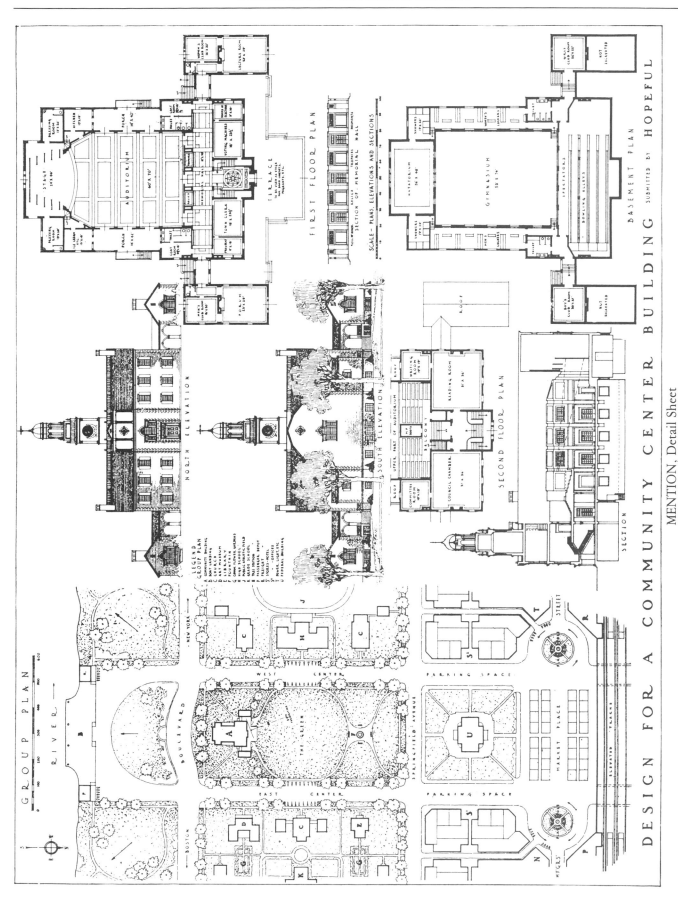

DESIGN FOR A COMMUNITY CENTER BUILDING

MENTION, Detail Sheet

Submitted by Carl C. Tallman and R. Douglas Steele, Auburn, New York

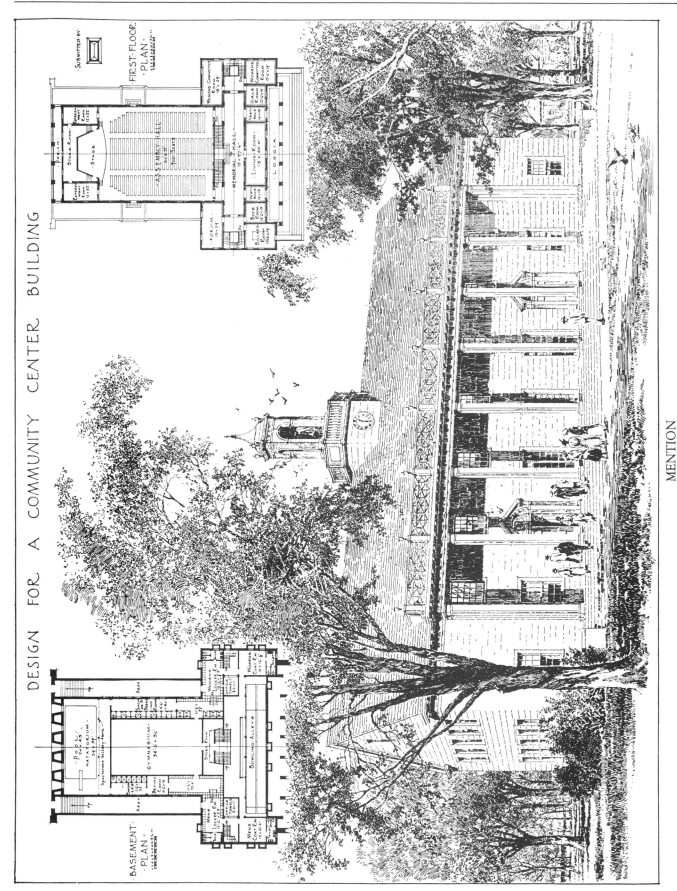

DESIGN FOR A COMMUNITY CENTER BUILDING

FIRST-FLOOR-PLAN-

BASEMENT-PLAN-

MENTION

Submitted by E. J. Maier, T. E. King and F. Lange, Toledo, Ohio

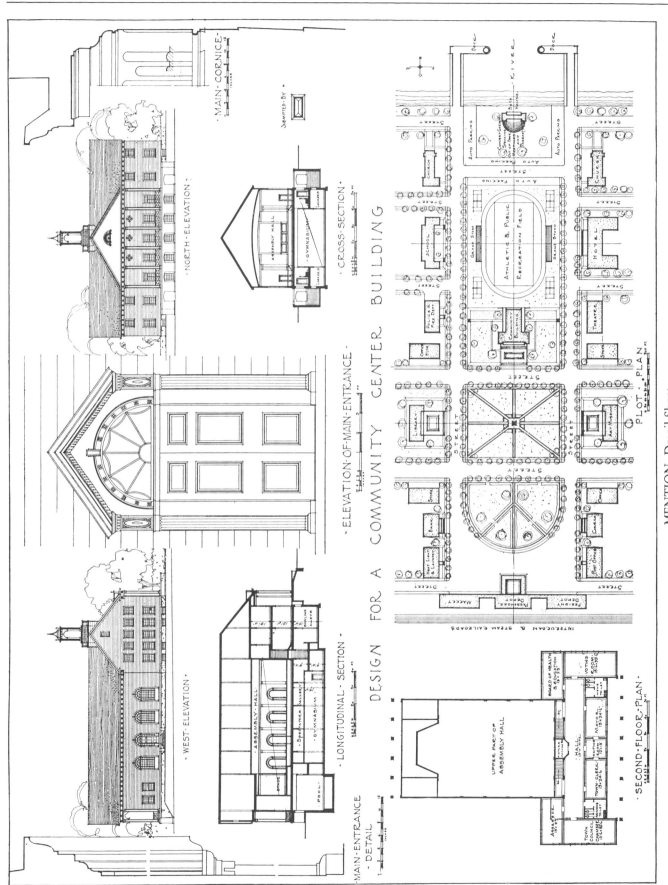

· DESIGN · FOR · A · COMMUNITY · CENTER · BUILDING ·

· NORTH · ELEVATION ·

· MAIN · CORNICE ·

· CROSS · SECTION ·

· ELEVATION · OF · MAIN · ENTRANCE ·

· WEST · ELEVATION ·

· LONGITUDINAL · SECTION ·

· MAIN · ENTRANCE · DETAIL ·

· PLOT · PLAN ·

· SECOND · FLOOR · PLAN ·

MENTION, Detail Sheet

Submitted by E. J. Maier, T. E. King and F. Lange, Toledo, Ohio

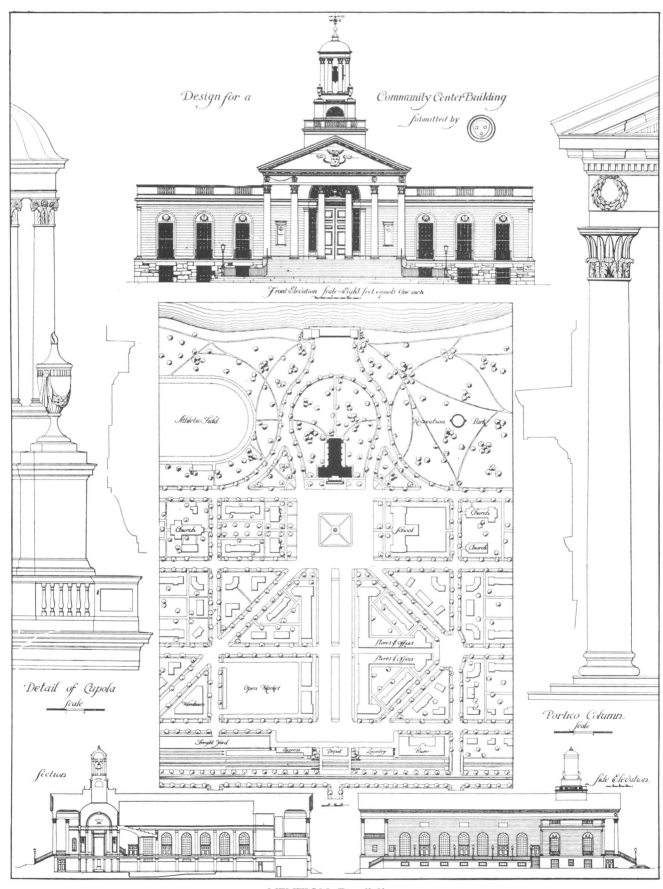

Design for a *Community Center Building*
submitted by

Front Elevation scale~Eight feet equals One inch

Detail of Cupola
scale

Portico Column
scale

section

side Elevation

MENTION, Detail Sheet
Submitted by Charles Mink and O. R. Eggers, New York, New York

Design for a Community Center Building

submitted by

MCMXIX

Basement

First Floor

Scale for Plans

MENTION

Submitted by Charles Mink and O. R. Eggers, New York, New York

square, the authors have saved a large area for a broad lawn, beyond the Community Building, sloping to the river, for pageantry, athletics and the other outdoor activities of community life. The Community Center Building has a well lighted, well balanced plan. The various services are well placed, and the entrances and exits are particularly well arranged for the several uses to which the building will be put. We find the character of the building and its presentation altogether delightful. The exigencies of wood construction, if not of structural ethics, probably allow the two-story rotunda to float lightly on the top of the bowling alleys and corridors of the basement. Nevertheless, we ourselves, in a building of this presumable simplicity, would have preferred to discard the interior rotunda if it became in any sense an architectural misfit.

SECOND PRIZE DESIGN. In the design awarded second place the distinct atmosphere of a New England village is maintained and the design both subordinates itself and characterizes the atmosphere. The group plan, while convenient and logical, does not depart from the scale of a New England village subdivision as to streets, size of buildings or of open spaces. The commercial facilities are grouped around the station, and the Community Center Building, as the important focal point, is at the base of the composition and opposite the entrance to the village. In this design as well as in a number of others, the river front is used to advantage. Under the conditions of the problem, it is the opinion of the Jury that the river is quite as important a feature as the railroads, and those designers who have developed that possibility have secured a very favorable consideration by the Jury. The plan of the Community Center Building is straightforward, convenient and logical. The features of the plan are evident and do not need special mention—with one exception: that is, the position of the voting booths, to which reference has already been made.

THIRD PRIZE DESIGN. The design placed as third is not as successful as the first two on account, among other things, of the separation of the community center from the business center by a park, which seems to result in the subdivision of the entire tract into four separate spots. The business center seems too formal for a village of this population. The two converging main streets are well located and would afford pleasing vistas to the river. The location of the public playgrounds and the athletic fields is good, but the Jury regrets that the author

has not taken greater advantage of the possible development of the river front. To be specific, in a small detail the balancing of a church with a power plant is not fortunate.

The exterior of the building is highly pleasing and thoroughly expresses the idea of a village community center, and is, moreover, entirely appropriate to its use. The plan of the building is one of the strongest features of the design. The position of the auditorium is correct and it is well proportioned. The gymnasium is well lighted and ventilated. The wing of the building adjacent to the general living room and women's rooms is also well designed, and the porches at each end are very attractive features. The position of the voting booths is good, though more light would be desirable, and the separation of the town offices in the second floor of the central part of the building is very good, indeed.

FOURTH PRIZE DESIGN. The fourth prize design is an interesting variant. It is noteworthy principally for the admirable community use it makes of the river frontage. A riverside park, bathing beach, tennis courts and athletic field are here provided. The conception of the author appears to have been that the Community Center Building should be placed in close relation to the river front, and would seem to have been so planned as to command views up and down the river. The plan of the building is interesting, but the *poché* does not express a frame building. The treatment of the ends of the two wings, while it would undoubtedly be impressive if executed in stone, would be exceedingly bleak in clapboards. In the general plan an effort seems to have been made to plant out these two uninteresting ends, a device which should have been made unnecessary.

SPECIAL MENTION. While the programme did not call for any first mention, the solution was so good in this case that the Jury felt it to be worthy of special commendation. The principal criticism of the group plan is the lack of scale in some particulars, and the plans of the building, while workable, are amateurish. With these exceptions, it is an excellent expression of a Community Center Group, has the charm of a New England town, and the Community Building is unmistakably a wooden structure.

WALTER H. KILHAM
H. VAN BUREN MAGONIGLE   } Jury
DWIGHT H. PERKINS   } of
E. J. RUSSELL   } Award
WADDY B. WOOD

A Roadside Tavern

Report of the Jury of Award
Given May 14 and 15, 1920
Originally published in 1920 as White Pine Monograph
Volume VI, Number 4

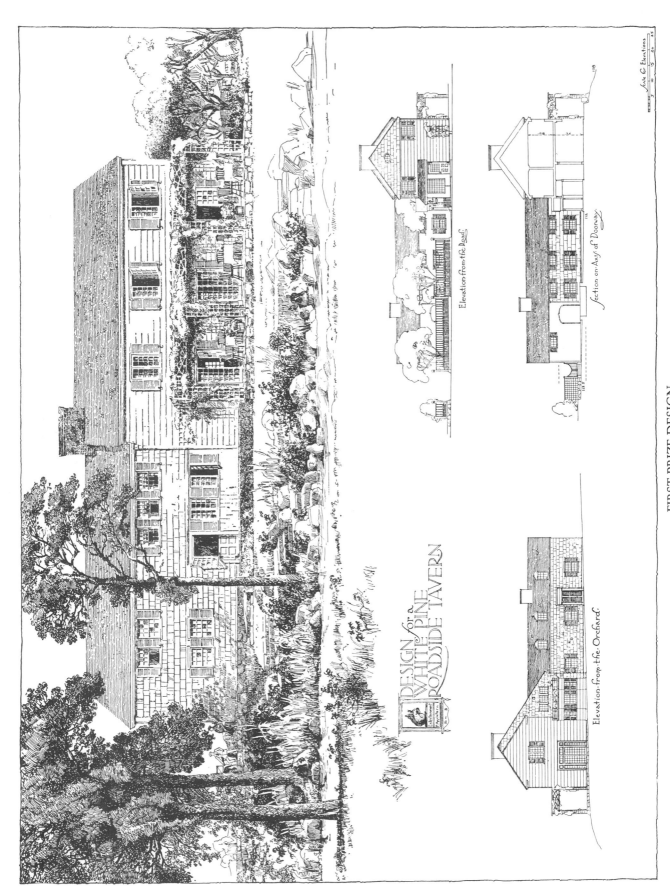

DESIGN for a WHITE PINE ROADSIDE TAVERN

Elevation from the Road.

Section on Axis of Doorway.

Elevation from the Orchard.

FIRST PRIZE DESIGN

Submitted by Joseph, Hudnut and Carl D. Montgomery, New York, New York

A ROADSIDE TAVERN

Report of the Jury of Award of the Fifth Annual White Pine Architectural Competition

Judged at the Biltmore, New York, NY, May 14 and 15, 1920

PROBLEM: The design of a roadside tavern, to be built of White Pine, which is for all year round use, and which is to include a restaurant, and living quarters for the people who run it. The requirements are as follows: A dining-room, area 750 square feet, and of such shape that the removal of tables would permit it to be used for dancing; men's dining-room, area 200 square feet; private dining-room, area 175 square feet; private dining-room, area 100 square feet; reception-room, area 250 square feet; adequate lavatories and toilet-rooms for both men and women; kitchen and service portion, area 500 square feet; chauffeurs' dining-room, area 150 square feet; living-room for proprietor's family, area 300 square feet; two main bedrooms, area 225 square feet each, and one bath; four servants' bedrooms, area 80 square feet each, and one bath; a space for the sale of candies and soft drinks, area 125 square feet, with direct access from the highway. These rooms may be disposed in one, two, or three stories, as the competitor may elect. Floor heights should not be less than 8 feet, nor exceed 12 feet. Cellar will be required for heating purposes only, and need not be indicated on drawings. No piazzas other than an entrance porch are required. The problem shall include a layout of the plot indicated herewith, showing development of the property as a whole. The competitor shall design an appropriate hanging sign for the entrance, which, drawn at a scale of ½ inch to the foot, shall be his *nom de plume* or device. The architectural style is optional.

THE problem presented in the Fifth Annual Architectural Competition conducted by THE WHITE PINE SERIES OF ARCHITECTURAL MONOGRAPHS involved a study of a Roadside Tavern, and its grounds, and the Jury of Award, in making its decisions, considered the general layout, the plan of the building to meet the needs of guests, and the character of the building within and without as designed to attract the motoring public, not only to stop, but to return.

A hundred designs were submitted, and the members of the Jury were almost overwhelmed with the very large number which were good— so good that they could not be readily or quickly eliminated. It is one of the most encouraging indications of the progress of architecture in this country to find in a general competition of this kind such a very large number of good designs. Older members of the profession, who look back twenty-five or thirty years, can see the very extraordinary advance not only in draughtsmanship but in thoughtful, intelligent design that has marked these years. Men who

could render as well as half of these hundred competitors were rare and eagerly sought after simply as renderers. Men who could design with the head as well as the hands were rarer still in architects' offices. In the last analysis, a large number of the designs may be fairly looked upon as worthy of any of the best offices in the country. It is more and more borne in upon the architects of the country that however much they may themselves contribute to the training of their draughtsmen, it is the draughtsmen themselves who make a very substantial contribution to the reputation of the office in which they work, and the Jury wishes to take this opportunity of emphasizing and acknowledging the debt which the architects owe to their draughtsmen. In architecture, more than in any other of the great arts, the best achievement is due to many minds working together, and no one man can claim credit for the masterpieces of architecture which have put this country in the forefront in architectural achievement.

The programme required that the tavern should contain rooms convenient for the entertainment of the public for meals, but not for the night, and should have accommodations for motor cars and chauffeurs, for the servants of the tavern, and for the proprietor's family.

FIRST PRIZE DESIGN. The design placed first has a good general plan. The building, "L" shaped, is close to the road, thus wasting none of the small lot in space for motors to enter or park, and reserving the front on the stream and the apple orchard for the use of the guests. The entrances, both from the court and direct from the street, are well placed to serve the public rooms, the main dining-room occupying the best corner, while the service portion occupies the wing. The exterior expresses the character and the use of the building. Simple and dignified, it is yet distinctly a tavern and not a private house, and the use of differing materials on the outside expresses very cleverly the main public parlors and the service wing. The dining-room French windows open on the terrace, of which more might well have been made. The little shop is admirably located near the street and yet is a part of the composition. The detail sheet shows thorough understanding and both exterior and interior are charming, and though distinctly borrowed, are none the less evidences of judgment and good taste. Incidentally, one questions the use of large beams running lengthwise of the dining-room, but this perhaps is being hyper-critical of a design that is excellent and which would undoubtedly look better rather than worse in execution.

SECOND PRIZE DESIGN. The design placed second came very near that placed first, and perhaps the only reason for this order of one and two was the fact that each of the jurymen independently placed first the one awarded first place, and all independently placed this design second. Both, however, are very good, and this design has its special merits. The general plan lets motors through to the rear, but the guests are landed direct from the street, and no space is wasted. The orchard and stream are preserved for the enjoyment of the guests. All the dining-rooms face this pleasant outlook, and the proprietor's living-rooms are equally well taken care of. The exterior is good in character, simple but full of charm, with a delightful hooded entrance and a portico which connects the front with the dining-rooms at the rear. The interior is simple and dignified, and other details show a thorough knowledge of design. The wrought-iron work is well designed and judiciously used where it gives the best effect. The building as a whole is so planned as to be equally attractive from any approach.

THIRD PRIZE DESIGN. The design placed third is totally different in conception from either one or two, for the author has deliberately and very wisely taken advantage of the contours of the land, and utilized both the first floor and the basement for rooms looking out on the stream. The general plan is admirable. The building is set close to the road; the easy approach and the view of the building are so attractive as to demand immediate attention; but the approach from the other direction, which is not shown, is equally attractive, and is not the least interesting part of the plan. The two-story plan already referred to simplifies the concentration of service, and dining-rooms are well placed for convenience of service. The details of the designs placed first and second are excellent examples of thorough classical knowledge; the details here are equally convincing as examples of good use of the very simplest forms. The wise use of simple material and simple forms is another sign of good taste which is rapidly coming into popular favor. It is somewhat remarkable that a country like ours, new in matters of the Fine Arts, with little or no tradition and no great examples before us, should have so completely avoided the pitfalls of over-loaded ornament and of the straining after something new, which has injured the architecture of both France and England, and absolutely vulgarized any shred of good taste in Germany. The affectations of England and the "New Art" of France never have touched our architects, and we are today doing the most restrained and most conservative work. The third design shows this restraint.

FOURTH PRIZE DESIGN. The design placed fourth was so placed unanimously, and yet the Jury regretted that the terms prevented giving equal or almost equal recognition to another design. In fact, closely following the four leaders there were others who "also ran." The general plan of the fourth prize design is simple and straightforward. The building is placed frankly where it belongs, near the highway, and all the land behind and by the stream is reserved for the guests. The proprietor, rather than the guests, enjoys the outlook over the stream. However, the plan is good and logical, with the guests' portion in the centre, the service on one side and the proprietor on the other; the private dining-rooms are upstairs over the centre portion, with the servants' rooms also upstairs. The proprietor's bedrooms are isolated in the right-hand wing. The interior and exterior details are quiet and restrained, and show a thorough knowledge which is admirable.

(Continued on page 150)

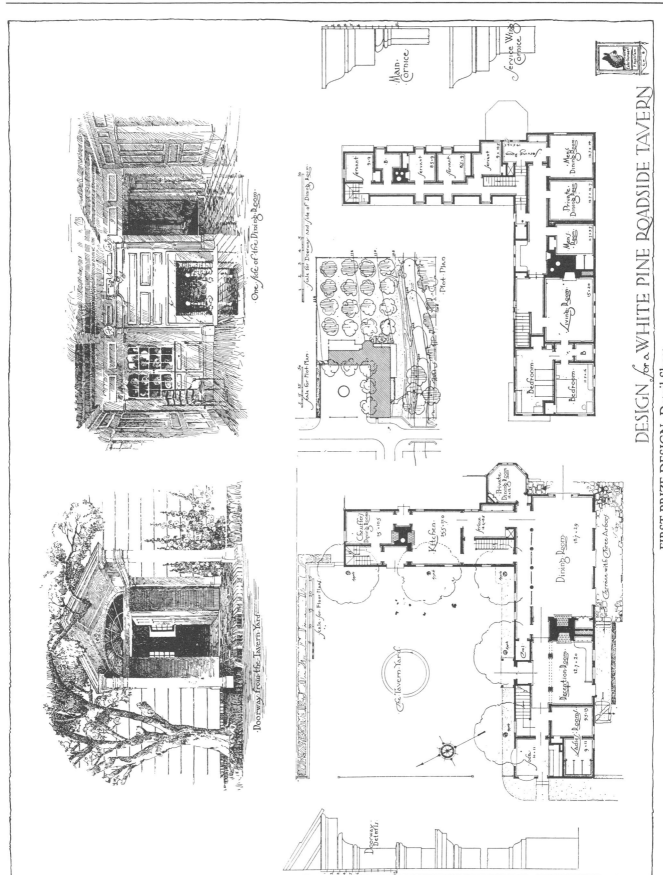

Main Cornice

Service Wing Cornice

One Side of the Dining Room

Scale for Doorway and Side of Dining Room

Plot Plan

Scale for Plot Plan

Servant 9·9

B

Servant 8·5·9

Servant 8·5·9

Servant 9·2·9

Serving Room

Men's Dining Room 18·7·31

Private Dining Room 18·7·31

Men's Dining Room 8·3·7

Living Room 15·7·26

Bedroom

Bedroom

B

Doorway from the Tavern Yard

Scale for Floor Plan

Chauffeur Dining Room 15·10·5

Kitchen 15·5·17·0

Service Entrance

Private Dining Room

The Tavern Yard

Dining Room 15·7·22·9

Coat

Reception Room 12·7·20

Hall

Ladies Room 5·5·15

Lobby 10·11

Terrace with Three Arbors

Doorway Detail

DESIGN for a WHITE PINE ROADSIDE TAVERN

FIRST PRIZE DESIGN, Detail Sheet

Submitted by Joseph Hudnut and Carl D. Montgomery, New York, New York

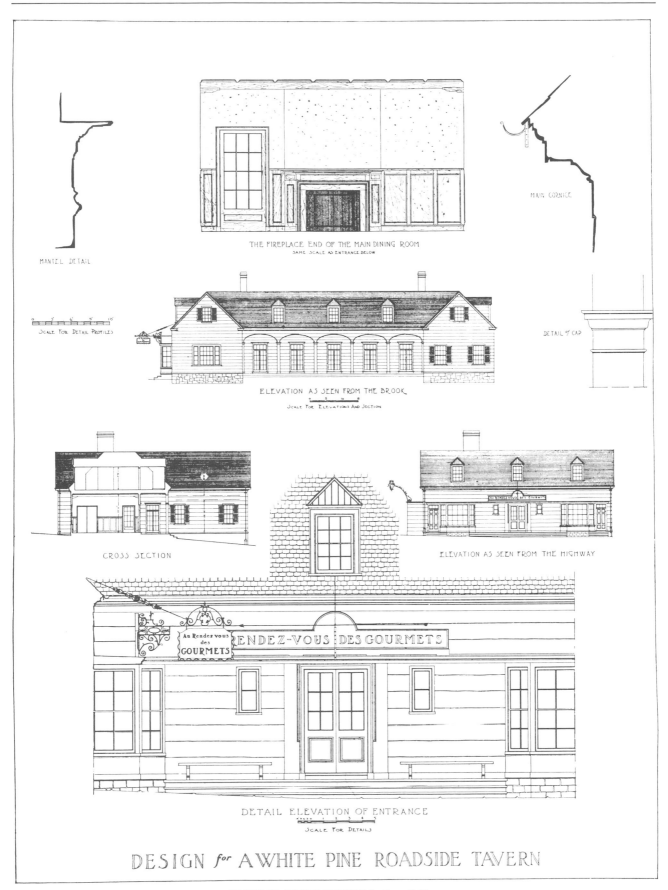

MANTEL DETAIL

THE FIREPLACE END OF THE MAIN DINING ROOM
SAME SCALE AS ENTRANCE BELOW

MAIN CORNICE

SCALE FOR DETAIL PROFILES

ELEVATION AS SEEN FROM THE BROOK
SCALE FOR ELEVATIONS AND SECTION

DETAIL OF CAP

CROSS SECTION

ELEVATION AS SEEN FROM THE HIGHWAY

Au Rendez-vous des GOURMETS

RENDEZ-VOUS DES GOURMETS

DETAIL ELEVATION OF ENTRANCE
SCALE FOR DETAILS

DESIGN for A WHITE PINE ROADSIDE TAVERN

SECOND PRIZE DESIGN, Detail Sheet
Submitted by Robbins L. Conn, New York, New York

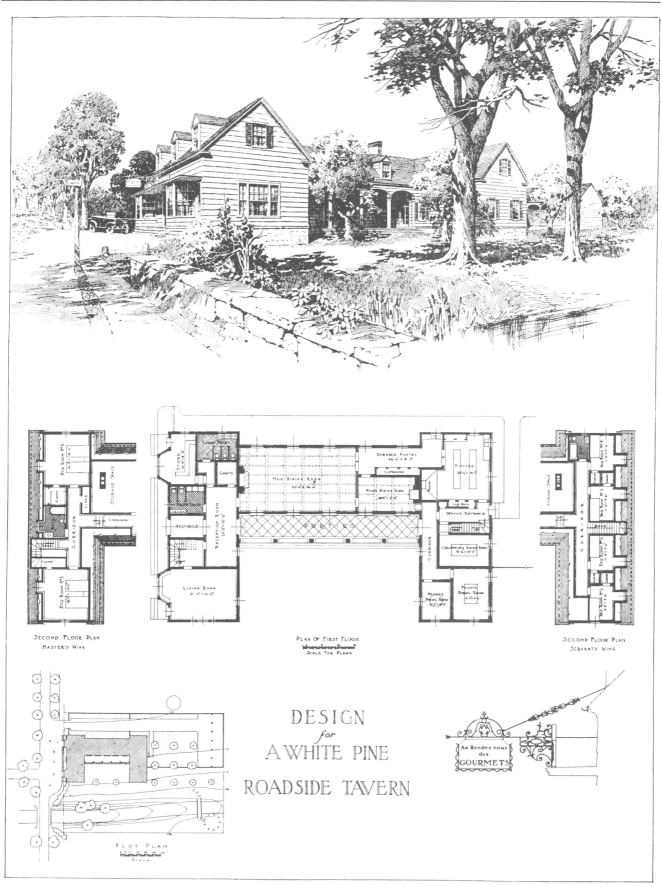

DESIGN
for
A WHITE PINE
ROADSIDE TAVERN

SECOND PRIZE DESIGN
Submitted by Robbins L. Conn, New York, New York

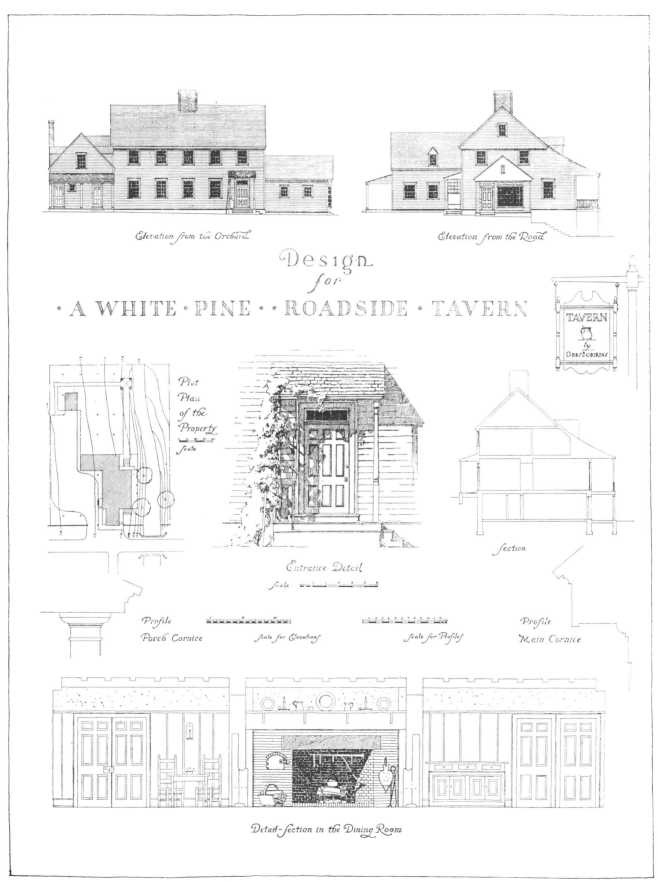

Elevation from the Orchard

Elevation from the Road

Design
for
· A WHITE · PINE · · ROADSIDE · TAVERN

TAVERN
by
Odds Bodikins

Plot
Plan
of the
Property
scale

Entrance Detail
scale

Section

Profile
Porch Cornice

scale for Elevations

scale for Profiles

Profile
Main Cornice

Detail-Section in the Dining Room

THIRD PRIZE DESIGN, Detail Sheet
Submitted by Thomas Bond Owings and Henry Herbert Dean, New York, New York

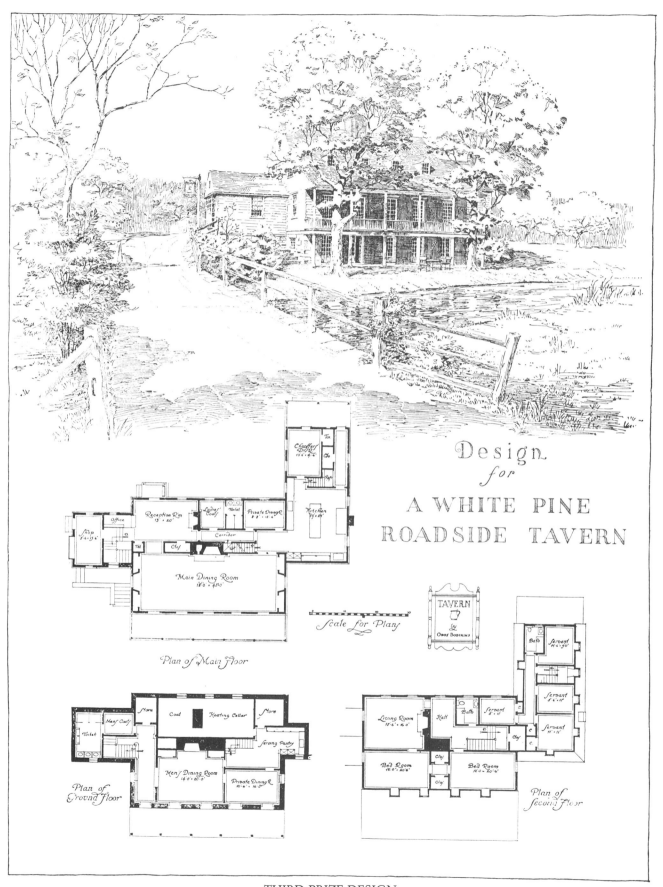

Design
for
A WHITE PINE
ROADSIDE TAVERN

Plan of Main Floor

Scale for Plans

Plan of Ground Floor

Plan of Second Floor

THIRD PRIZE DESIGN
Submitted by Thomas Bond Owings and Henry Herbert Dean, New York, New York

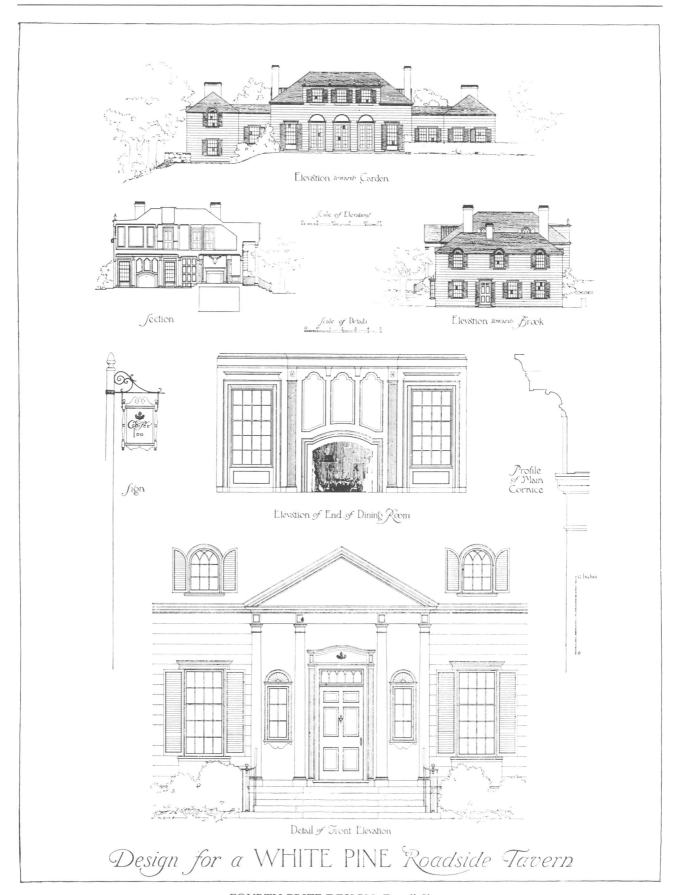

Elevation towards Garden

Scale of Elevations

Section

Scale of Details

Elevation towards Brook

Sign

Elevation of End of Dining Room

Profile of Plain Cornice

Detail of Front Elevation

Design for a WHITE PINE Roadside Tavern

FOURTH PRIZE DESIGN, Detail Sheet
Submitted by P. Donald Horgan, William J. Mooney, and Harold A. Rich, Boston, Massachusetts

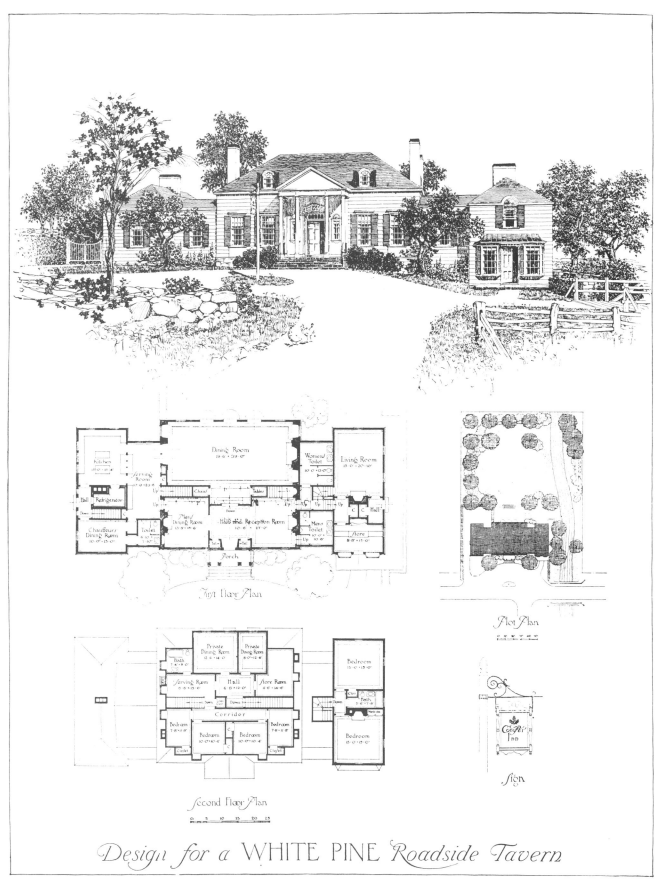

Design for a WHITE PINE *Roadside Tavern*

FOURTH PRIZE DESIGN

Submitted by P. Donald Horgan, William J. Mooney, and Harold A. Rich, Boston, Massachusetts

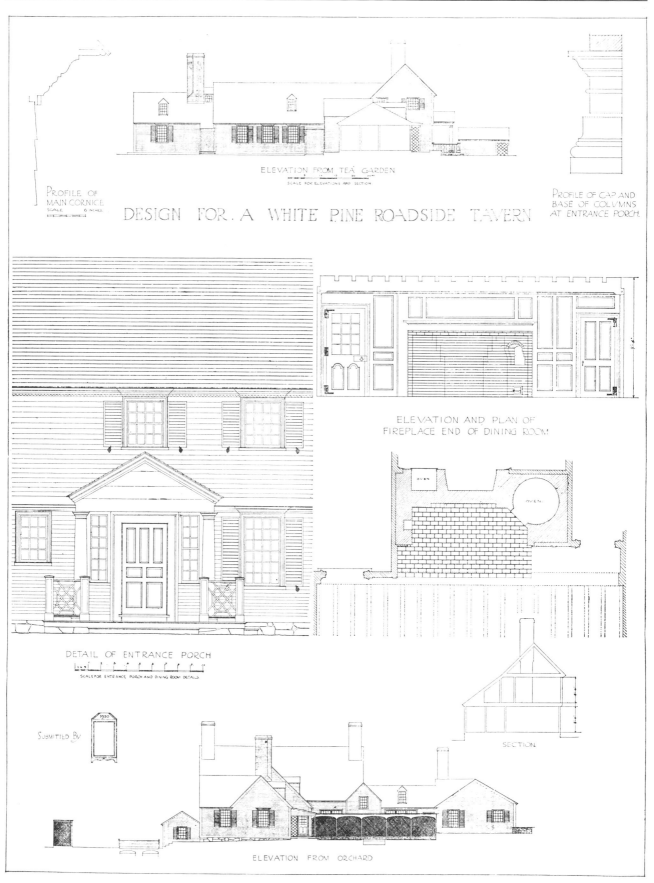

ELEVATION FROM TEA GARDEN
SCALE FOR ELEVATIONS AND SECTION.

PROFILE OF
MAIN CORNICE
SCALE   6 INCHES.

DESIGN FOR A WHITE PINE ROADSIDE TAVERN

PROFILE OF CAP AND
BASE OF COLUMNS
AT ENTRANCE PORCH.

ELEVATION AND PLAN OF
FIREPLACE END OF DINING ROOM

DETAIL OF ENTRANCE PORCH
SCALE FOR ENTRANCE PORCH AND DINING ROOM DETAILS

SECTION

SUBMITTED BY

ELEVATION FROM ORCHARD

FIRST MENTION, Detail Sheet
Submitted by Richard M. Powers and Joseph G. McGann, Boston, Massachusetts

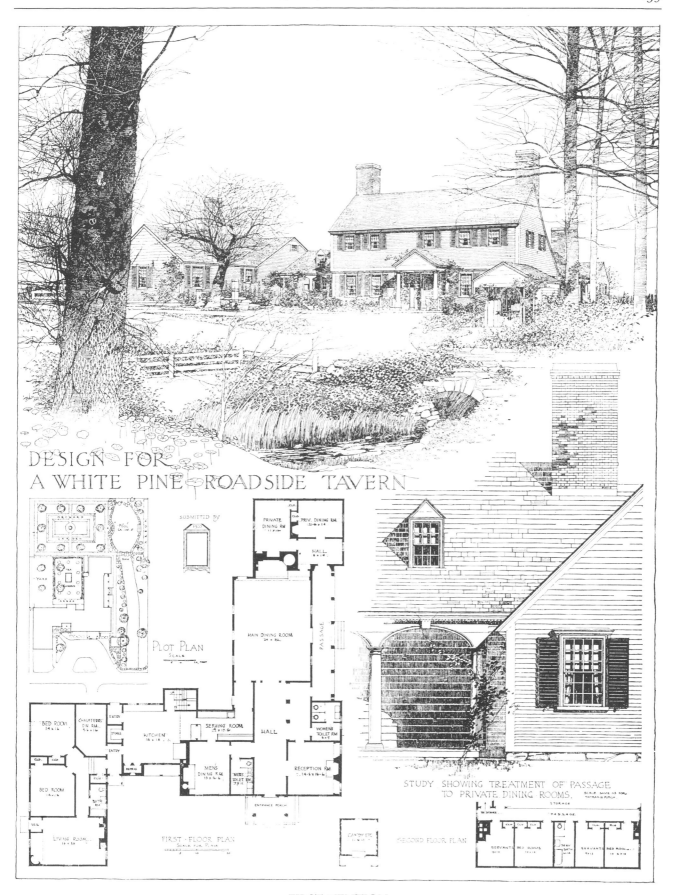

DESIGN FOR
A WHITE PINE ROADSIDE TAVERN

PLOT PLAN

FIRST·FLOOR PLAN

STUDY SHOWING TREATMENT OF PASSAGE
TO PRIVATE DINING ROOMS.

SECOND FLOOR PLAN

FIRST MENTION
Submitted by Richard M. Powers and Joseph G. McGann, Boston, Massachusetts

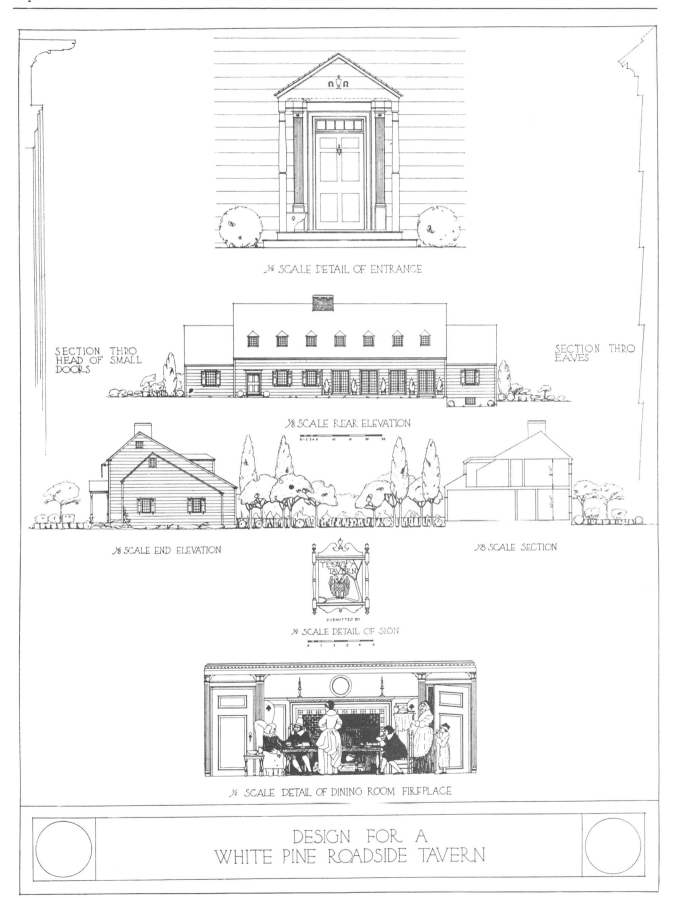

½ SCALE DETAIL OF ENTRANCE

SECTION THRO HEAD OF SMALL DOORS

SECTION THRO EAVES

⅛ SCALE REAR ELEVATION

⅛ SCALE END ELEVATION

⅛ SCALE SECTION

½ SCALE DETAIL OF SIGN

½ SCALE DETAIL OF DINING ROOM FIREPLACE

DESIGN FOR A
WHITE PINE ROADSIDE TAVERN

SECOND MENTION, Detail Sheet
Submitted by Atwell John King and Henry V. Capel, New York, New York

DESIGN FOR A
WHITE PINE ROADSIDE TAVERN

YE
OWL
TAVERN

SECOND FLOOR PLAN

FIRST FLOOR PLAN

SECOND MENTION

Submitted by Atwell John King and Henry V. Capel, New York, New York, New York

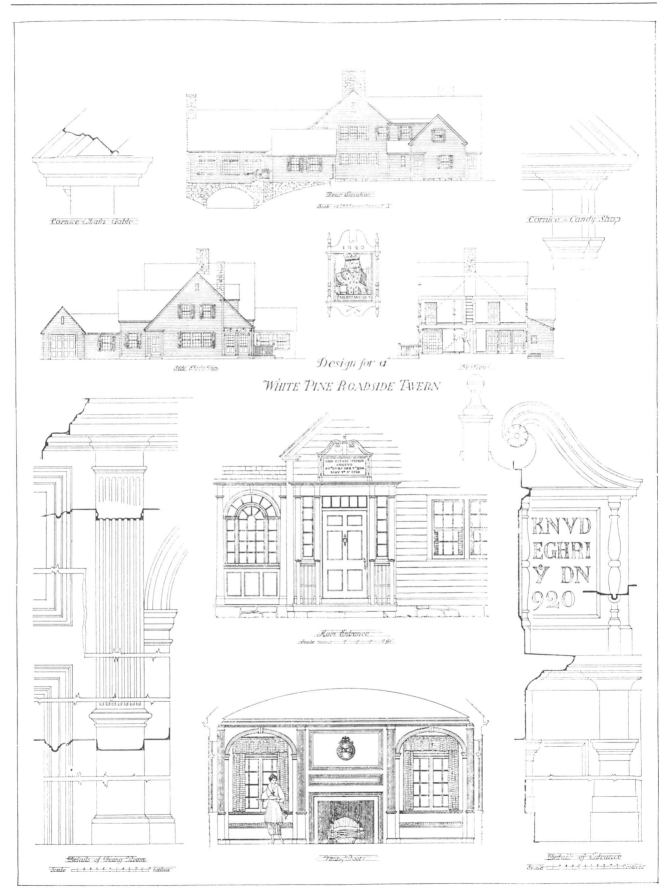

MENTION, Detail Sheet
Submitted by Donald Robb, Boston, Massachusetts

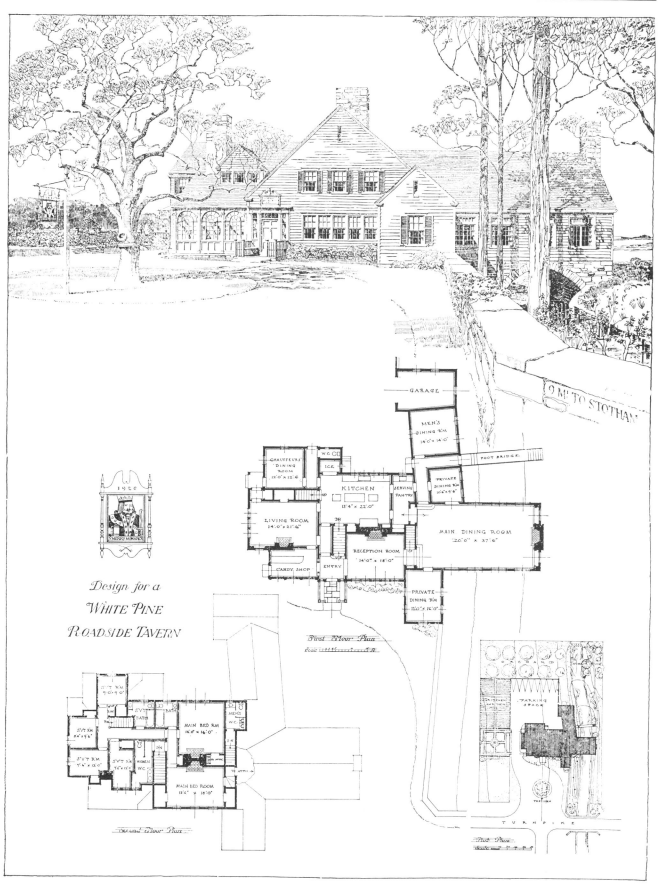

Design for a
White Pine
Roadside Tavern

MENTION
Submitted by Donald Robb, Boston, Massachusetts

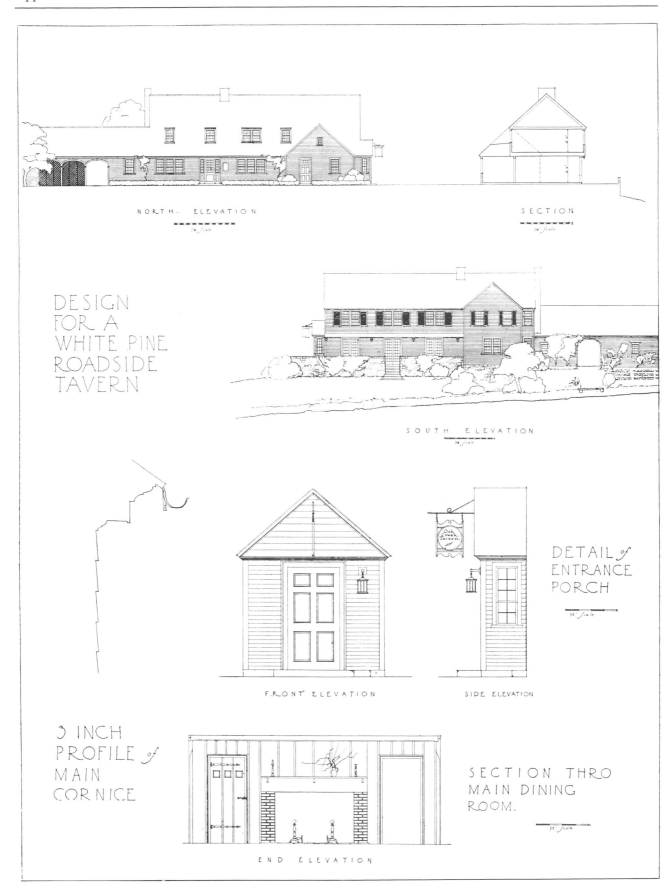

NORTH. ELEVATION

SECTION

DESIGN
FOR A
WHITE PINE
ROADSIDE
TAVERN

SOUTH ELEVATION

DETAIL of
ENTRANCE
PORCH

FRONT ELEVATION

SIDE ELEVATION

3 INCH
PROFILE of
MAIN
CORNICE

SECTION THRO
MAIN DINING
ROOM.

END ELEVATION

MENTION, Detail Sheet
Submitted by Bernhard Dirks, Chicago, Illinois

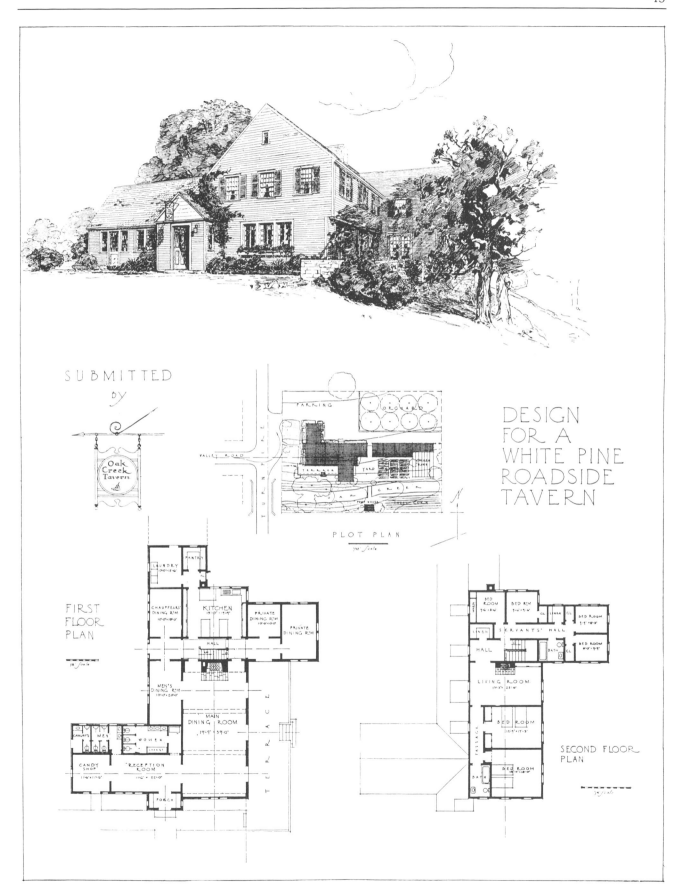

SUBMITTED
by

Oak
Creek
Tavern

PLOT PLAN

DESIGN
FOR A
WHITE PINE
ROADSIDE
TAVERN

FIRST
FLOOR
PLAN

SECOND FLOOR
PLAN

MENTION
Submitted by Bernhard Dirks, Chicago, Illinois

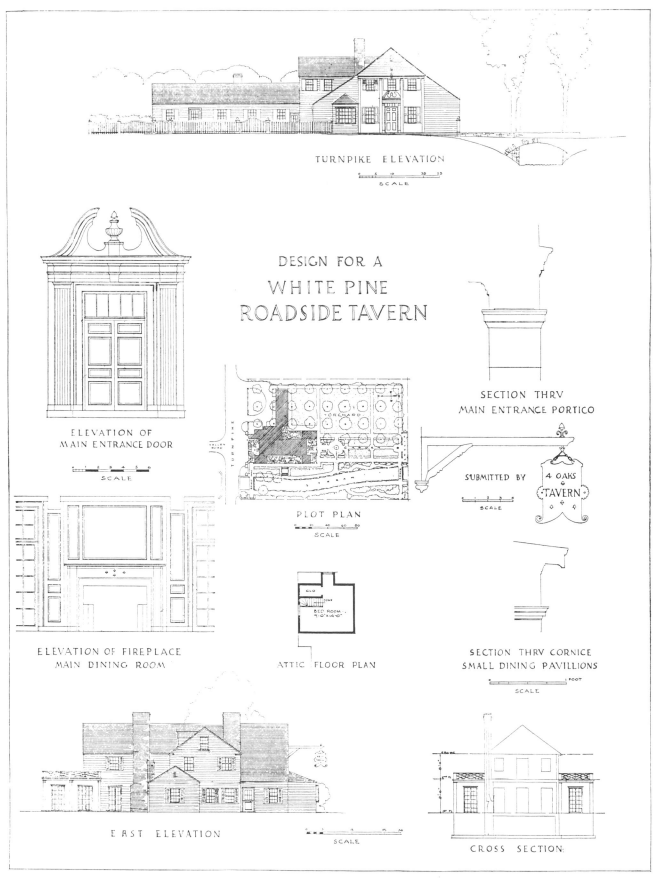

TURNPIKE ELEVATION
SCALE

DESIGN FOR A
WHITE PINE
ROADSIDE TAVERN

ELEVATION OF
MAIN ENTRANCE DOOR
SCALE

SECTION THRU
MAIN ENTRANCE PORTICO

PLOT PLAN
SCALE

SUBMITTED BY

4 OAKS
TAVERN

SCALE

ELEVATION OF FIREPLACE
MAIN DINING ROOM

ATTIC FLOOR PLAN

SECTION THRU CORNICE
SMALL DINING PAVILLIONS
SCALE

EAST ELEVATION
SCALE

CROSS SECTION

MENTION
Submitted by Wilmer Bruce Rabenold, New York, New York

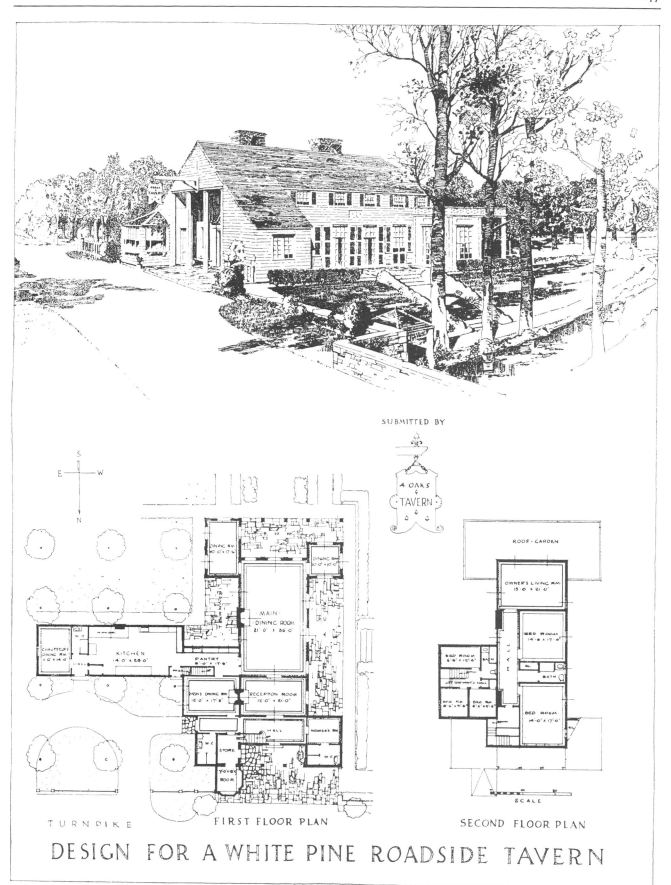

SUBMITTED BY

4 OAKS TAVERN

TURNPIKE   FIRST FLOOR PLAN   SECOND FLOOR PLAN

DESIGN FOR A WHITE PINE ROADSIDE TAVERN

MENTION, Detail Sheet
Submitted by Wilmer Bruce Rabenold, New York, New York

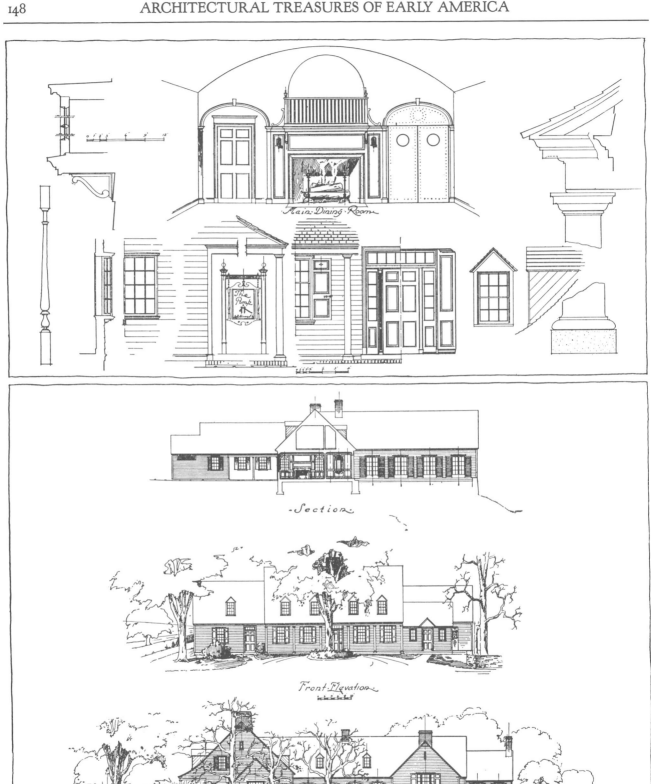

Main Dining Room

The Pump

Section

Front Elevation

Side Elevation

~Design for a White Pine Roadside Tavern~

Submitted by "The Pump"

MENTION, Detail Sheet
Submitted by R. J. Wadsworth, Philadelphia, Pennsylvania

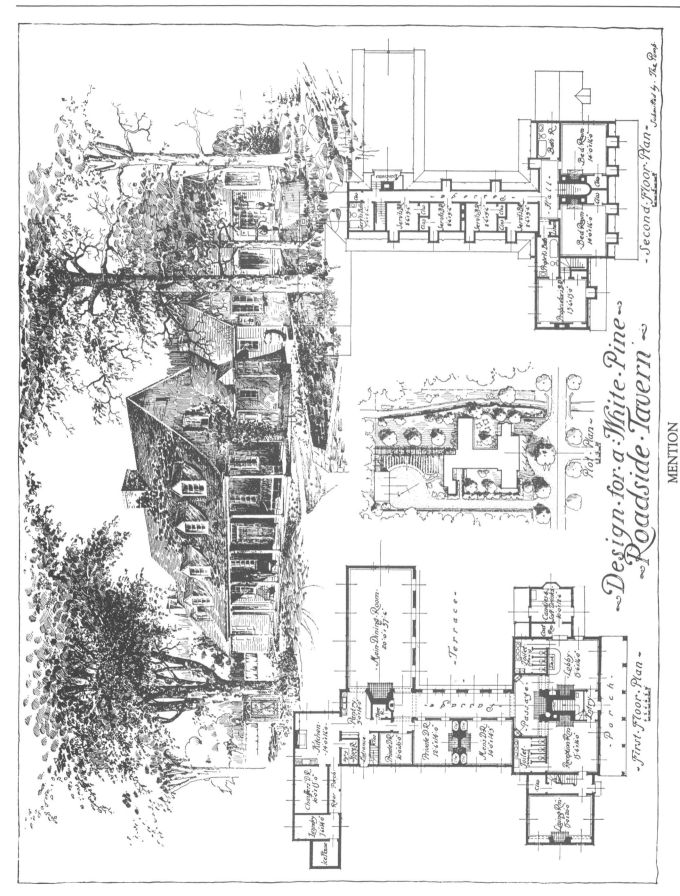

Design for a White Pine Roadside Tavern

MENTION

Submitted by R. J. Wadsworth, Philadelphia, Pennsylvania

The designs awarded mentions are all good, but two stand out a little apart from the others, and are so near the first four as to deserve special mention.

The First Mention has a good general plan, which places the building near the road, and reserves the stream and orchard for the guests of the tavern. The main building is rectangular in mass, with wings for dining-room, for service, and for the proprietor. Perhaps here is the one weak point, for the public dining-rooms are really the key-note of the tavern, and not an appendage. Apart from this, the general layout, the plan, and the elevations and details without and within are charming, and the rendering is such as we can all envy.

One may say here, perhaps, that throughout all the drawings there is a draughtsmanship which is most encouraging for the future of the draughtsmen. If we have such draughtsmanship as is shown in this competition, we may rest assured that the presentation of architectural designs will lose nothing in the rendering. While speaking of rendering, it is not out of place to refer also to lettering. All of this is good, and some of really unusual beauty, as for example that on the drawings given the fourth prize. Good lettering is, after all, the last word in draughtsmanship. A man who can letter beautifully can draw anything.

The design given Second Mention has a general plan which sacrifices perhaps too much to the entrance, but is thoughtfully and well studied. The plan of the building is straightforward, simple, and convincing. The exterior is so quiet and so simple as to have the charm which goes with all restrained work, and the Jury feel that the simplicity of this design is a most hopeful sign of the general tendency toward appreciation of the beauty of proportion. The rear elevation was accidentally drawn the wrong way round, to speak colloquially. This, however, is a draughtsman's error, which happens in the best regulated offices.

The four designs given mentions are good, and each has so many assets as to make it rather invidious to attempt to rank them. There are good points and bad points in each, but all are creditable to those who presented them.

CASS GILBERT
CHAS. Z. KLAUDER
HOWARD SHAW   } *Jury*
R. CLIPSTON STURGIS, *Chairman*   } *of*
F. R. WALKER   } *Award*

A Three-Teacher Rural School

Report of the Jury of Award
Given May 6 and 7, 1921
Originally published in 1921 as White Pine Monograph
Volume VII, Number 4

Design for
A WHITE PINE
THREE TEACHER
RURAL SCHOOL

Submitted by

PLAN OF SCHOOL
Scale

SIDE ELEVATION

FRONT ELEVATION

Scale of Detail

ENTRANCE FEATURE OF SCHOOL

FIRST PRIZE DESIGN
Submitted by Antonio DiNardo and W. Frank Hitchens, Pittsburgh, Pennsylvania

A THREE-TEACHER RURAL SCHOOL WITH TEACHERS' COTTAGE

Report of the Jury of Award of the Sixth Annual White Pine Architectural Competition

Judged at Yama Farms, Napanoch, NY, May 6 and 7, 1921

PROBLEM: **A.** The design of a three-teacher rural school building to be built of wood—all outside finish to be of White Pine. The school property is level and contains about five acres. It is located on the east side of the main street of the village, which runs north and south, and between two minor roads, making a frontage of the property of three hundred feet on the main street and a depth of seven hundred feet to a property line. The building is to be kept well back from the main street and the front portion of the property developed and used as a small Park or Village Green. The requirements are as follows:

Building to be one story with or without a basement, or with basement partially excavated for boiler and fuel rooms.

Three standard class rooms, each with an area of 720 square feet, and seating 40 pupils each. Two of these rooms separated by folding partitions.

Ceiling heights not less than 12′ 0″ in clear.

Class rooms lighted from left side only. Windows in one long bank. Heads of windows as close to ceiling as possible. Net glass area of windows to equal not less than 20% of the class room floor area.

Adjoining each class room shall be provided a coat room for the pupils' clothing.

An industrial art room shall be provided for boys, equal in area from ½ to ¾ of a class room. Net glass area to be same proportion as called for in class room, but windows may be on one or two sides of the room.

A domestic science room for girls, equal in area from ½ to ¾ of a class room. Net glass area to be same proportion as called for in class room, but windows may be on one or two sides of room.

A room for library, 150 to 200 square feet.

A teachers' room with toilet accommodations and about the same size as library.

Toilet room for boys, containing two W. C.'s and three urinals and two lavatories.

Toilet rooms for girls, containing four W. C.'s and two lavatories.

A play room for boys, equal to about a class room in area.

A play room for girls, equal to about a class room in area.

These play rooms may be either in the basement or on main floor. In any case, they must be adjacent to and the toilet rooms made available, as these play rooms are used before and after school and in summer time when the main portion of school is closed. Toilet rooms should also be easily accessible from the main part of school building. Play rooms must be directly accessible from outside of building and also accessible to main portions of building from the inside.

Two or more entrances must be provided.

A flag-pole, higher than the school building, must be located on the property in a dignified position.

The building will be heated and ventilated by a hot-air furnace or steam boiler. Therefore, a furnace room and a fuel room are necessary, also a small general storage room, janitor's room, etc.

Electricity, water and sewerage facilities are supplied by the village. For this reason the school will not have the usual outside drinking pumps, toilets, etc., but will have modern city conveniences.

The architectural style is optional.

B. The design of a teachers' cottage—construction materials similar to those of school building. The requirements are as follows:

Living room with fireplace, area 225 square feet.

Dining room, area about 150 square feet.

Kitchen and accessories, area about 130 square feet.

Three teachers' bedrooms with clothes closets, area about 125 square feet each.

Bath room; closet for trunks; and a porch.

The teachers' cottage may be one story or two stories in height, at the option of the designer. It should have a domestic character, but correspond in general architectural style to the school building.

THE programme for the Sixth Annual Architectural Competition, instituted by the Editor of *The White Pine Series of Architectural Monographs*, called for a school building and teachers' cottage, to be erected in a progressive community, where the desire was for buildings which would be expressive of the purpose for which they were to be used, and which would set a high standard of good taste and architectural beauty.

The author of the programme realized that this type of building was one not often encountered in the average architectural practice, and that, therefore, the contestant would have to exercise a greater degree of ingenuity than when working out a problem for which there was ample precedent. The specific conditions of the problem, therefore, necessarily were made fairly precise and definite. If it had been possible to make the programme a little "looser," and thereby have allowed a greater latitude of thought and a greater degree of imagination, perhaps it might have made for an even more interesting problem. If the somewhat inelastic terms of the programme intimidated a number of possible contestants, or if the majority of designers lack initiative to solve an unfamiliar problem, we would consider it a most unfortunate augury for the future of the architectural profession.

Eighty-four sets of drawings were submitted in the competition, and, while none of the designs was highly imaginative in conception nor strikingly original in character, yet a fair average in plan and elevation was maintained, making the task of differentiation a not altogether agreeable or satisfying one to the Jury of Award, but making it a pleasure for the Jury to comment favorably upon several designs, which, in the process of selection, did not fall into the "Premiated" nor "Mention" classes.

FIRST PRIZE DESIGN. Submitted by Antonio DiNardo and W. Frank Hitchens, of Pittsburgh, Pa. Architecture, being a three-dimensional subject, cannot be considered otherwise, and, therefore, it becomes not a question of plan *or* elevation, but a question of plan *and* elevation. This design had a well articulated plan which functioned admirably, and an elevation possessing the charm of light and shade and shadow. The "porch," both as a practical and as an æsthetic feature, is attractive.

SECOND PRIZE DESIGN. Submitted by William D. Foster, of New York, N. Y. As between the design placed first and that placed second, there was no great difference in merit. The ample sunlit corridor presents an attractive feature excelled by no competitor. The plan turns the most attractive elevation of the building away from the Village Green. The location of the play rooms and their correlation with the out-of-door play spaces and toilets, the location of the special rooms with respect to the class rooms, are admirable features of this fine open plan.

The one-story teachers' cottage is attractive exteriorly, but not well studied as to plan, the living room being turned, necessarily, into a runway, interfering with its use as a center of social life. The kitchen is not any too well equipped with pantries or storage closets.

THIRD PRIZE DESIGN. Submitted by Chauncey F. Hudson, of Buffalo, N. Y. This plan fell into the interior corridor type, and so loses somewhat of the attractiveness of the first and second prize designs. Nor do the toilet and play rooms, as to arrangement, quite reach the standard set by those designs. The location of the special rooms—industrial arts and domestic

science—is not as good as in the two preceding plans. The character of the exterior is rich in quiet, rural charm, lacking in too many of the designs submitted.

FOURTH PRIZE DESIGN. Submitted by Robbins L. Conn, of New York, N. Y. Like the design placed third, a long interior corridor was introduced into this design. The relation of the play rooms and toilets to the special rooms is good, as is also the correlation of the library and of the teachers' room with the class rooms. Also, like the third prize design, the elevations adequately express that which is most characteristic of rural surroundings, a leisurely charm.

FIRST MENTION. Submitted by Alfred Cookman Cass, of New York, N. Y.

SECOND MENTION. Submitted by David W. Carlson and Emil A. Lehti, of New York, N. Y. Of the designs to receive Mention, of which there were six, two seemed worthy of being given a definite place, and the Jury takes pleasure in according them this recognition. The First Mention is quite "academic" in design, that is, suggestive of the old "academies," yet rural in character; while the Second Mention has a decidedly free and picturesque quality. The interior toilet in connection with the teachers' room in this design is a blemish in the plan which a bit of practical surgery might remove. The setting of the "academic" design is attractive.

MENTIONS. The four remaining designs to receive mention were submitted by William J. Mooney and Harold A. Rich, of Boston, Mass.; Charles H. Dornbusch and Erick N. Kaeyer, New York, N. Y.; Leon H. Hoag, Bloomfield, N. J.; and Paul Hyde Harbach, Buffalo, N. Y.

The design submitted by Messrs. Mooney and Rich was the simplest and most appropriate of the designs which featured a tower, of which there were six in the competition. The plan is compact and well arranged, its principal weakness, except for the cramped vestibule, lying in the dark corridor terminating in the toilet rooms rather than in points of light. An otherwise dark corridor may be saved and even made attractive by opening up the ends to the light.

The design submitted by Messrs. Dornbusch and Kaeyer, while extremely attractive in its terraced approaches, suffers from a lack of relationship between the wings, and a central feature which is attenuated and inadequate. The corridor is satisfying. Mr. Harbach's design is good of its type, with a well considered plan, and an

(Continued on page 166)

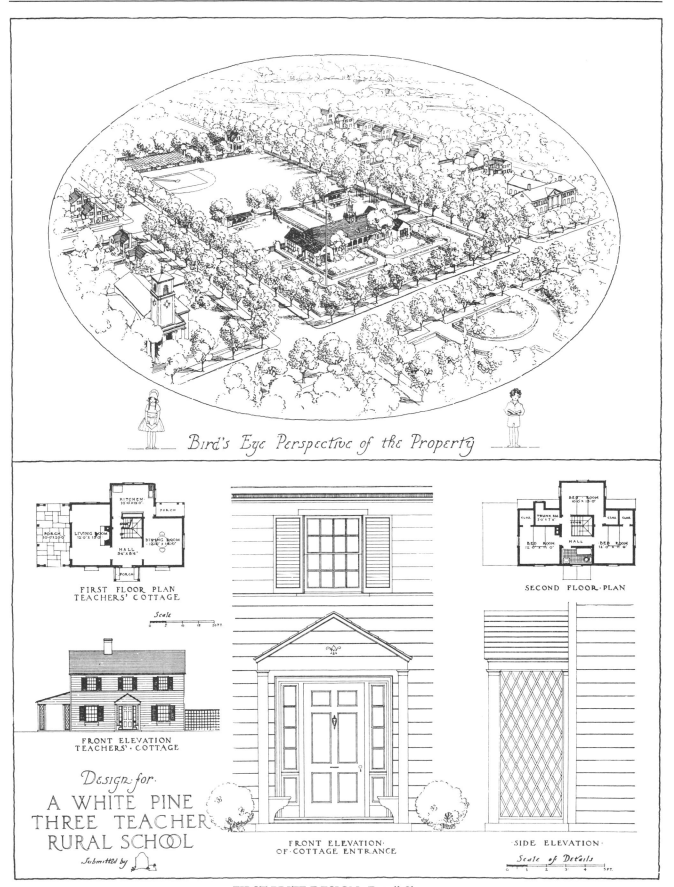

Bird's Eye Perspective of the Property

FIRST FLOOR PLAN
TEACHERS' COTTAGE

Scale

FRONT ELEVATION
TEACHERS' COTTAGE

Design for
A WHITE PINE
THREE TEACHER
RURAL SCHOOL
Submitted by

FRONT ELEVATION
OF COTTAGE ENTRANCE

SECOND FLOOR PLAN

SIDE ELEVATION

Scale of Details

FIRST PRIZE DESIGN, Detail Sheet
Submitted by Antonio DiNardo and W. Frank Hitchens, Pittsburgh, Pennsylvania

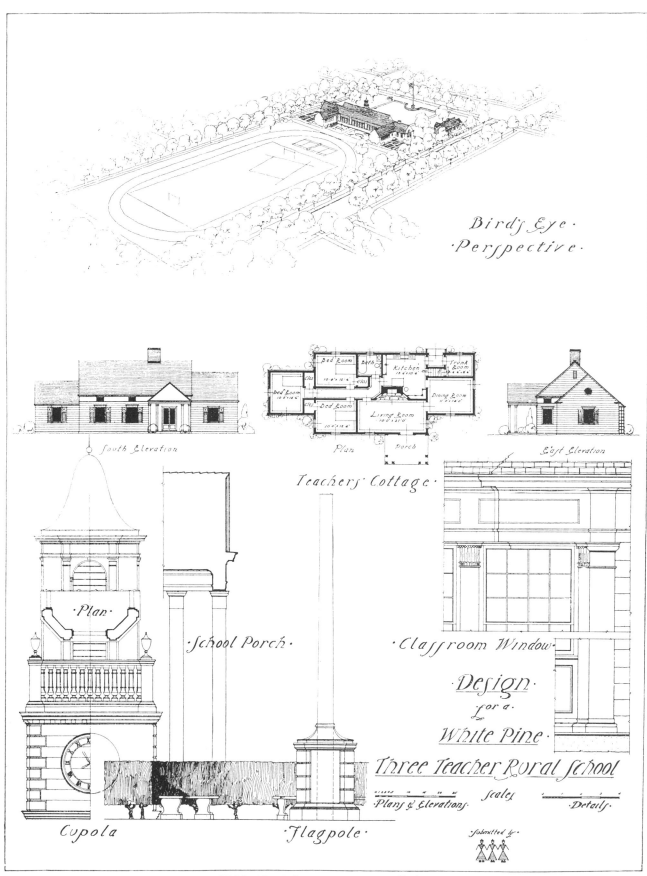

Birds Eye Perspective

South Elevation

Plan   Porch

Teachers Cottage

East Elevation

Plan

School Porch

Classroom Window

Cupola   Flagpole

Design for a White Pine Three Teacher Rural School

Plans & Elevations   Scales   Details

submitted by

SECOND PRIZE DESIGN, Detail Sheet
Submitted by William D. Foster, New York, New York

West Elevation

South Elevation

Design
for a
White Pine
Three Teacher Rural School
scale

Submitted by

SECOND PRIZE DESIGN
Submitted by William D. Foster, New York, New York

THIRD PRIZE DESIGN, Detail Sheet
Submitted by Chauncey F. Hudson, Buffalo, New York

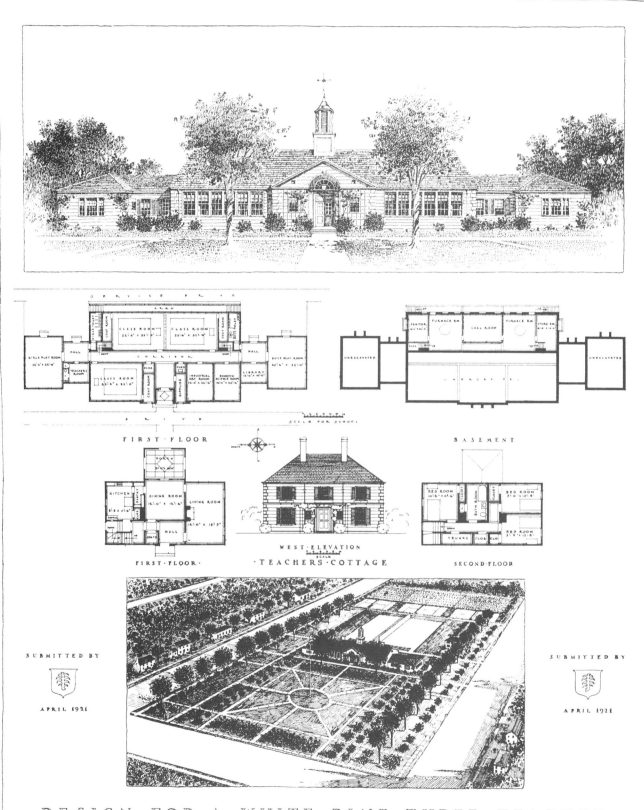

DESIGN FOR A WHITE PINE THREE TEACHER
RURAL SCHOOL

THIRD PRIZE DESIGN
Submitted by Chauncey F. Hudson, Buffalo, New York

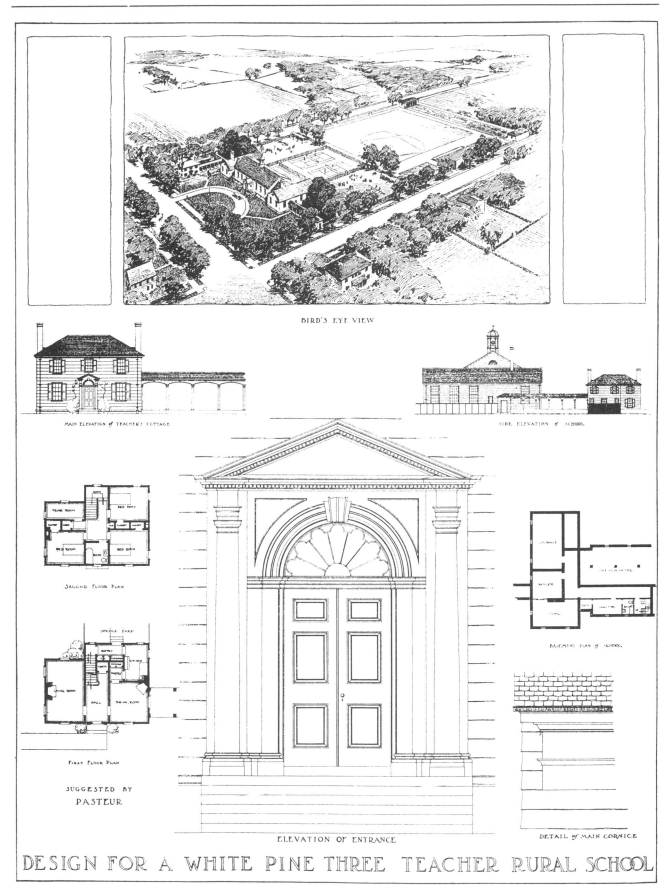

BIRD'S EYE VIEW

MAIN ELEVATION of TEACHER'S COTTAGE

SIDE ELEVATION of SCHOOL

SECOND FLOOR PLAN

FIRST FLOOR PLAN

SUGGESTED BY
PASTEUR

BASEMENT PLAN of SCHOOL

ELEVATION OF ENTRANCE

DETAIL of MAIN CORNICE

DESIGN FOR A WHITE PINE THREE TEACHER RURAL SCHOOL

FOURTH PRIZE DESIGN, Detail Sheet
Submitted by Robbins L. Conn, New York, New York

PERSPECTIVE

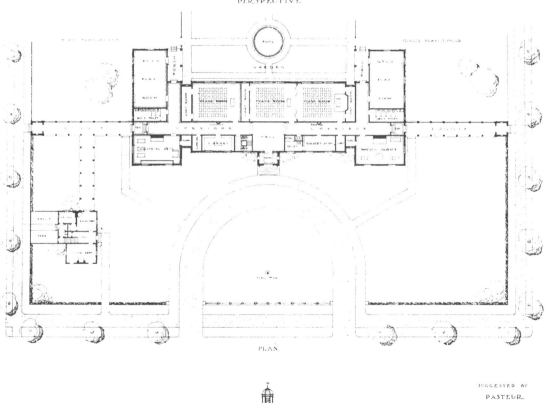

PLAN

ELEVATION

DESIGN FOR A WHITE PINE THREE TEACHER RURAL SCHOOL

FOURTH PRIZE DESIGN
Submitted by Robbins L. Conn, New York, New York

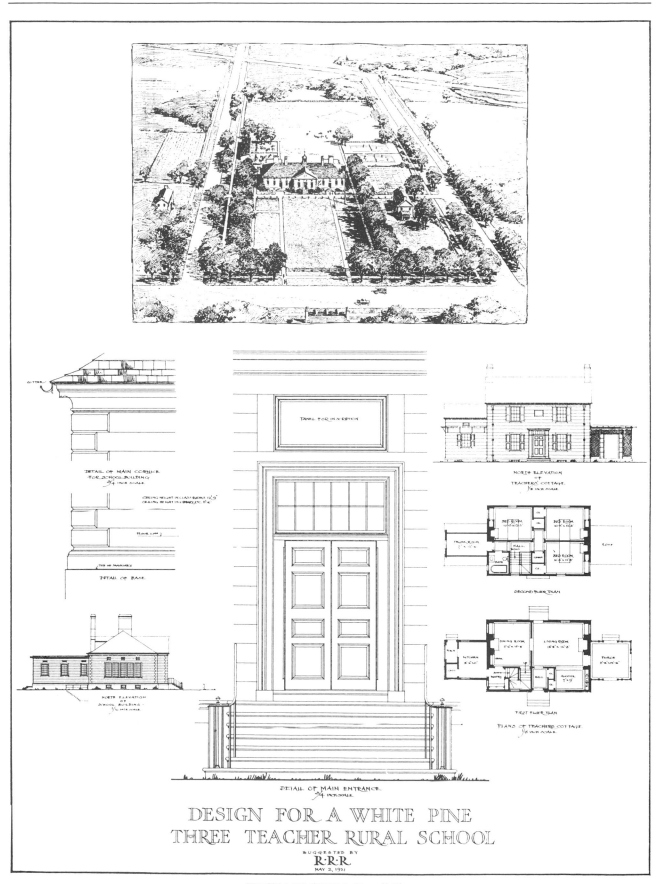

DESIGN FOR A WHITE PINE
THREE TEACHER RURAL SCHOOL

SUGGESTED BY
R·R·R
MAY 2, 1921

FIRST MENTION, Detail Sheet
Submitted by Alfred Cookman Cass, New York, New York

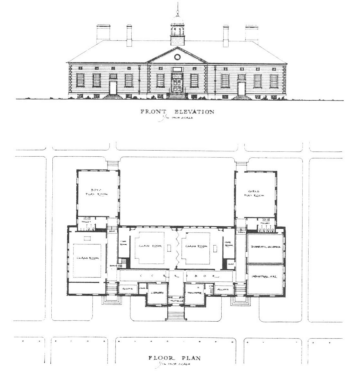

FRONT ELEVATION

FLOOR PLAN

DESIGN FOR A WHITE PINE
THREE TEACHER RURAL SCHOOL

SUGGESTED BY
R·R·R
MAY 2, 1921

FIRST MENTION
Submitted by Alfred Cookman Cass, New York, New York

Design for a
WHITE PINE
THREE TEACHER
RURAL SCHOOL
Submitted By
US

SECOND

Submitted by David W. Carlson and

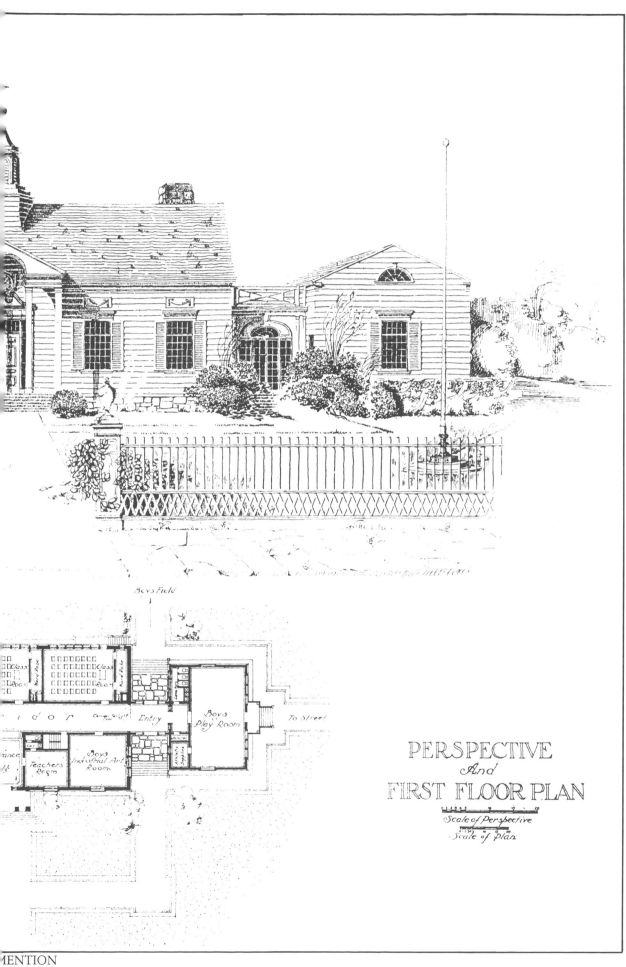

PERSPECTIVE
And
FIRST FLOOR PLAN

Scale of Perspective
Scale of Plan

Emil A. Lehti, New York, New York

exterior well balanced, but not too replete with points of interest. Mr. Leon H. Hoag's design, concluding the list of those to receive mention, has many good points in plan, together with an exterior which would have been much more attractive and effective had its rather ænemic porch been made to hold its own with the unnecessarily expansive grouped windows of the corridor.

These ten designs noted above and recognized with prizes and mentions were not alone in merit among the eighty-four exhibits. It may not be invidious to mention certain others, which, while not reaching the standard set by the "Premiated" and "Mentioned" designs, in the matter of exterior treatment and in the character of the block plans present school-house and cottage plans almost, if not quite, on a par with those submitted by their more fortunate competitors. Thus, the design submitted by Ralph H. Hannaford, of Boston, Mass., presents a plan with a sunlit corridor and terraced forecourt which functioned most satisfactorily. Its exterior seemed to be too monumental in character to fit the material and the conditions. A plan in a manner similar, though not so attractively presented nor conceived, was submitted by George Marshall Martin, of Louisville, Ky. Messrs. Wicks and Hopkins and Ernest Crimi, of Buffalo, N. Y., submitted a compact plan, with an interior corridor, which develops into a too austere and shadeless exterior. The scheme presented by Messrs. Ralph T. Walter and Fred R. Lorenz, of New York, N. Y., has an interior, end lighted, spacious corridor, with well arranged rooms. The open porches in connection with the play rooms might well have been adopted by others. The absence of a teachers' toilet, called for in the programme, is a fault.

A review of the designs discloses the fact, or the seeming fact, that previous issues of the White Pine publications have been studied to some effect. What has been presented in previous competitions, as well as what has been built of white pine from Colonial times down, has made its impress. The general uniformity in the designs betokens a subservience to tradition which rather has hindered the flow of originality which competitions of this character might well be counted upon to bring out.

JAMES O. BETELLE
WM. B. ITTNER
GUY LOWELL   *Jury*
ARTHUR I. MEIGS   *of*
IRVING K. POND, *Chairman*   *Award*

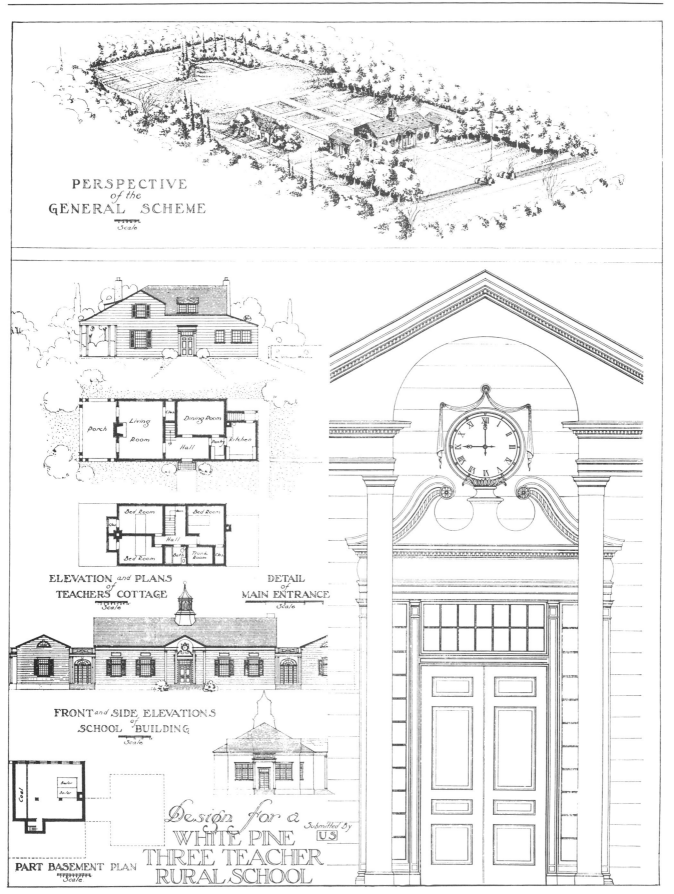

PERSPECTIVE
of the
GENERAL SCHEME
Scale

ELEVATION *and* PLANS
of
TEACHERS' COTTAGE
Scale

DETAIL
of
MAIN ENTRANCE
Scale

FRONT *and* SIDE ELEVATIONS
of
SCHOOL BUILDING
Scale

PART BASEMENT PLAN
Scale

Design for a
WHITE PINE
THREE TEACHER
RURAL SCHOOL

Submitted By
US

SECOND MENTION, Detail Sheet
Submitted by David W. Carlson and Emil A. Lehti, New York, New York

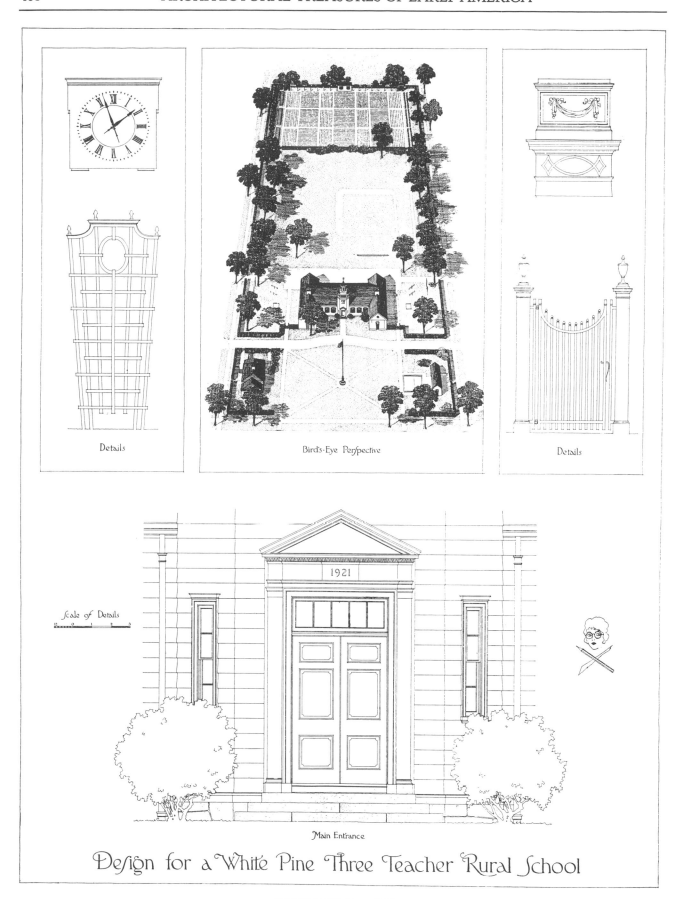

Details

Bird's-Eye Perspective

Details

1921

Scale of Details

Main Entrance

Design for a White Pine Three Teacher Rural School

MENTION, Detail Sheet
Submitted by William J. Mooney and Harold A. Rich, Boston, Massachusetts

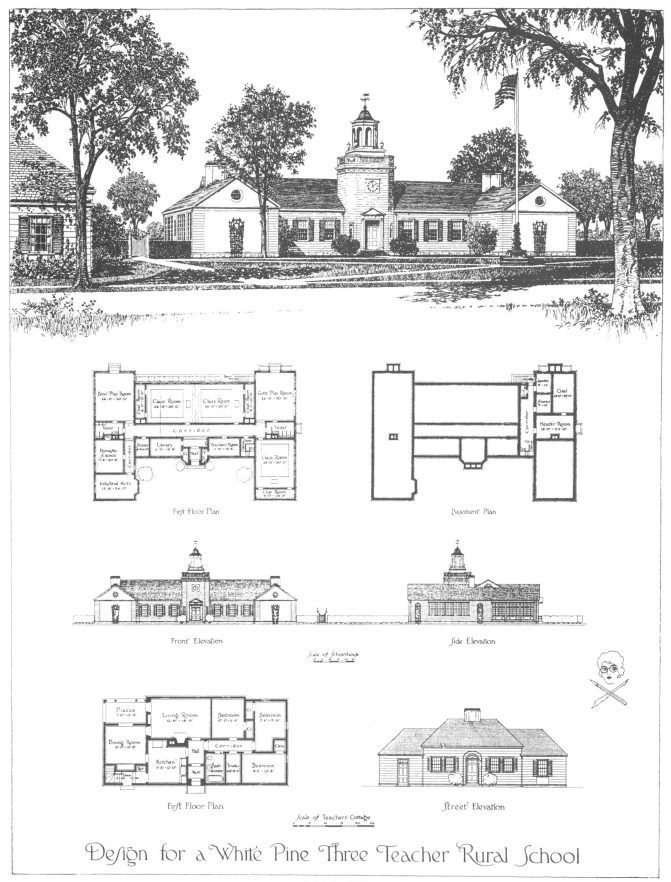

First Floor Plan

Basement Plan

Front Elevation

Side Elevation

Scale of Schoolhouse

First Floor Plan

Street Elevation

Scale of Teachers' Cottage

Design for a White Pine Three Teacher Rural School

MENTION

Submitted by William J. Mooney and Harold A. Rich, Boston, Massachusetts

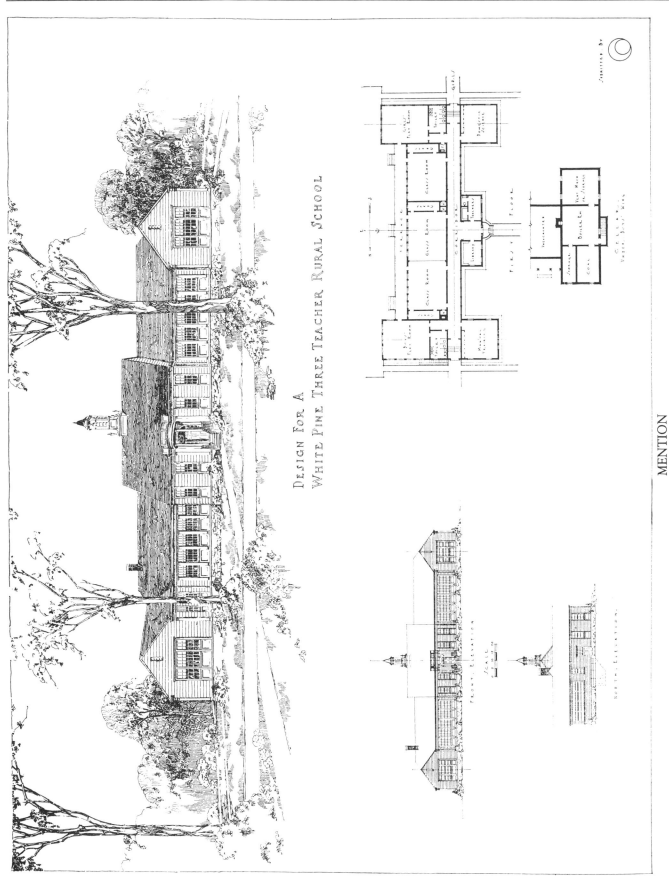

DESIGN FOR A
WHITE PINE THREE TEACHER RURAL SCHOOL

MENTION

Submitted by Leon H. Hoag, Bloomfield, New Jersey

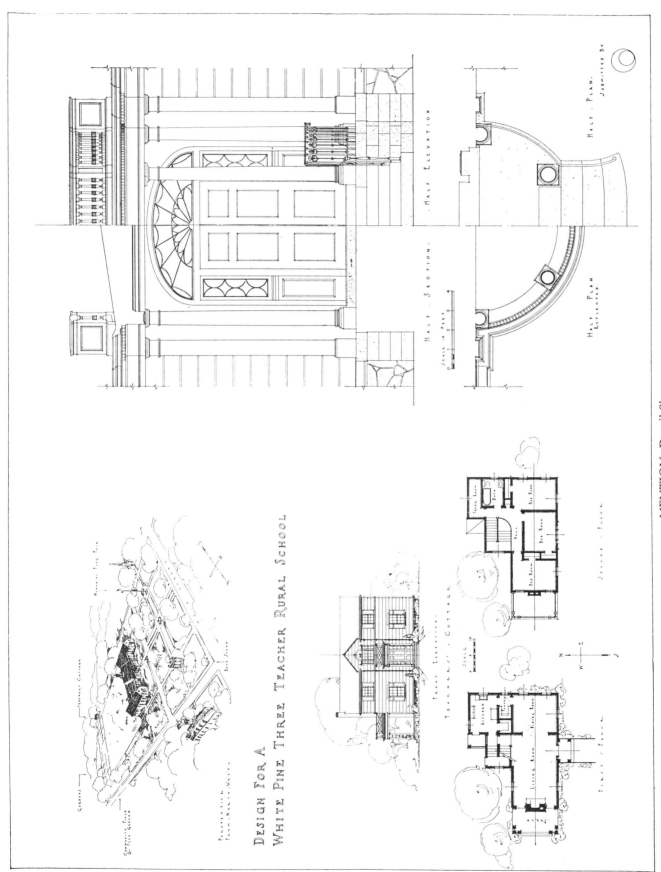

DESIGN FOR A
WHITE PINE THREE TEACHER RURAL SCHOOL

MENTION, Detail Sheet
Submitted by Leon H. Hoag, Bloomfield, New Jersey

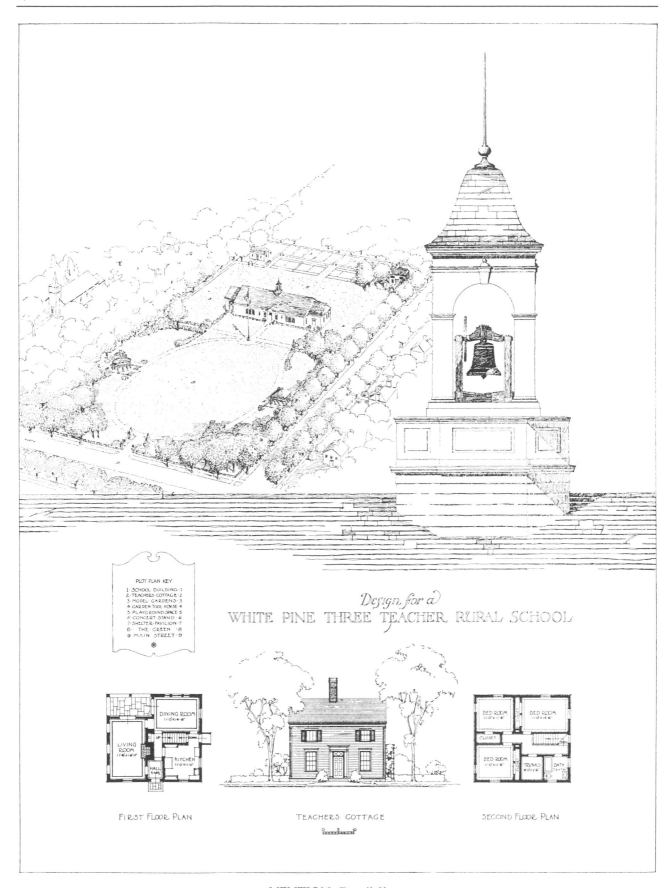

PLOT PLAN KEY

1 · SCHOOL · BUILDING · 1
2 · TEACHERS · COTTAGE · 2
3 · MODEL · GARDEN · 3
4 · GARDEN · TOOL · HOUSE · 4
5 · PLAYGROUND · SPACE · 5
6 · CONCERT · STAND · 6
7 · SHELTER · PAVILION · 7
8 · THE · GREEN · 8
9 · MAIN · STREET · 9

Design for a
WHITE PINE THREE TEACHER RURAL SCHOOL

FIRST FLOOR PLAN   TEACHERS COTTAGE   SECOND FLOOR PLAN

MENTION, Detail Sheet
Submitted by Paul Hyde Harbach, Buffalo, New York

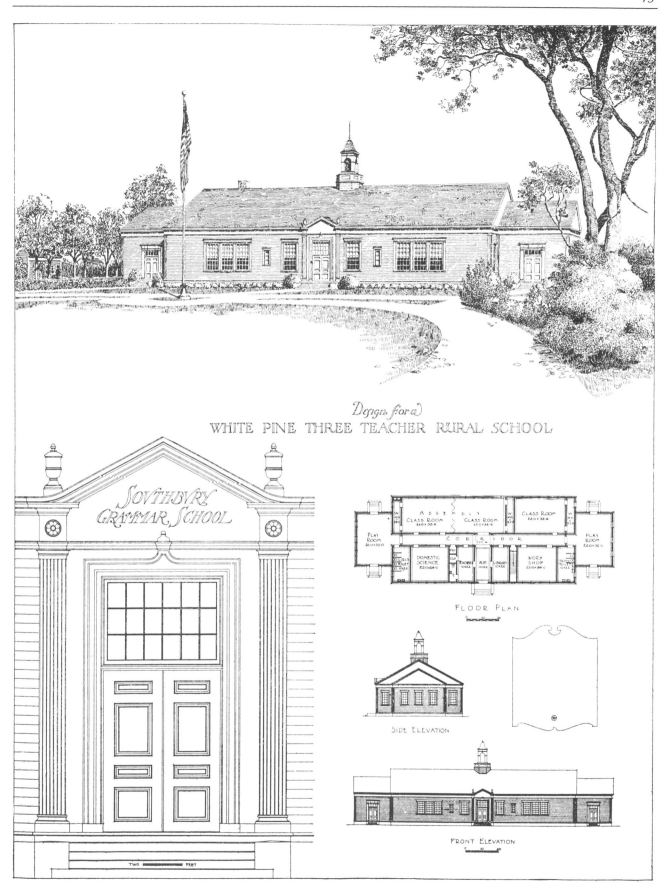

Design for a
WHITE PINE THREE TEACHER RURAL SCHOOL

SOVTHBVRY
GRAMMAR SCHOOL

TWO FEET

FLOOR PLAN

SIDE ELEVATION

FRONT ELEVATION

MENTION
Submitted by Paul Hyde Harbach, Buffalo, New York

DESIGN FOR A WHITE PI...

Boys Play Ground

Boys'
Play Room

Class Room   Class R...

Boys

Industrial Arts

Front Elevation

MEN
Submitted by Charles H. Dornbusch a...

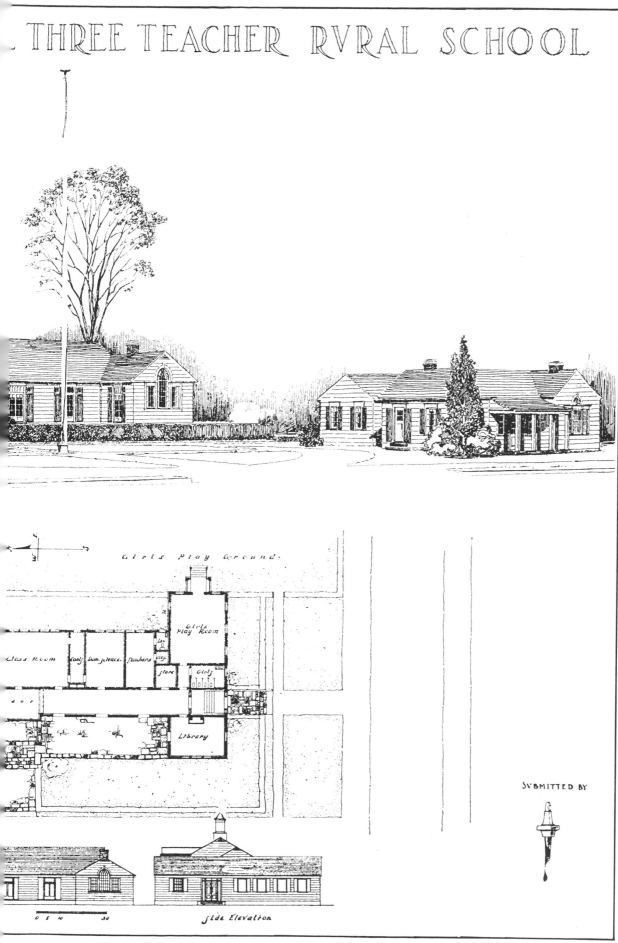

Girls Play Ground.

Girls Play Room

Class Room Cloak Lum. Science. Teachers
Store
Girls
dor
Library

SVBMITTED BY

0 5 10   50   Side Elevation

ick N. Kaeyer, New York, New York

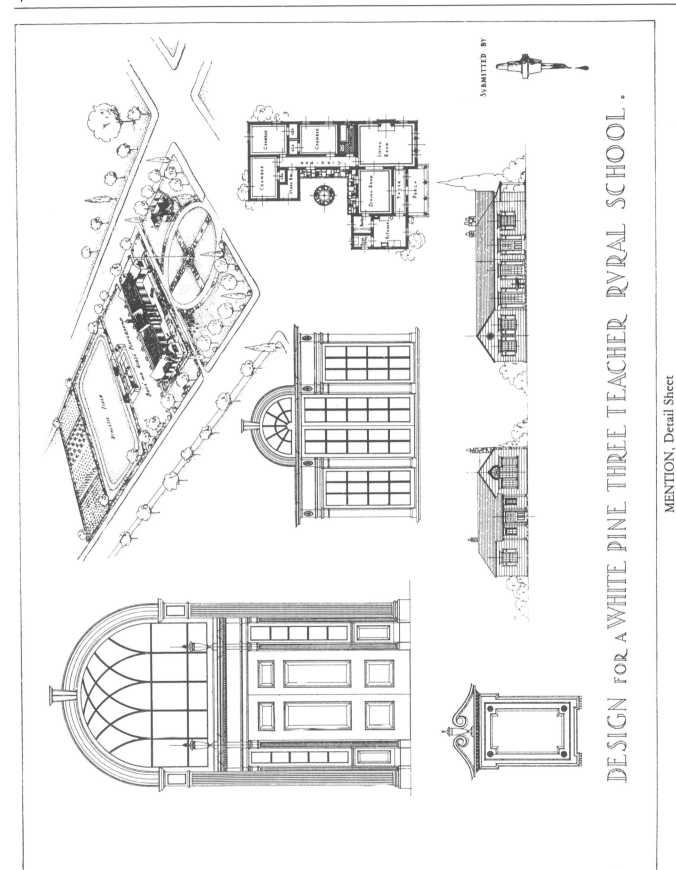

DESIGN FOR A WHITE PINE THREE TEACHER RVRAL SCHOOL.

MENTION, Detail Sheet

Submitted by Charles H. Dornbusch and Erick N. Kaeyer, New York, New York

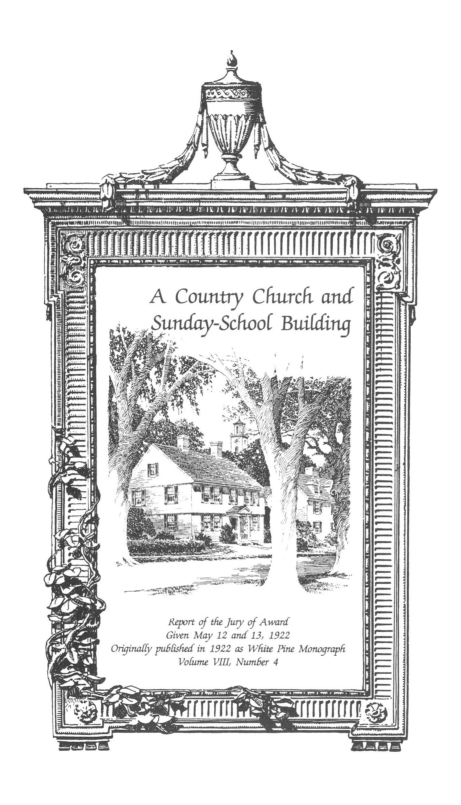

A Country Church and Sunday-School Building

Report of the Jury of Award
Given May 12 and 13, 1922
Originally published in 1922 as White Pine Monograph
Volume VIII, Number 4

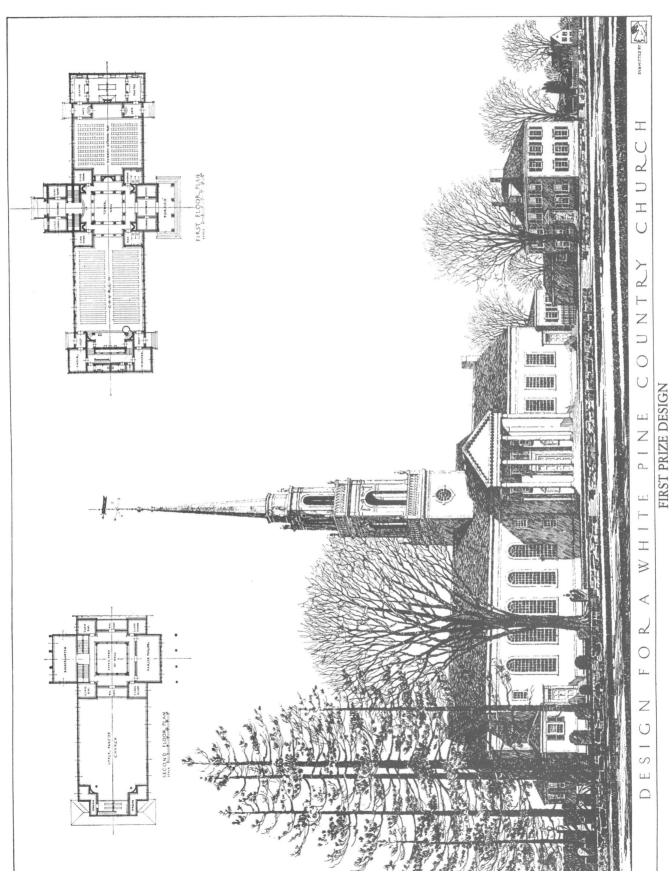

DESIGN FOR A WHITE PINE COUNTRY CHURCH

FIRST PRIZE DESIGN

Submitted by Ralph H. Hannaford and Hampton F. Shirer, Boston, Massachusetts

A COUNTRY CHURCH AND SUNDAY-SCHOOL BUILDING WITH RESIDENCE FOR THE MINISTER

Report of the Jury of Award of the Seventh Annual White Pine Architectural Competition

Judged at Yama Farms, Napanoch, NY, May 12 and 13, 1922

PROBLEM: A Church building proper, to seat approximately 350, and to contain a gallery large enough to accommodate a double quartette. This gallery may be at either end of the auditorium. Convenient to the Choir Gallery, a Choir Practice Room, with coat room and toilets for men and women. A Minister's Room, 150 square feet, should adjoin the Chancel and be provided with coat closet and toilet.

A Sunday-school Building directly connected with the Church, but not necessarily arranged to open into it. Main Auditorium to seat approximately 225, with stage suitable for simple entertainments. Eight classrooms, 100 square feet each, will be needed for the various grades of the Sunday-school. These may be partitioned from the main seating space by curtains or by folding screens, or may be in separate rooms. In addition to this, a Kindergarten, 350 square feet, with a sunny exposure; a room of approximately the same size, which may be used both as a Men's Bible Class Room and as a Parish Parlor. Toilets and coat rooms for men and women. A Kitchen and Pantry, 800 square feet, connected with the Auditorium.

A Manse, or residence for the minister, to contain, on the ground floor, Living-room, Study, Dining-room, Kitchen, and Pantry. On the second floor, four Bedrooms and two Baths. The attic shall be unfinished, but should be large enough for one Bedroom and Bath and a small Store-room. A one-car Garage.

All the outside finish for the three buildings, including siding and corner boards, window-sash, frames and casings, outside blinds, all exposed porch and balcony lumber, cornice boards, brackets, ornaments, mouldings, etc., *not* including shingles, is to be of White Pine.

The ancient burial-ground at the corner of the property, although not now in use, should not be disturbed; and the competitor is requested to spare as many of the fine elms and white pines as possible.

Accommodations for automobiles should be provided at the rear of the lot.

As the site is an important one and the church the principal one in the village, it is suggested that a tower, with or without a spire, be incorporated in the design.

The grade is approximately level, and about 2½ feet above the sidewalk. All corners of the lot are right angles except the two on Perkins' Lane. The stone retaining-wall on two sides of the property is to be kept, but the entrance steps may be moved if the competitor so desires.

AN unusually small number of designs, less than fifty, were entered in the latest of the admirable and enterprising competitions conducted by the Editor of *The White Pine Series of Architectural Monographs*. Possibly the programme was thought to be difficult, or else it was perceived as especially challenging to ecclesiastical draughtsmen, which would be an unhappy conclusion, for it is proper to record the Jury's disappointment at the comparatively inferior standard of the work. It might even be recorded that for a time there was question of the propriety of withholding certain of the prizes.

The adoption of the Colonial style was not a mandatory requirement of the programme, though it appears to have been so regarded, one competitor only having had the temerity to try his luck with a very flamboyant scheme of Gothic clapboarding. The approach to the problem has been distinctly timid and unventuresome, in spite of what appeared to be an unusual opportunity for an interesting exploitation of a very charming historical architecture. The pervasiveness of familiar towers, cupolas, and façades throughout the designs was anticipated, but the Jury was over-sanguine in expecting that a nice feeling for the genius of the material might have had a larger exercise in modifying the

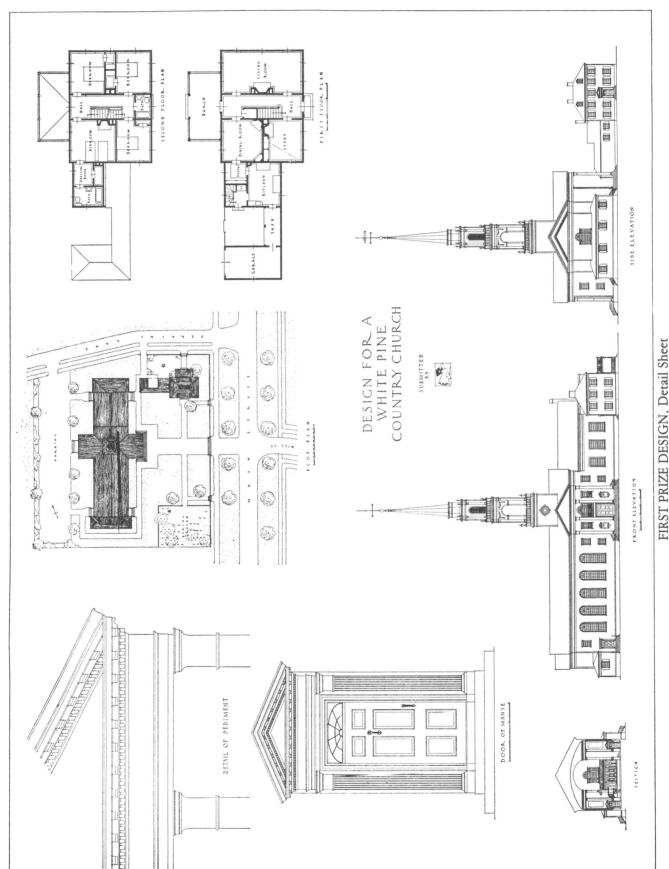

DESIGN FOR A
WHITE PINE
COUNTRY CHURCH

SUBMITTED
BY

FIRST PRIZE DESIGN, Detail Sheet

Submitted by Ralph H. Hannaford and Hampton F. Shirer, Boston, Massachusetts

archæology of these examples. One design, that awarded Fourth Prize, had recourse to the earlier and more naïve phases of the tradition, and a more interesting handling of this would have placed it high in the award.

The problem consisted in the bringing of three unequal and traditionally self-contained units of a formal architecture into picturesque and convincing composition. Seldom was this accomplished with high measure of success. The relation of the secondary mass to that of the church was particularly troublesome. The Sunday-school building was frequently introduced so as to mask by its awkward bulk the perspective view of the church. Occasionally, recourse was had to the gambrel-roof for a lower and less competitive sky-line. The organic relation of these two elements in one architectural unit was rarely tried, and yet a successful attempt at this made for the quiet composition which finally won the first place in the Jury's opinion.

The competitors were obviously embarrassed by the implications of "Perkins' Lane," which promised dignified presence for the church, while its southerly situation no less invited the rectory. Considerable ingenuity seems to have been expended in the effort to provide a corner lot for both.

Only a few found suggestion in the burying-ground, which lies, therefore, as an unrelated incident on most of the plans, making little direct contribution to the general effect. The design placed second, however, is notable for the very effective way in which this important asset of the problem has been persuaded to an architectural result of singular picturesqueness.

FIRST PRIZE DESIGN. A bold "orientation," but fairly vindicated. The correlation of church and Sunday-school on the same axis, if unusual and somewhat reminiscent of medieval types on exterior, is in principle thoroughly straightforward and logical, and in full accord with the programme. What with the tower, which arises out of the common foyer, and the portico at its base with axial outlook in Mill Street, the chief interests of the problem are already satisfied and simplicity of composition assured. The manse has a full Colonial dignity, and is well set in pleasing and agreeably distant opposition to the cemetery. There is a certain gaucherie, however, about its effort to effect actual contact with the church by means of the low ell and fence, and, however good the intention, this is the weakest part of the design. A less rigid plan of its upper stage would give the tower a decided gain in gracefulness. Whatever minor shortcomings there may be in the design

would undoubtedly be disclosed in the south elevation of the Sunday-school, where, for instance, the lowered ridge line would undoubtedly suggest also a slight narrowing of its plan, were it only to permit of its cornice being received within the line of the church. As detailed, the portico is rather bald, and dry in character.

SECOND PRIZE DESIGN. Reference has elsewhere been made to the charming way in which the approach to the church has here been contrived. A free and interesting type of portico, which deserves to be surmounted by a better tower. The applied arcade on the Sunday-school recognizes a problem without successfully solving it. The school is still short of successful relation either with the church or the rather involved rectory.

THIRD PRIZE DESIGN. A quaint and interesting type of church, but the Sunday-school across the rather contracted court is poorly conceived. The juncture with it of the connecting cloister (in itself a good feature) is unsatisfactory, and only aggravates the fact that the large auditorium mass had no special relation with anything. At least a hint of the manse should have appeared in the perspective of the church.

FOURTH PRIZE DESIGN. This design, which in spirit is so thoroughly admirable, has been referred to elsewhere. Its author has an excellent feeling for the limitations of his material.

When he eschews the sophisticated types of Colonial for this early phase, it is a pity that something of this refinement of feeling does not appear in the presentation, which does something less than justice to its merit. Intrinsically, the design has decided faults; the plan encroaches too far on the east line of the property. Were this line only farther away, so as to permit of the manse being pushed fifty feet farther back, its askewness, which is now somewhat gratuitous, would be admirable in character. Its present placing is objectionable.

The fenestration of the Sunday-school might be improved. The exterior generally, which would be appropriately rendered in stain rather than in paint, has a certain hardness which could readily be eliminated by study of detail.

FIRST MENTION. One of the very few good renderings. No more beautiful belfry tower than this could have been employed. The continuity of the series of square gallery windows around the façade of the church is unfortunate.

(Continued on page 200)

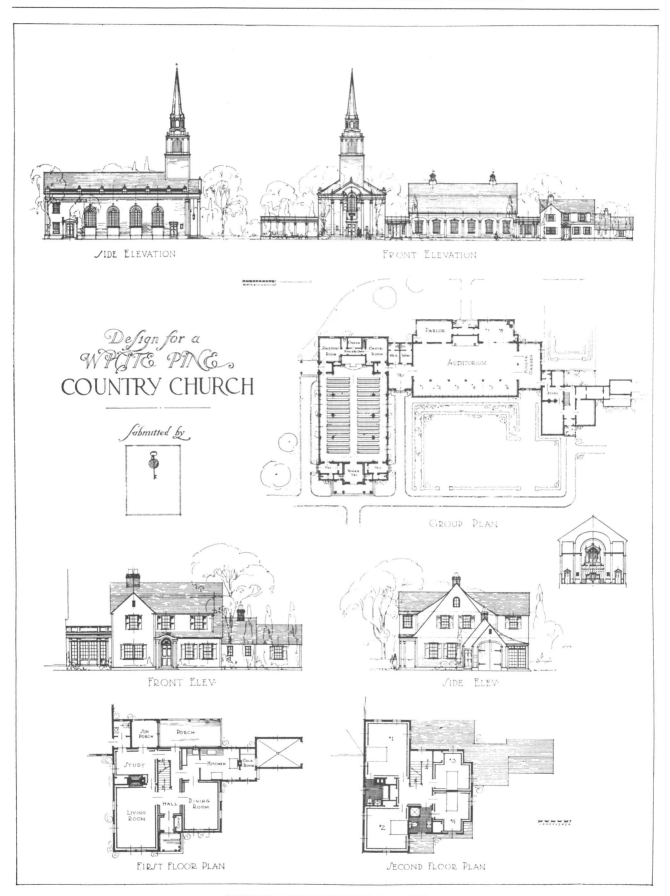

SIDE ELEVATION

FRONT ELEVATION

Design for a
WHITE PINE
COUNTRY CHURCH

Submitted by

GROUP PLAN

FRONT ELEV·

SIDE ELEV·

FIRST FLOOR PLAN

SECOND FLOOR PLAN

SECOND PRIZE DESIGN, Detail Sheet
Submitted by Paul Forrester Taylor, Philadelphia, Pennsylvania

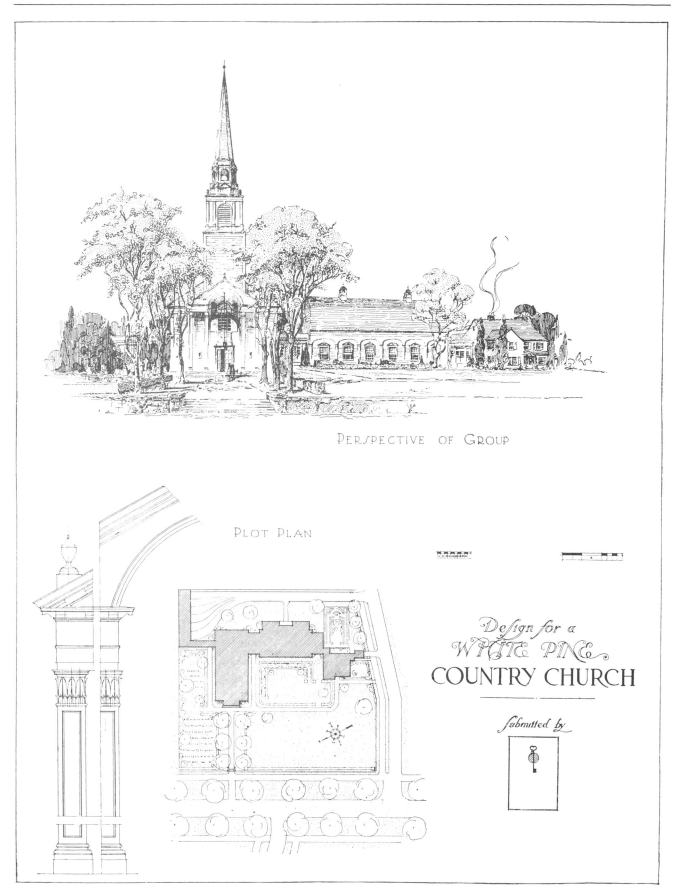

PERSPECTIVE OF GROUP

PLOT PLAN

Design for a
WHITE PINE
COUNTRY CHURCH

submitted by

SECOND PRIZE DESIGN
Submitted by Paul Forrester Taylor, Philadelphia, Pennsylvania

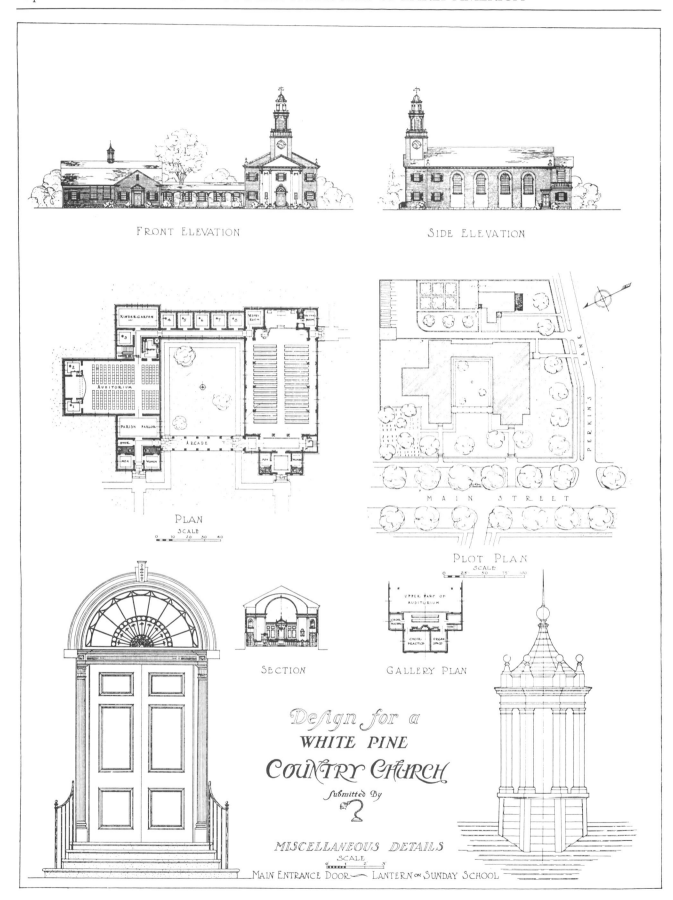

FRONT ELEVATION

SIDE ELEVATION

PLAN

SCALE

PLOT PLAN

SCALE

SECTION

GALLERY PLAN

Design for a
WHITE PINE
COUNTRY CHURCH
Submitted By

MISCELLANEOUS DETAILS
SCALE

MAIN ENTRANCE DOOR — LANTERN ON SUNDAY SCHOOL

THIRD PRIZE DESIGN, Detail Sheet
Submitted by D. R. Cochran, Boston, Massachusetts

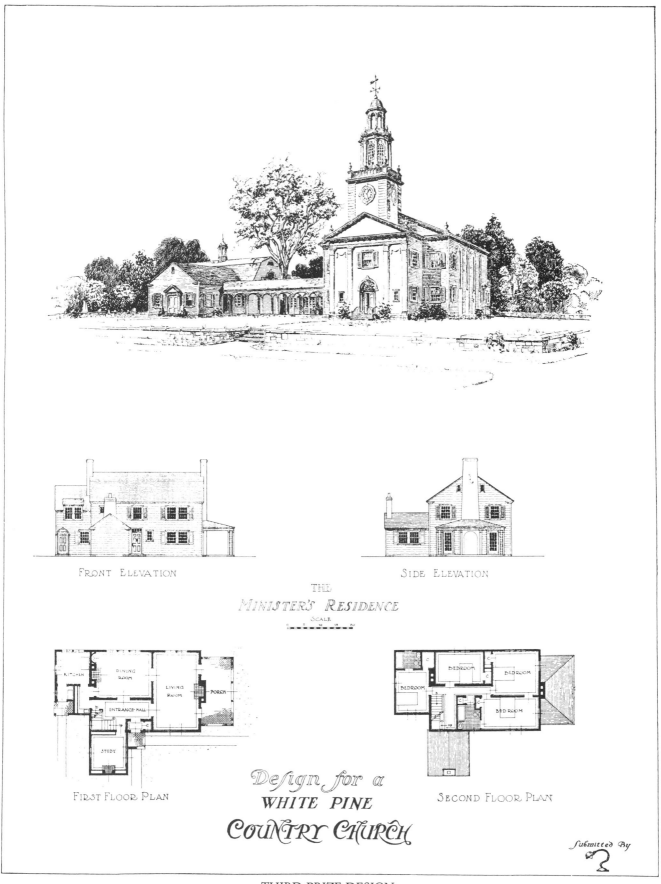

FRONT ELEVATION

SIDE ELEVATION

THE
MINISTER'S RESIDENCE
SCALE

FIRST FLOOR PLAN

SECOND FLOOR PLAN

Design for a
WHITE PINE
COUNTRY CHURCH

Submitted By

THIRD PRIZE DESIGN
Submitted by D. R. Cochran, Boston, Massachusetts

FOURTH PRIZE DESIGN, Detail Sheet
Submitted by Duke W. Rowat, New York, New York

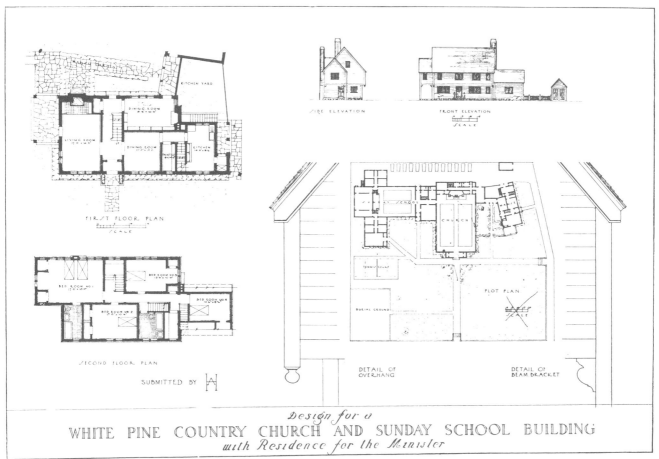

Design for a
WHITE PINE COUNTRY CHURCH AND SUNDAY SCHOOL BUILDING
with Residence for the Minister

FOURTH PRIZE DESIGN
Submitted by Duke W. Rowat, New York, New York

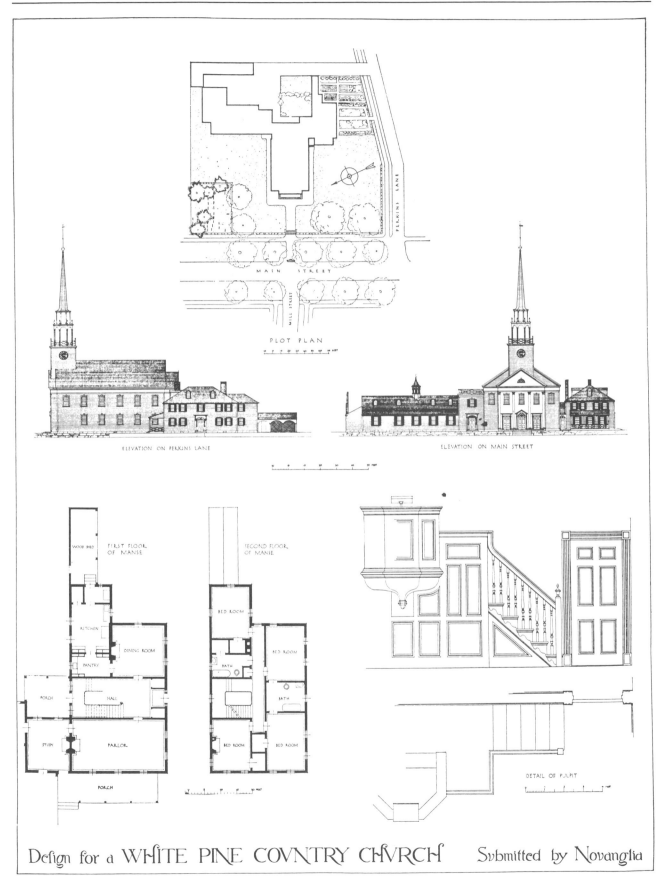

Design for a WHITE PINE COVNTRY CHVRCH   Svbmitted by Novanglia

FIRST MENTION, Detail Sheet
Submitted by O. H. Murray, James Perry Wilson, and Felix Wedgwood Bowen, Newark, New Jersey

Defign for a WHITE PINE COVNTRY CHVRCH   Svbmitted by Novanglia

FIRST MENTION

Submitted by O. H. Murray, James Perry Wilson, and Felix Wedgwood Bowen, Newark, New Jersey

MAIN CORNICE

CHURCH PORCH CORNICE

FRONT ELEVATION OF GROUP   SIDE ELEVATION OF MANSE   SIDE ELEVATION OF GROUP

SCALE OF GROUP

LAVS DEO ET DOM·
FIRST COMBINED CHURCH
MDCCXC   MCMXXII

CHURCH ENTRANCE DOOR

MAIN STREET

PERKINS LANE

PLOT PLAN

ENTRANCE DOOR OF MANSE

SCALE OF PLANS

FIRST FLOOR PLAN   SECOND FLOOR PLAN

FRONT ELEVATION OF MANSE

DESIGN FOR A WHITE PINE COUNTRY CHURCH

SECOND MENTION, Detail Sheet
Submitted by Leroy J. White and Reah deBourg Robinson, Wilmington, Delaware

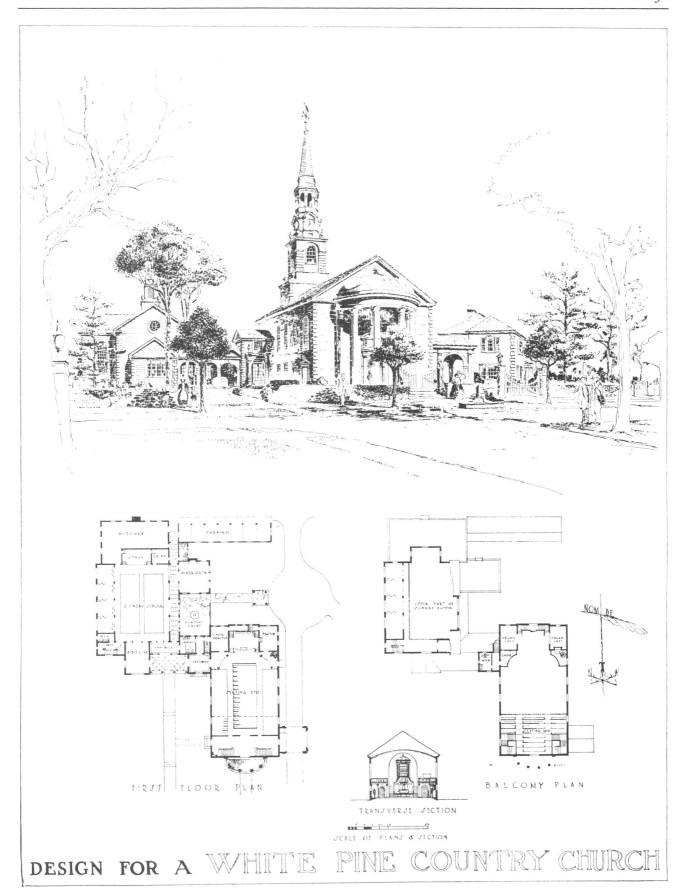

FIRST FLOOR PLAN

TRANSVERSE SECTION

SCALE OF PLANS & SECTION

BALCONY PLAN

DESIGN FOR A WHITE PINE COUNTRY CHURCH

SECOND MENTION
Submitted by Leroy J. White and Reah deBourg Robinson, Wilmington, Delaware

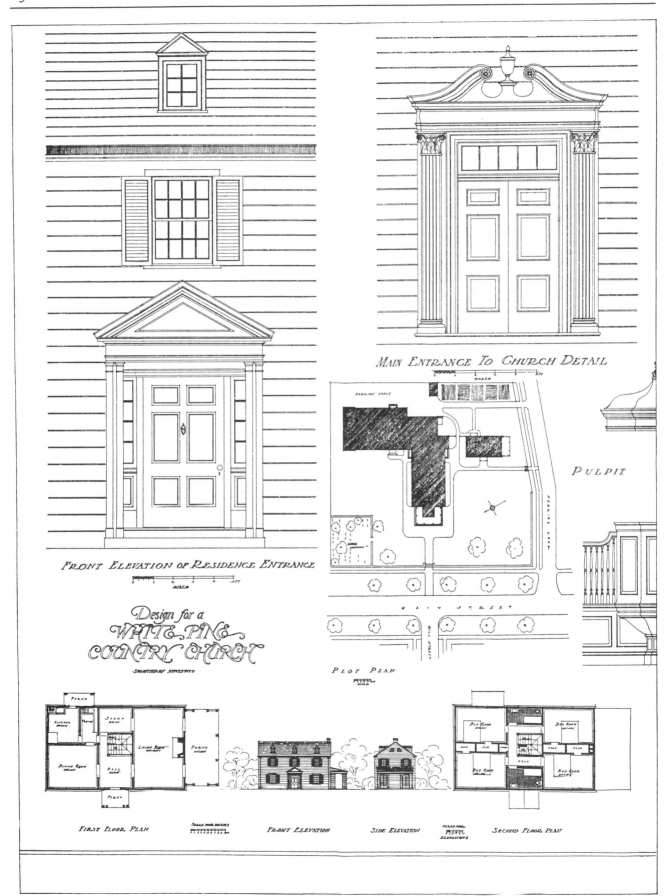

MAIN ENTRANCE TO CHURCH DETAIL

PULPIT

FRONT ELEVATION OF RESIDENCE ENTRANCE

Design for a
WHITE PINE
COUNTRY CHURCH

PLOT PLAN

FIRST FLOOR PLAN   FRONT ELEVATION   SIDE ELEVATION   SECOND FLOOR PLAN

THIRD MENTION, Detail Sheet
Submitted by F. E. Brinkmann, Columbus, Ohio

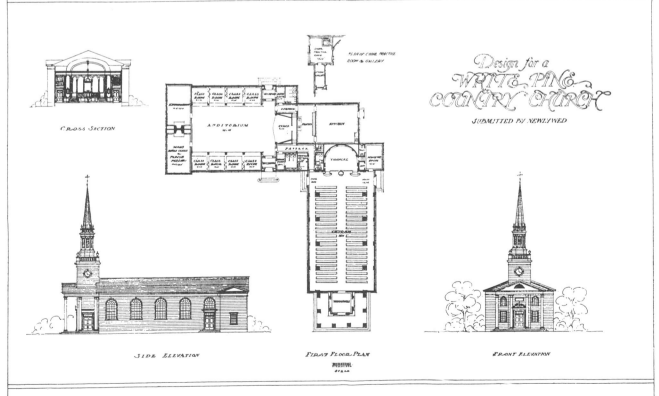

CROSS SECTION

PLAN OF CHOIR PRACTICE ROOM & GALLERY

Design for a WHITE PINE COUNTRY CHURCH

SUBMITTED BY NEWLYWED

SIDE ELEVATION

FIRST FLOOR PLAN

FRONT ELEVATION

THIRD MENTION
Submitted by F. E. Brinkmann, Columbus, Ohio

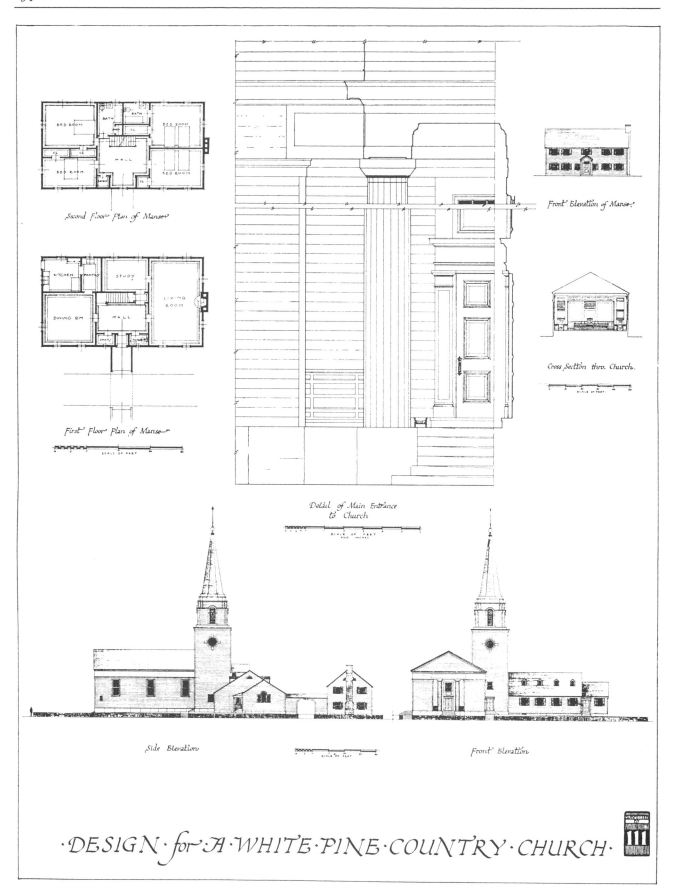

Second Floor Plan of Manse

First Floor Plan of Manse

Front Elevation of Manse

Cross Section thro. Church.

Detail of Main Entrance to Church

Side Elevation

Front Elevation

·DESIGN· for ·A·WHITE·PINE·COUNTRY·CHURCH·

FOURTH MENTION, Detail Sheet
Submitted by Elliott L. Chisling and George C. Stiles, Brooklyn, New York

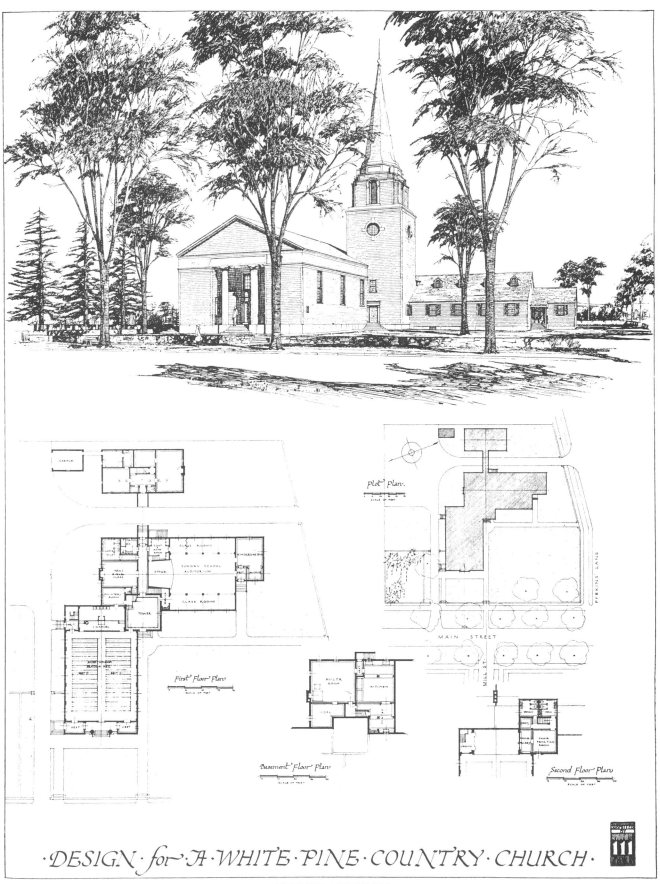

·DESIGN· for· A ·WHITE· PINE· COUNTRY· CHURCH·

FOURTH MENTION
Submitted by Elliott L. Chisling and George C. Stiles, Brooklyn, New York

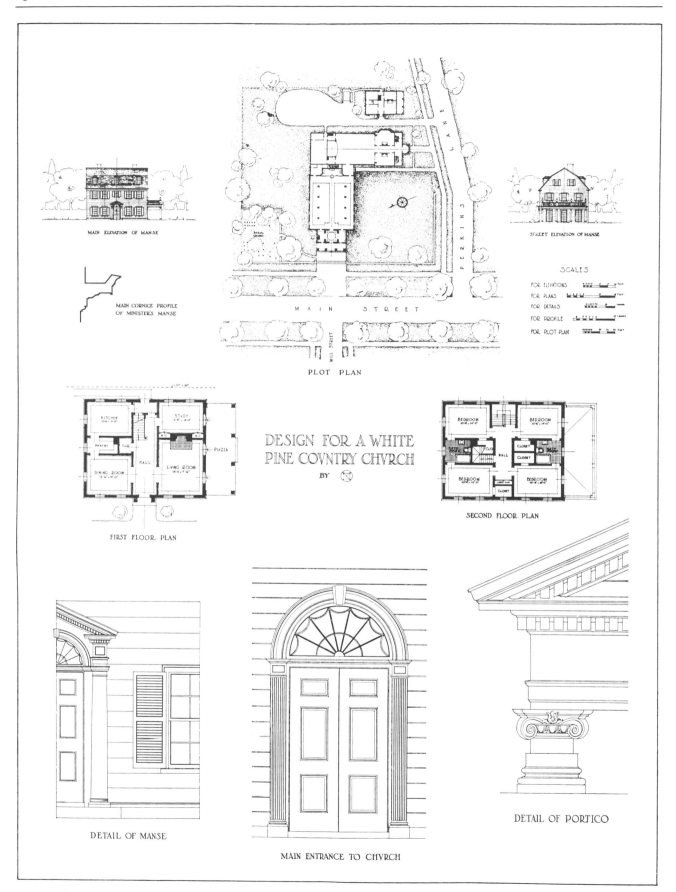

MAIN ELEVATION OF MANSE

MAIN CORNICE PROFILE
OF MINISTER'S MANSE

STREET ELEVATION OF MANSE

PLOT PLAN

SCALES

FOR ELEVATIONS

FOR PLANS

FOR DETAILS

FOR PROFILE

FOR PLOT PLAN

DESIGN FOR A WHITE
PINE COVNTRY CHVRCH

BY

FIRST FLOOR PLAN

SECOND FLOOR PLAN

DETAIL OF MANSE

MAIN ENTRANCE TO CHVRCH

DETAIL OF PORTICO

FIFTH MENTION, Detail Sheet
Submitted by Florian A. Kleinschmidt, Boston, Massachusetts

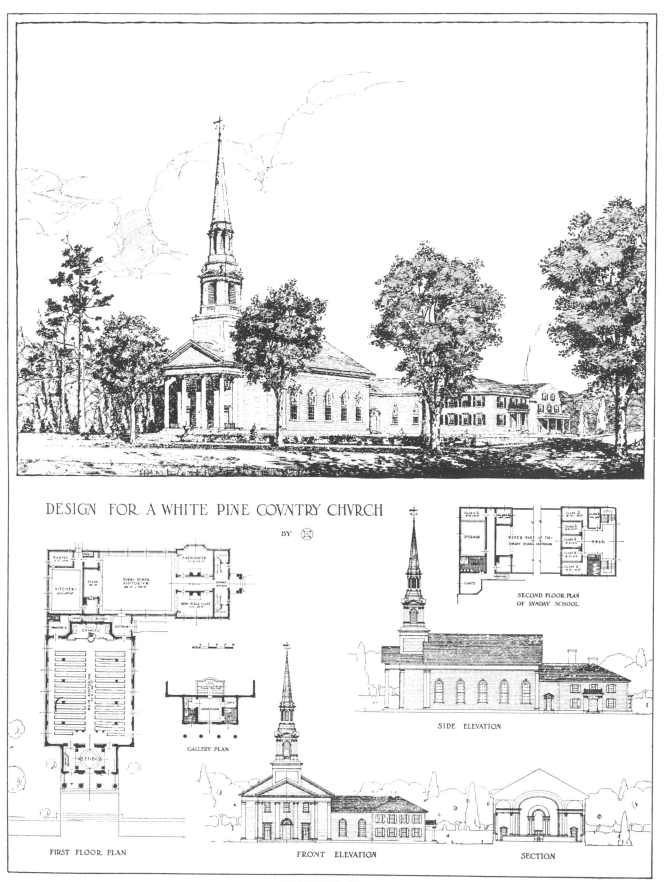

DESIGN FOR A WHITE PINE COUNTRY CHURCH

BY

SECOND FLOOR PLAN
OF SUNDAY SCHOOL

FIRST FLOOR PLAN

GALLERY PLAN

SIDE ELEVATION

FRONT ELEVATION

SECTION

FIFTH MENTION
Submitted by Florian A. Kleinschmidt, Boston, Massachusetts

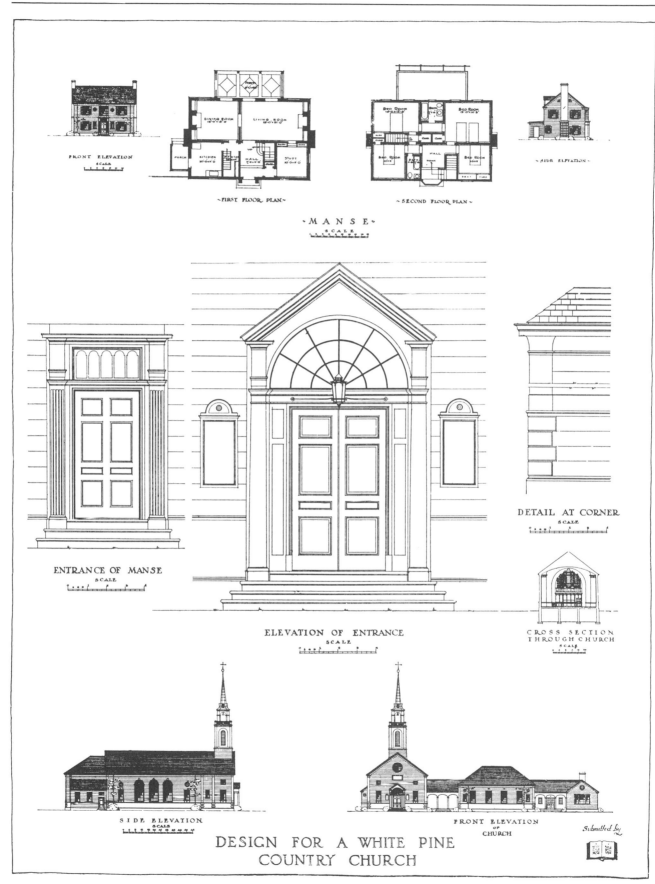

DESIGN FOR A WHITE PINE
COUNTRY CHURCH

SIXTH MENTION, Detail Sheet
Submitted by Daniel Neilinger, New York, New York

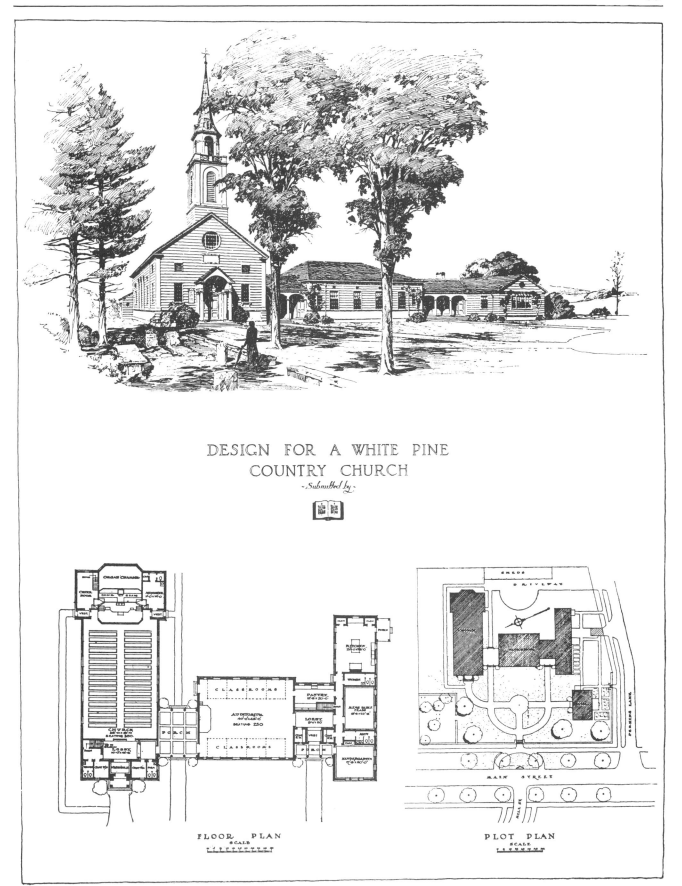

DESIGN FOR A WHITE PINE
COUNTRY CHURCH
- Submitted by -

FLOOR PLAN
SCALE

PLOT PLAN
SCALE

SIXTH MENTION
Submitted by Daniel Neilinger, New York, New York

The manse is not successfully related, and, on the north side, the composition tapers off rather weakly.

SECOND MENTION. Too sophisticated for the programme. Suggests a brick group of a London suburb. The manse is not agreeably placed, is not of agreeable form, and cuts off an important perspective of the church.

THIRD MENTION. The upper part of tower is poor and the lower has too many entrances. The gables at the end of the Sunday-school and church are weak and the latter quite meaningless.

FOURTH MENTION. This shows a nice feeling for the composition, but is the work of one unfamiliar with the implications of the clapboard and the tenpenny nail, which is, here at least, so far a pity that, if given its right rendering, so admirable a plan would have made the going for first prize much harder. As it is, the design is too suggestive of stone architecture.

FIFTH MENTION. The treatment of the Sunday-school wing is unsatisfactory, giving it the suggestion of a manse, and this places the minister at the disadvantage of appearing to occupy a neighbor's house.

SIXTH MENTION. Exterior in modest vein, and so far excellent. The advanced plane of the Sunday-school distinctly takes from the emphasis of the church in perspective, without itself being sufficiently ingratiating to justify its axial position. The effort, moreover, to establish the right relation of this plane between the Sunday-school and church is labored and unconvincing.

BERTRAM G. GOODHUE
EDWARD B. GREEN
THOMAS R. KIMBALL, *Chairman*
CHARLES D. MAGINNIS, *Secretary*
C. C. ZANTZINGER

Jury of Award

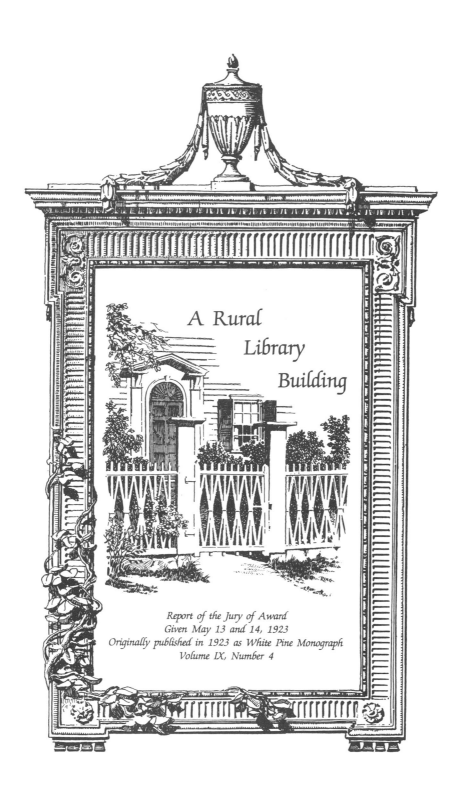

A Rural
Library
Building

Report of the Jury of Award
Given May 13 and 14, 1923
Originally published in 1923 as White Pine Monograph
Volume IX, Number 4

FIRST PRIZE DESIGN

Submitted by Richard M. Powers and Albert C. MacLellan, Boston, Massachusetts

A RURAL LIBRARY BUILDING

Report of the Jury of Award of the Eighth Annual White Pine Architectural Competition

Judged at Yama Farms, Napanoch, NY, May 13 and 14, 1923

PROBLEM: The design of a Rural Library Building, for a progressive and growing community with a present population of 2000, located "somewhere in the United States." The lot is on a corner with a frontage of 100 feet on the main street and 200 feet on the secondary street. The land is level. Main Street runs north and south.

The architectural style is optional, and the plan arrangement left to the ingenuity of the designer.

All the outside finish for the building, including siding and corner boards, window sash, frames and casings, outside blinds, cornice boards, brackets, ornaments, mouldings, etc., *not* including shingles, is to be of White Pine.

The Library Building shall contain: Delivery Room (not less than 225 square feet), Adult Reading Room (not less than 375 square feet, seating capacity 20), Reference Room (not less than 275 square feet, seating capacity 6), Children's Reading Room (about 475 square feet, seating capacity 20), Librarian's Office and Work Room (175 to 200 square feet, capacity 500 volumes), space for Auditorium uses with small platform (seating capacity 125). By "Room" is meant space devoted to the purpose designated rather than an area enclosed within partitions. Shelving shall be provided for 8000 volumes, either in a Book Room or on wall and floor bookcases in the Reading Room, or by a combination of both methods.

If consistent with the design, attic space may be devoted to a Local Historical Museum (not less than 400 square feet).

The building will be heated and ventilated by a hot air furnace or, steam boiler. Therefore, a furnace room and a fuel room are necessary, also a small general storage room and janitor's work room. There should be a storage room for books not in constant use, and a toilet room and lavatory for the use of the Librarian and her staff. No public toilets and no drinking fountains will be required.

The Librarian's Office shall contain ample space for a desk and table, a wash basin, coat closet, supply cupboard, wall shelving, and a lift from the unpacking room in the basement. Privacy must be secured by shutting this room off from the rest of the building.

There must be good natural light at all points and especially at the Loan Desk in the Delivery Room. Avoid skylights.

Not more than two persons, and usually only one, will be responsible for the supervision of the entire library when it is open to borrowers and readers. In many recent successful buildings partitions have been omitted and low bookcases have served to mark divisions.

A part of the building must be devoted entirely to the children. For a limited number of hours much of the activity of the library focuses in the Children's Room. The books, the card catalogue, and reference or school collection will be assembled here. Shelving must be adapted to their convenience. A bulletin board, a few shelves behind glass doors for the exhibit of 50 to 100 illustrated books are desirable features for a Children's Room. A fireplace may be planned in this room if it is in keeping with the general scheme of the room.

Space must be provided for a general bulletin board, the card catalogue, a magazine rack, conveniently accessible to the public.

Two or more entrances should be provided.

The competitor shall design an appropriate sign for the building, which, drawn to scale of ½ inch to the foot, shall be his *nom de plume*.

THE material submitted in this year's competition was of unusual and encouraging merit. One hundred and one sets of drawings in all were received and judged. These came from all sections of the country; twenty-four states being represented. There were also several submissions from Canada. The percentage of really good designs was much higher than in former competitions, well over one-half being worthy of the most careful consideration and study.

The general high standard and good taste displayed particularly in the large scale details were remarkable. These were thoroughly consistent with the style and period chosen. Many of them showed a real knowledge and experience. The usual following of dull "cold Vignola" seems to have been purposely avoided, and a lively interest and distinction given by a refreshing individuality of treatment. A study of many of these details would be rewarding to any practising architect.

The plot plans, as a whole, were also of an exceedingly high standard. The treatment in most cases being thoughtful, distinctive and sympathetic. The buildings generally were set far back from the main street to insure quiet. The development of the rear of the lot into an intimate secluded garden for out-door reading in warm weather being admirably arranged. The general indication of paths, trees and planting showed a surprising understanding of landscape facility.

The standard of the perspectives, as a whole, was less good than the details and plot plans, although often a part of the same drawing.

The rural character called for in the problem was considered by the Jury to be of major consequence. Quite a number of otherwise able and attractive designs failed to produce this essential quality, being frankly urban or suburban. The Jury felt that they could not make an award to what was in effect a two-story town residence or to very formal types of architecture, better suited to stone treatment and more appropriate for location in the wealthy suburbs of some large city.

The intensive use of a small compact plan, capable of easy supervision by one person, was considered the second essential. There were a number of rambling "country club" schemes with alluring porticos and arcades that failed to satisfy this fundamental requirement.

FIRST PRIZE DESIGN: A very simple and admirable plan. Of all the plans submitted this seemed to the Jury to best meet the requirements of the programme. It is practical, convenient and easily supervised. The auditorium annex could easily be omitted, if for reasons of economy it be considered not essential, without impairing the design or the general effect of the building. The basement space could then become valuable and the building would probably be better served if it were wholly utilized. The exterior possesses a high degree of both beauty and form in its ensemble and in all its naïve details and the scale is highly consistent. A study of these details discloses a rare choice of simple forms suitable for execution in wood. The wood pickets beside the steps, the lattice, the profile of mouldings, the detail of the lantern and the direct way in which these forms are used make a pleasing variety and a harmonious design.

The rendering of the perspective, while not affecting the award, is commended by the Jury as a most delightful example of draughtsmanship; marvelous understanding and beautiful work.

SECOND PRIZE DESIGN: An excellent plan, very similar to that of the First Prize, with just a shade less suavity. The basement is utilized to good advantage and the attic space is adapted for a small historical museum. The design meets the requirements of the programme to a marked degree. The exterior, highly appropriate for a rural community, is original in treatment, of good proportions and simple in detail. The very frank use of one-inch boards gives an "early American" feeling to the whole composition. The groups of high windows over the bookcases give excellent light and add to the character of the building. The lighting of the museum by large studio windows in each gable is efficient and sensible. The chimney, which can be made a feature of prime interest, does not appear and the iron railing on the front steps seems a little out of keeping with the agricultural character of the building. The spirit of this design breathes economy and husbandry.

THIRD PRIZE DESIGN: A very lovely design which combines with its distinctly rural quality an admirable dignity. The plan, while simple and well arranged, suggests a larger building than called for by the programme. Its outline redeems this fault in part, the simplification of certain details with which the plan appears crowded would tend to bring the design into scale. The presentation, while admirable, does not sufficiently focus the mind on the essentials. The large scale details are beyond criticism; and the elevations, save a slight forcing of the scale, are in the best of 18th Century taste.

FOURTH PRIZE DESIGN: The plan of this building appealed very strongly to the Jury. In some ways perhaps an ideal solution of the problem. Excellent judgment is displayed in its location on the lot and in its unsymmetrical arrangement, constituting its chief charm. The large well designed windows are varied to fit the needs of the rooms; the bay window and long window to the floor making the children's room very cheerful and attractive. The separate entrance to the basement auditorium, the placing of the book room, storage and heating apparatus are carefully worked out and the first floor plan is ideal in every respect. The exterior is simple and dignified, although one feels that too much emphasis is given to the roof. The details lack a certain *savoir faire*. (Continued on page 224)

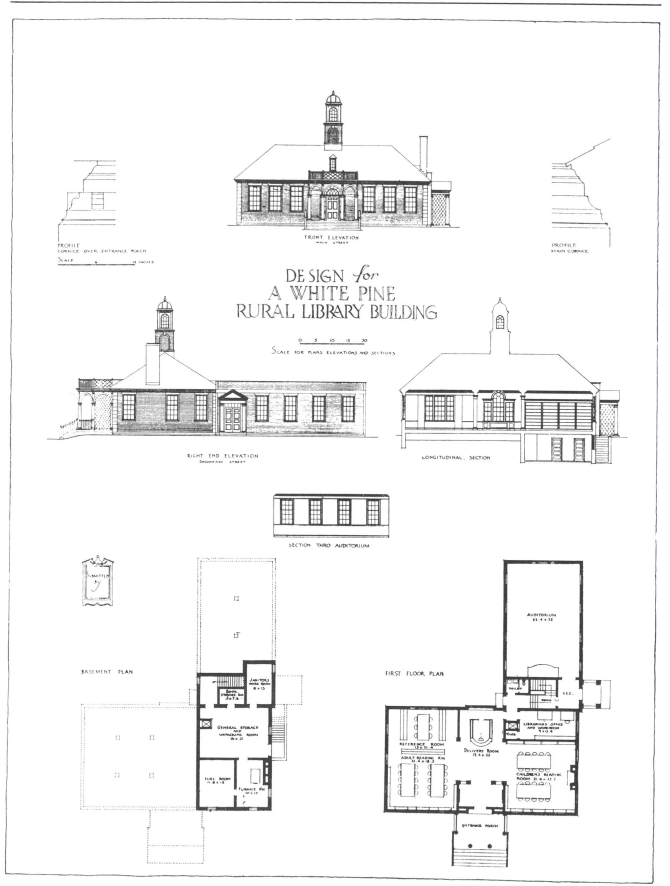

DESIGN for
A WHITE PINE
RURAL LIBRARY BUILDING

FIRST PRIZE DESIGN, Detail Sheet
Submitted by Richard M. Powers and Albert M. MacLellan, Boston, Massachusetts

SECTION

FRONT ELEVATION

SIDE ELEVATION

SIGN

DESIGN FOR
WHITE PINE
RURAL LIB-
RARY BUILD-
ING

PLOT PLAN

LA CROIX
PUBLIC LIBRARY

LA CROIX
PUBLIC
LIBRARY
&
LECTURE
ROOM

SIDE ENTRANCE

¾ SCALE DETAIL OF FRONT ENTRANCE

SECOND PRIZE DESIGN, Detail Sheet
Submitted by H. A. Salisbury and Frederick S. Stott, Omaha, Nebraska

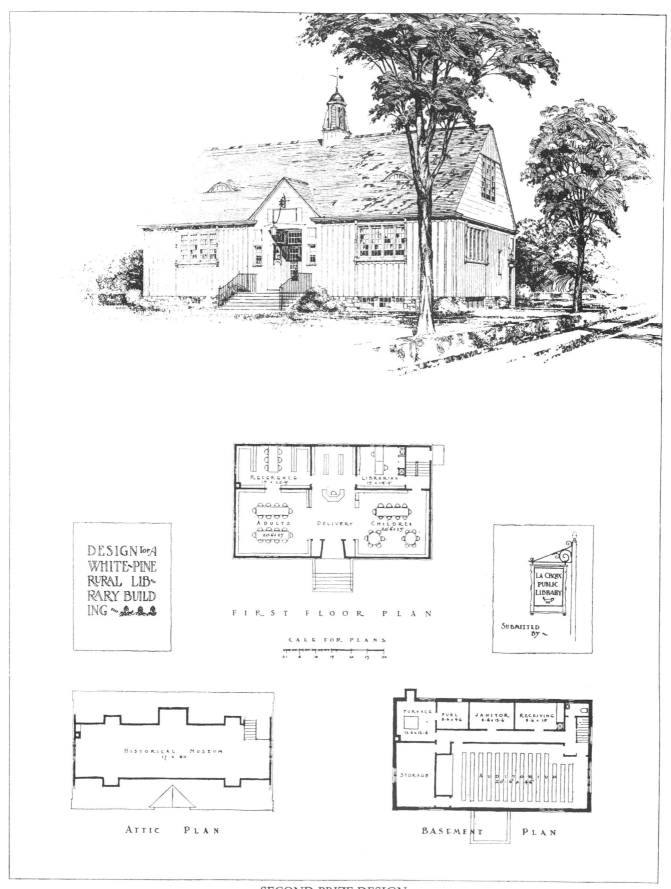

DESIGN for A
WHITE~PINE
RURAL LIB~
RARY BUILD
ING ~

REFERENCE
LIBRARIAN
ADULTS
DELIVERY
CHILDREN

FIRST FLOOR PLAN

SCALE FOR PLANS

LA CROIX
PUBLIC
LIBRARY

SUBMITTED
BY ~

HISTORICAL MUSEUM
17 x 60

ATTIC PLAN

FURNACE
12.6 x 12.6
FUEL
8.6 x 9.6
JANITOR
8.6 x 13.6
RECEIVING
8.6 x 18

STORAGE
AUDITORIUM
20.6 x 40

BASEMENT PLAN

SECOND PRIZE DESIGN
Submitted by H. A. Salisbury and Frederick S. Stott, Omaha, Nebraska

FRONT ELEVATION

SIDE ELEVATION

LANTERN

SPVRWINK
PVBLIC
LIBRARY
BVILT A·D·1924

PLOT PLAN

DETAIL of MAIN ENTRANCE

SCALE of ENTRANCE & LANTERN

DETAIL AT CORNER

PLAN

TYPICAL WINDOW JAMB

PILASTER BASE

DOORWAY & MAIN CORNICE

RAIL, POST & NOSING

DESIGN FOR A
WHITE PINE
RVRAL LIBRARY BVILDING

THIRD PRIZE DESIGN, Detail Sheet
Submitted by Ralph H. Hannaford, Boston, Massachusetts

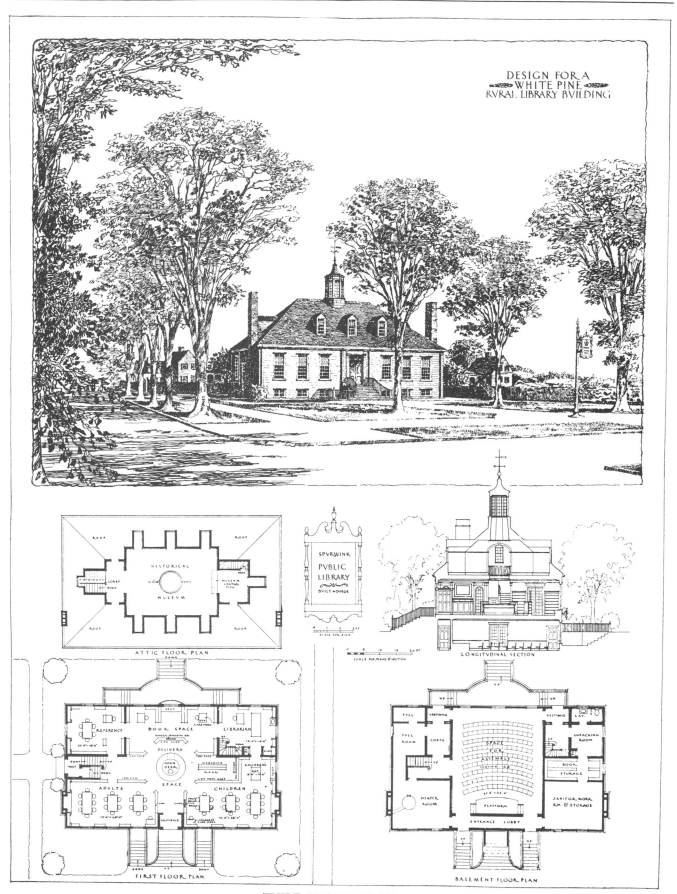

DESIGN FOR A
WHITE PINE
RVRAL LIBRARY BVILDING

ATTIC FLOOR PLAN

SPVRWINK
PVBLIC
LIBRARY
BVILT A·D 1924

LONGITVDINAL SECTION

FIRST FLOOR PLAN

BASEMENT FLOOR PLAN

THIRD PRIZE DESIGN
Submitted by Ralph H. Hannaford, Boston, Massachusetts

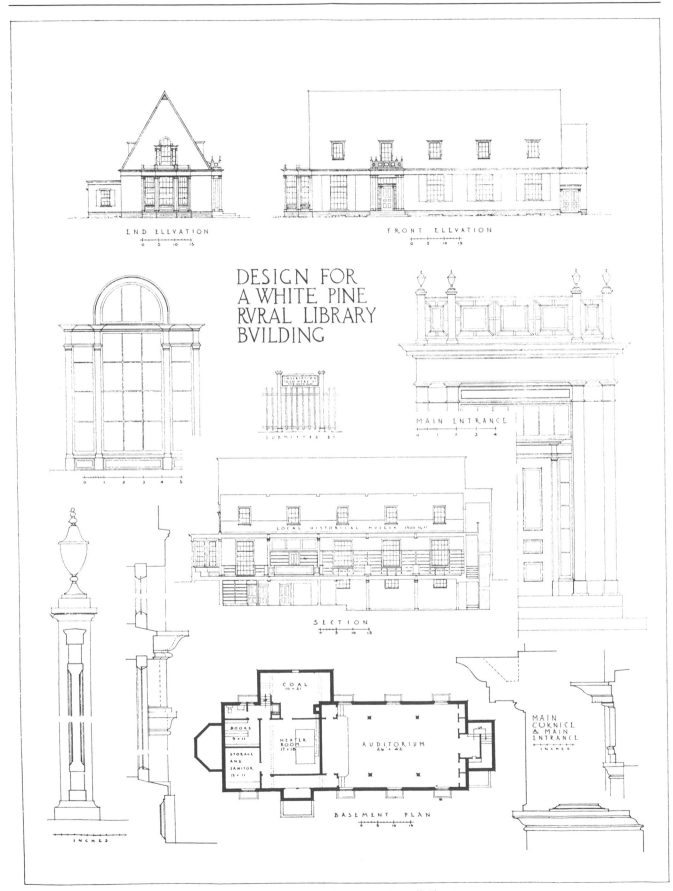

END ELEVATION

FRONT ELEVATION

DESIGN FOR
A WHITE PINE
RVRAL LIBRARY
BVILDING

MAIN ENTRANCE

SECTION

COAL

BOOKS

HEATER
ROOM

STORAGE
AND
JANITOR

AUDITORIUM

MAIN
CORNICE
& MAIN
ENTRANCE

BASEMENT PLAN

FOURTH PRIZE DESIGN, Detail Sheet
Submitted by Merton G. Kingsley, Lakewood, Ohio

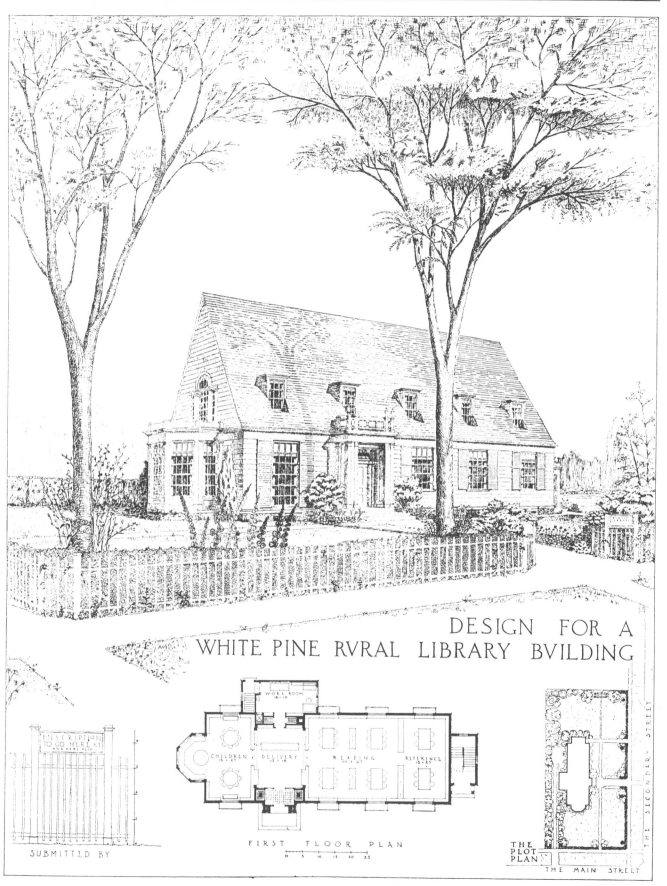

DESIGN FOR A
WHITE PINE RVRAL LIBRARY BVILDING

FIRST FLOOR PLAN

SUBMITTED BY

THE PLOT PLAN

FOURTH PRIZE DESIGN
Submitted by Merton G. Kingsley, Lakewood, Ohio

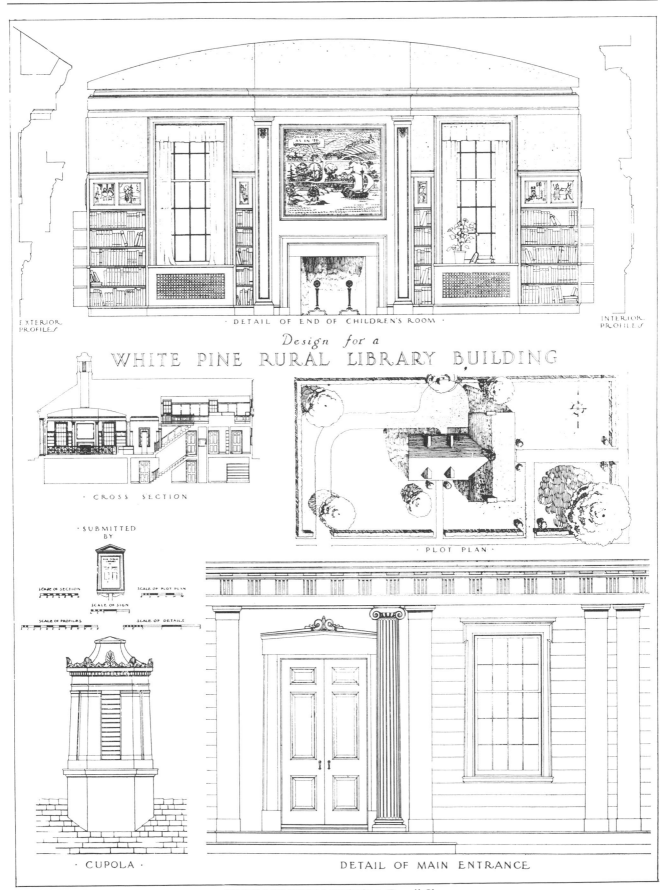

· DETAIL OF END OF CHILDREN'S ROOM ·

EXTERIOR PROFILES

INTERIOR PROFILES

Design for a

WHITE PINE RURAL LIBRARY BUILDING

· CROSS SECTION ·

· SUBMITTED BY ·

SCALE OF SECTION

SCALE OF PLOT PLAN

SCALE OF SIGN

SCALE OF PROFILES

SCALE OF DETAILS

PLOT PLAN

· CUPOLA ·

DETAIL OF MAIN ENTRANCE

FIRST MENTION DESIGN, Detail Sheet
Submitted by Charles M. Stotz and Milton B. Steinman, New York, New York

Design for a
WHITE PINE RURAL LIBRARY BUILDING

· FRONT ELEVATION ·   SUBMITTED BY   SIDE ELEVATION

BASEMENT PLAN   · MAIN FLOOR PLAN ·   MUSEUM PLAN

FIRST MENTION DESIGN, Detail Sheet
Submitted by Charles M. Stotz and Milton B. Steinman, New York, New York

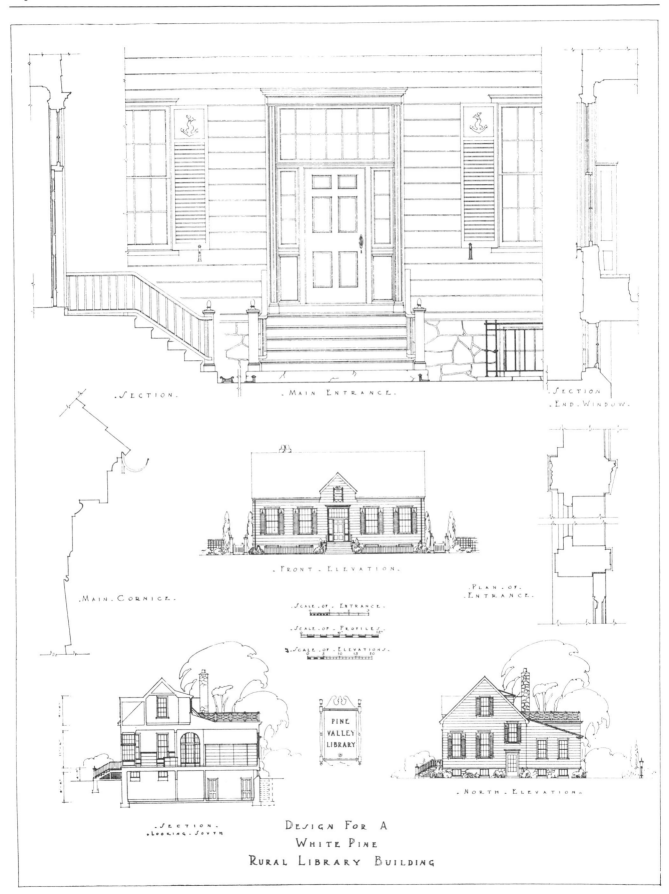

.SECTION.

.MAIN.ENTRANCE.

.SECTION.
.END.WINDOW.

.MAIN.CORNICE.

.FRONT.ELEVATION.

.SCALE.OF.ENTRANCE.

.SCALE.OF.PROFILES.

.SCALE.OF.ELEVATIONS.

.PLAN.OF.
.ENTRANCE.

PINE
VALLEY
LIBRARY

.SECTION.
.LOOKING.SOUTH.

.NORTH.ELEVATION.

DESIGN FOR A
WHITE PINE
RURAL LIBRARY BUILDING

SECOND MENTION DESIGN, Detail Sheet
Submitted by Leon H. Hoag, Bloomfield, New Jersey

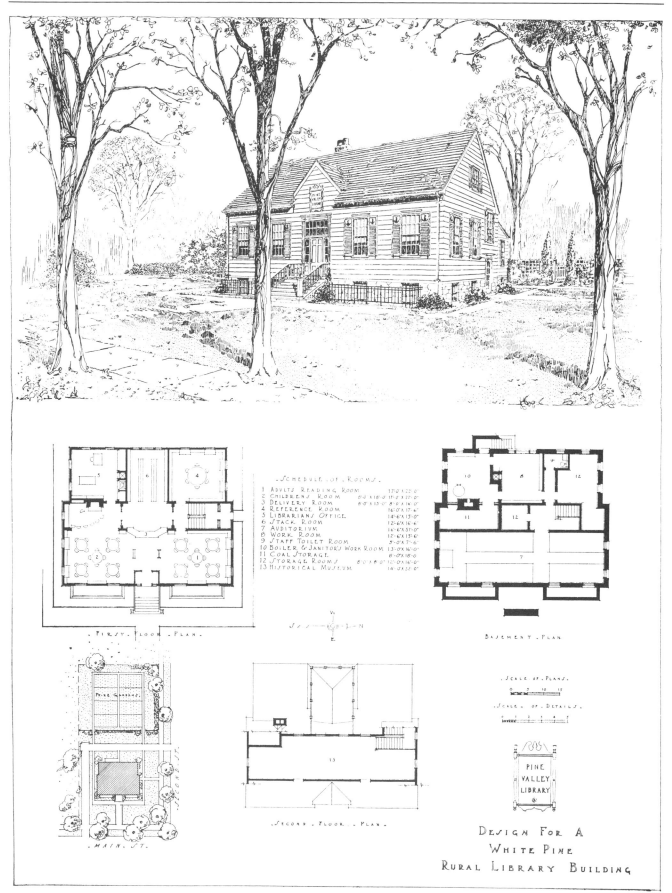

.SCHEDULE .OF .ROOMS.
1 ADULTS READING ROOM   17'-0" X 25'-0"
2 CHILDRENS ROOM   8'-0" X 18'-0" 17'-0" X 22'-0"
3 DELIVERY ROOM   8'-0" X 13'-0" 8'-0" X 16'-0"
4 REFERENCE ROOM   16'-0" X 17'-6"
5 LIBRARIANS OFFICE   14'-6" X 15'-0"
6 STACK ROOM   12'-6" X 16'-6"
7 AUDITORIUM   16'-6" X 51'-0"
8 WORK ROOM   12'-6" X 15'-6"
9 STAFF TOILET ROOM   5'-0" X 7'-6"
10 BOILER & JANITOR'S WORK ROOM 13'-0" X 16'-0"
11 COAL STORAGE   8'-0" X 16'-0"
12 STORAGE ROOMS   8'-0" X 8'-0" 12'-0" X 16'-0"
13 HISTORICAL MUSEUM   14'-0" X 52'-0"

. FIRST. FLOOR. PLAN.

. BASEMENT . PLAN.

. SCALE OF. PLANS.
0 5 10 15

. SCALE OF . DETAILS.

PINE
VALLEY
LIBRARY

. MAIN . ST.

. SECOND . FLOOR . PLAN.

DESIGN FOR A
WHITE PINE
RURAL LIBRARY BUILDING

SECOND MENTION DESIGN
Submitted by Leon H. Hoag, Bloomfield, New Jersey

SIDE ELEVATION
SCALE FOR ELEVATIONS & SECTION

FRONT ELEVATION

SECTION

SIGN

PROFILE OF
MAIN ENTRANCE

MAIN ENTRANCE
SCALE FOR DETAILS

PROFILE OF PORTICO
AND MAIN CORNICE

END OF REFERENCE ROOM

DESIGN FOR A WHITE PINE RURAL LIBRARY BUILDING

THIRD MENTION DESIGN, Detail Sheet
Submitted by Frank C. Burke, Watertown, Massachusetts

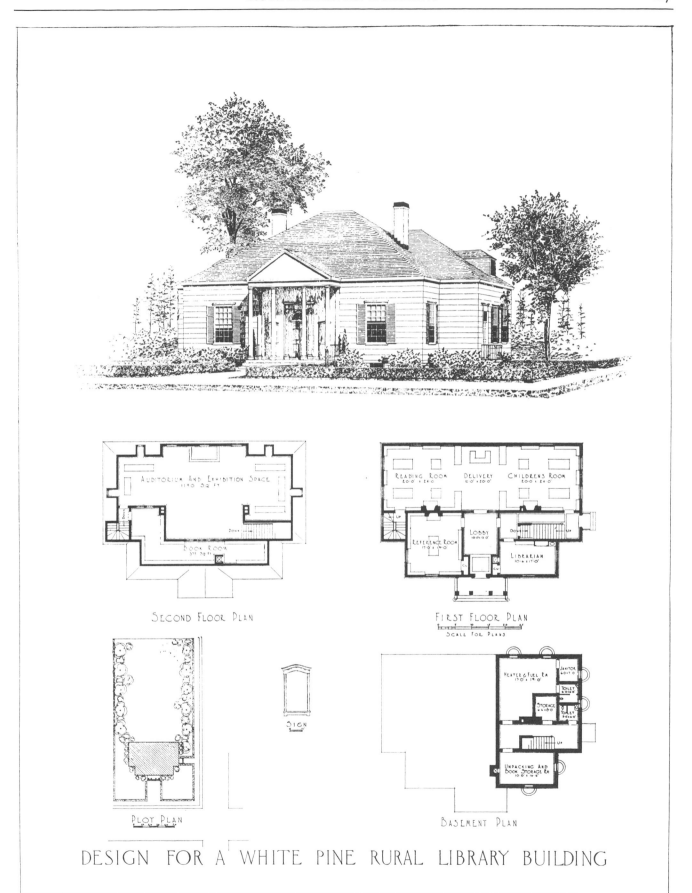

SECOND FLOOR PLAN

FIRST FLOOR PLAN

PLOT PLAN

SIGN

BASEMENT PLAN

DESIGN FOR A WHITE PINE RURAL LIBRARY BUILDING

THIRD MENTION DESIGN

Submitted by Frank C. Burke, Watertown, Massachusetts

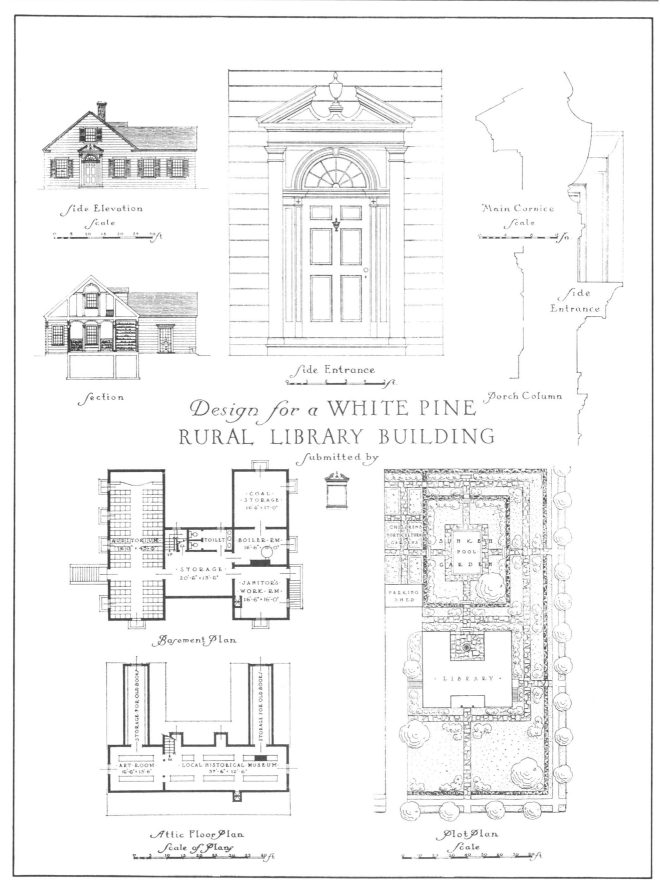

Side Elevation
Scale

Section

Main Cornice
Scale

Side
Entrance

Porch Column

Side Entrance

Design for a WHITE PINE
RURAL LIBRARY BUILDING
Submitted by

COAL STORAGE
16'-6" × 17'-0"

AUDITORIUM
16'-0" × 43'-0"

TOILET

BOILER RM.
16'-6" × 11'-0"

STORAGE
20'-6" × 13'-6"

JANITOR'S WORK RM.
16'-6" × 16'-0"

Basement Plan

CHILDRENS HORTICULTURAL GARDEN

SUNKEN POOL GARDEN

PARKING SHED

LIBRARY

STORAGE FOR OLD BOOKS

STORAGE FOR OLD BOOKS

ART ROOM
16'-6" × 13'-6"

LOCAL HISTORICAL MUSEUM
37'-6" × 12'-6"

Attic Floor Plan
Scale of Plans

Plot Plan
Scale

FOURTH MENTION DESIGN, Detail Sheet
Submitted by Leslie W. Devereux and Almus Pratt Evans, New York, New York

Design for a WHITE PINE
RURAL LIBRARY BUILDING

Submitted by

First Floor Plan

Front Elevation
Scale

Front Entrance
Scale

FOURTH MENTION DESIGN
Submitted by Leslie W. Devereux and Almus Pratt Evans, New York, New York

Side Elevation

Section

Front Elevation

Scale for Elevations & Section

Design for

A WHITE PINE

Rural Library Building

Sign
Scale

Detail of
Cornice
Above
Main
Entrance

Detail of
Main
Cornice

Detail of Main Entrance

Scale

Scale for Details

FIFTH MENTION DESIGN, Detail Sheet
Submitted by William Rankin and Charles Kenneth Clinton, New York, New York

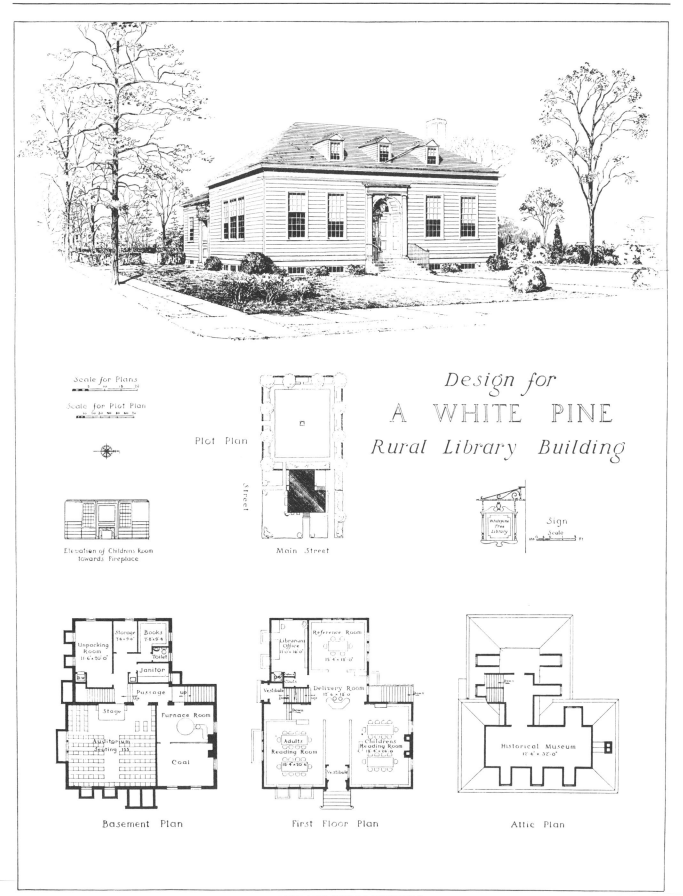

Scale for Plans

Scale for Plot Plan

Plot Plan

Street

Main Street

Elevation of Childrens Room
towards Fireplace

Design for
A WHITE PINE
Rural Library Building

Whitepine
Free
Library

Sign
Scale

Basement Plan

Unpacking
Room
11·6"×20'·0"

Storage
7·6×9·6'

Books
7·8×9·4

Toilet

Janitor

Passage   up

Stage

Auditorium
Seating 125

Furnace Room

Coal

First Floor Plan

Librarians
Office
11·6×16·0'

Reference Room
15·4×18·0'

Vestibule

Delivery Room
12·6×18·0

Adults
Reading Room
18·4×20·6'

Childrens
Reading Room
18·4×20·0

Vestibule

Attic Plan

Historical Museum
12·6"×32'·0"

FIFTH MENTION DESIGN
Submitted by William Rankin and Charles Kenneth Clinton, New York, New York

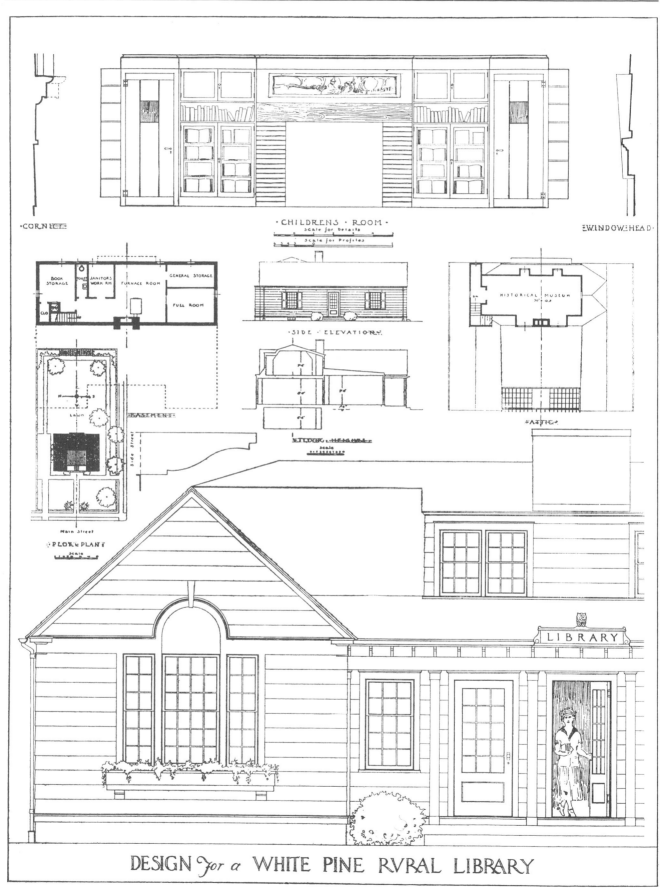

·CORNICE· ·CHILDRENS · ROOM · ·WINDOW·HEAD·

·BASEMENT· ·SIDE · ELEVATION· ·ATTIC·

· PLOT & PLAN ·

DESIGN for a WHITE PINE RVRAL LIBRARY

SIXTH MENTION DESIGN, Detail Sheet
Submitted by Einar A. Wikander and John Floyd Yewell, New York, New York